NOLS
Wilderness
First Aid

Tod Schimelpfenig and Linda Lindsey
Illustrated by Joan Safford

third edition

A Publication of the
National Outdoor Leadership School
and
Stackpole Books

0 11557 02864 5

Published by
Stackpole Books
5067 Ritter Road
Mechanicsburg, PA 17055
www.stackpolebooks.com

Printed in the United States of America.

Cover photo by Randy Lincks / Sharpshooters

Library of Congress Cataloging-in-Publication Data

Schimelpfenig, Tod, 1954-
    NOLS wilderness first aid / Tod Schimelpfenig and Linda
Lindsey ; illustrated by Joan Safford.—3rd ed.
        p.   cm.
    "A publication of the National Outdoor Leadership School
and Stackpole Books."
    Includes bibliographic references and index
    ISBN 0-8117-2864-1 (pbk.)
    1. First aid in illness and injury. 2. Outdoor medical emer-
gencies. I. Lindsey, Linda, 1952-   . II. Title.

RC88.9.O95 S35 2000
616.02'52—dc21
                                                            00-036586

To the students at NOLS. We hope this text helps you to be better outdoor leaders.

To all NOLS instructors, who on a daily basis teach and practice first aid and safety in the wilderness and are the source of the practical experience that is the foundation of this text.

To our families: Betsy, Sam, Dave, Mark and Emily; and Michael, Laura, and Hannah for their support and patience during the time we devoted to this project.

—Tod and Linda

To the St. Michael's College Rescue Squad, where I first learned quality patient care.

—Tod

About NOLS

The National Outdoor Leadership School (NOLS) is a private, nonprofit school based in Lander, Wyoming. NOLS branch schools are located in the Rocky Mountains (Wyoming, Teton Valley), the Pacific Northwest (Washington), the Southwest (Arizona), Alaska, Canada (the Yukon), Kenya, Mexico, and Patagonia (Chile.) Since our founding in 1965, we have graduated more than 50,000 students.

The mission of the National Outdoor Leadership School is to be the leading source and teacher of wilderness skills and leadership that serve people and the environment.

Correspondence and catalog requests may be addressed to:

> The National Outdoor Leadership School
> 288 Main Street
> Lander, Wyoming 82520
> Telephone: (307) 332-5300
> www.nols.edu
> admissions@nols.edu

Other NOLS Publications

NOLS Wilderness Mountaineering (Stackpole Books, 2000)
NOLS Cookery (Stackpole Books, 1997)
Soft Paths (Stackpole Books, 1995)
The NOLS Wilderness Guide (Simon & Schuster, 1999)

THE AUTHORS

Tod Schimelpfenig is the past NOLS risk management director, founder of the wilderness risk managers committee, advisor to the Wilderness Medicine Institute, and current NOLS Rocky Mountain branch director. An EMT for 25 years, he has gained extensive experience in search and rescue and ambulance work. In 1990, he was named Wyoming EMT Instructor of the Year. Tod has been a NOLS instructor for 25 years. He teaches NOLS' Wilderness EMT and Wilderness First Responder courses and serves as a critical stress debriefer.

Linda Lindsey, RN, BSN, EMT, is NOLS human resources director and a board member of the Wilderness Medical Society. She is the former coordinator of the Colorado Outward Bound first aid program and has five years' experience as a staff nurse in obstetrics and neonatal intensive care.

CONTENTS

PREFACE

Traditional first aid programs are designed for the common medical problems, telephones, ambulances, and hospitals of urban areas. In wilderness medicine we take these practices and make them relevant to the medical problems we experience in the outdoors, factoring in the available equipment, transportation, and communication systems. Wilderness medicine training has become the standard for outdoor professionals and important training for the outdoor enthusiast. When the first edition of *NOLS Wilderness First Aid* appeared on bookshelves in 1991, the concept of wilderness medicine seemed clear. Today, its very definition, at least in North America, has blurred.

In 1991, the traditional definition of medical care, in remote locations with improvised gear and challenging environmental conditions, applied to many wilderness areas. Today, technology and growing popularity of outdoor pursuits has managed to effectively shrink many wilderness areas. The use of helicopters has largely replaced the need for multiday evacuations with improvised litters. Communication systems now offer the chance of quick transport from remote areas to medical care, and indeed, many wilderness visitors have come to expect such service. In fact, much of what we call wilderness medicine today is really a simple extension of modern emergency medical services into the wilderness by cell phone and helicopter.

This doesn't mean wilderness medicine is obsolete. There are still areas where a radio or a cell phone will not work and where quick rescue service is not available. Weather and terrain can still hamper rescue efforts. True wilderness medicine involves situations in which we don't have the advantages of modern medicine, such as access to medications, diagnostic equipment and procedures, rapid transport and specialty care. In reality, a medical emergency in the wilderness is a grave situation.

For 35 years, students and instructors on NOLS courses in remote locations around the world have received top-notch wilderness medical training in the outdoors. This book is an extension of those years of practical experience. It draws from the insights and experience of NOLS instructors and expedition leaders, who must occasionally assess patients and make decisions about medical treatment and urgency of transport, and from the experience of our staff, who volunteer as members of the Fremont County (Wyoming) Search and Rescue. It shows how skilled outdoors people who are not medical professionals make decisions and in what context. This decision-making process is informed by the NOLS database of field safety incidents, possibly the most extensive in the industry. The treatment and evacuation guidelines in this text are the same that guide the decisions of NOLS instructors in the field.

The third edition of *NOLS Wilderness First Aid* reflects the changing field of wilderness medicine. With this edition, NOLS further cements its reputation as an innovator and leader. NOLS and the people of NOLS provide the vision and action to move and grow with technology and to pool resources with others to provide the best possible medical care. In 1991, for example, there was no Wilderness Risk Managers Committee. In 1993, that group was started by one of this book's authors, Tod Schimelpfenig. Today, it has combined wilderness leadership, risk management, and wilderness medicine into one of the most important conferences of its type.

Another very important move by NOLS in the past decade was the acquisition, in 1999, of the Wilderness Medicine Institute. One of the nation's leading wilderness medical trainers, WMI of NOLS is now the foremost wilderness medicine training center in the western United States, with courses held in 15 states. It provides wilderness first aid, first responder, and emergency medical technician training to more than 3,000 students each year.

Practical experience. Innovation. Vision. These are qualities that have made NOLS and this text a success. But no medicine is better than prevention. The prevention theme runs throughout this book. You'll read about it in every chapter, with new additions on hygiene, gender, and cold injuries. You'll also read about it in the chapter on leadership, teamwork, and communication for small groups. Remember, though, that the foundation of wilderness medicine is competence in basic outdoor skills and leadership. You can't learn these from a book. You need to go on your own wilderness trips, or take a NOLS course.

John N. Gans
Executive Director

ACKNOWLEDGMENTS

We would like to thank the following people for their assistance in the preparation of this edition:

Shana Tarter of the Wilderness Medicine Institute at NOLS.

NOLS Field Program Supervisors Allen O'Bannon, Missy White, Pete Absolon, Kathy Brown, and Gary Cukjati for reviewing the chapters on cold injury, gender, and hygiene and helping to assure the text reflects what really happens in the wilderness.

Karl Weller, long time NOLS Rocky Mountain Branch chef, for his advice on hygiene and foodborne illness.

Molly Doran, NOLS Leadership project coordinator and assistant operations director, for her review of the chapter on leadership, curriculum, and teamwork.

Herb Ogden, M.D., NOLS Medical Adviser and Chair of the NOLS Risk Management Committee, for review of the new sections of the text, and his advice and support of NOLS instructors and students.

Louise Collins, M.D., for her assistance with the chapter on gender-specific concerns.

INTRODUCTION

Wilderness has no handrails, no telephones, and no simple solutions for complex emergency situations. Yet it does have dangers. Some are obvious: rockfall, moving water, stormy weather, avalanches, crevasses, and wild animals. Others are less obvious: boulder fields, deadfall, impure water, dehydration, and altitude illness.

Although these risks can be minimized with skill, experience and judgment, outdoor leaders know that despite their best efforts, accidents and illnesses will happen. They prepare for the challenge of providing emergency medical care in remote and hostile environments.

This book is designed as a field textbook for the wilderness first aid curriculum presented on NOLS semester courses. This curriculum is designed to train the student to 1) prevent, recognize, and treat common wilderness medical problems and 2) to stabilize a severely ill or injured patient for evacuation.

NOLS Wilderness First Aid may also be used as a basic text for wilderness first aid courses, as an information source for outdoor enthusiasts, or as a resource to tuck into your pack or kayak. It covers most, but not all, of the material commonly taught by reputable Wilderness First Responder (WFR) instructors or listed in the Wilderness Medical Society's recommended minimum WFR course topics. People using this as a WFR textbook should seek supplementary background information on medical-legal issues; common simple expedition problems; Cardio-Pulmonary Resuscitation (CPR); obstetrical, psychological, and behavioral emergencies; oxygen use and mechanical aids to breathing. Additionally, NOLS core curriculum gives the student weeks of instruction and experience in the critical WFR skills of living and traveling in wilderness, expedition planning, and emergency procedures.

While the majority of the practices discussed in this text are standard and accepted first aid, there are areas where wilderness medicine expands the scope of practice beyond what may be routinely done when a hospital or physician is nearby. For example, in remote settings it is appropriate to attempt to reduce dislocations, to clean wounds, and to consider clearing a potential spine injury. As well, wilderness leaders often make decisions on whether to seek the advice of a physician; decisions that are not made by ambulance personnel who routinely transport all patients; decisions that may end an expedition or place rescuers in jeopardy. Those leading trips or managing wilderness programs should be aware of the medical-legal issues in wilderness medicine and consider using written medical protocols, such as the *Practice Guidelines for Wilderness Emergency Care* (Wilderness Medical Society, 1995), and employing a physician medical adviser to guide the wilderness protocols specific for their program.

Chapters one through eight cover fundamental topics in first aid—patient assessment, shock, soft tissue injury, burns, fractures and dislocations, and chest, head, and abdominal injury. They prepare us to assess and treat seriously ill or injured persons. Chapters nine though fifteen present medical problems associated with heat, cold, water, altitude, and poisonous plants and animals.

The final seven chapters discuss a variety of topics—athletic injuries, hygiene, hydration, gender-specific medical concerns, dental emergencies, stress in the rescuer, and leadership skills. These concerns may not threaten life or limb, but our safety history has shown them to be common in the everyday medical experience of the wilderness leader. Hydration and hygiene are especially important to ensuring that backcountry trips are safe and healthy. Finally, summaries at the end of each chapter provide snapshot views of assessment, treatment, and key points. These may also serve as quick emergency reference.

There are many substantive changes in this new edition.

The patient assessment chapter has been written to be consistent with the patient assessment system presented in the U.S. Department of Transportation's recently revised national standard Emergency Medical Technician curriculum.

The cold injury chapter includes an expanded section on immersion foot and nonfreezing cold injury, an important topic many wilderness first aid courses lightly touch on, and many outdoor enthusiasts are unfamiliar with.

The head and spine injury chapter now includes a section on eye injury and presents the protocols for clearing the spine.

Gender-specific medical conditions has an expanded section on hygiene tips for wilderness trip leaders. Hygiene and water disinfection includes an expanded section on foodborne illness and hygiene tips for the wilderness kitchen.

Asthma, pneumonia, and chest pain have been added to the medical emergencies in the chapter on diabetes, seizures, and unconscious states.

The new final chapter weaves together the NOLS leadership skills curriculum with the authors' 25 years of field experience in wilderness medicine and current research in human factors in accidents to discuss the critical topic of leadership, teamwork, and communication among rescue groups. This chapter is unique within wilderness medical texts and curriculum and sets this text apart from others in the field.

Wilderness first aid is patient care in which communication with a physician and rapid transport are rarely possible. It is first aid with limited equipment, often requiring improvisation. It involves caring for the patient for long periods and protecting him from the weather.

The first step in safety and first aid is prevention. Wilderness first aid training, in addition to preparing us to deal with serious illness and injury and environmental emergencies, should also discuss prevention and treatment of common wilderness medical problems such as infected wounds, hygiene-associated illness, and treatment of athletic injuries. You will find prevention to be a recurring theme in this text.

An essential but often neglected component of wilderness

first aid is the ability to care for and lead others under adverse conditions. Developing the skills and experience to be safe and comfortable in the outdoors is what the NOLS core curriculum is all about.

Simply reading the text or successfully completing a NOLS course does not qualify a person to perform any procedure. The text is not a substitute for thorough, practical training, experience in emergency medicine and the outdoors, critical analysis of the needs of specific situations, or the continued education and training necessary to keep skills sharp.

Professionals who experience daily emergencies still train routinely. There is no substitute for knowing how to respond to a medical emergency, for the group knowing what needs to be done in an emergency, and for having the basics wired so you can make a sound decision on how best to treat a patient. Plan ahead for emergencies. Research emergency procedures prior to your wilderness trip. Carry a well-stocked first aid kit and consider your inventory of available splinting and litter equipment. Practice first aid and emergency skills with your group.

Paul Petzoldt asked students at the beginning of NOLS courses to look at the person sitting next to them. There is a chance, Paul said, that that person will not finish the course due to illness or injury. There is also a chance he or she will end up providing first aid for you in the wilderness.

At NOLS, we routinely use the term "expedition behavior" to refer to how we interact and care for one another. Being prepared for emergencies is an essential component of good outdoor leadership. It is also good expedition behavior. First aid classes, when compared to opportunities to climb, hike, paddle, or fish, may not be as fun, but by dedicating only a portion of the time spent working on technical skills to emergency preparedness, you will enhance the health and safety of your expedition.

CHAPTER 1

PATIENT ASSESSMENT

INTRODUCTION

Imagine yourself kneeling beside a fallen hiker, deep in the wilderness. As you begin to examine the victim, thoughts of your remoteness, the safety of your companions, the incoming weather, evacuation, communication, and shelter possibilities swirl through your brain. The telephone, the ambulance, and those images and expectations we have of prompt advanced medical care don't apply to this situation. You are about to make decisions and initiate a series of events that will greatly affect the safety and well-being of the patient, your group, and outside rescuers.

In the city, the patient could be quickly transported to a hospital. In the wilderness, patient care may be your responsibility for hours or days. You cope with improvised gear and inclement weather and take care of yourself, the other members of your group, and the patient. The rescue or evacuation may be strenuous and can jeopardize the safety of the group and the rescuers.

You need information to help you determine how to best care for and transport the patient. You will gather that information during the patient assessment, the foundation of your care.

SCENE SIZE-UP

Patient assessment—analyzing what happened in an accident or illness and what you should do about it—begins immediately upon encountering the first aid situation. Your observations of weather, terrain, bystanders, and the position of the patient are your first clues to how an injury occurred, the patient's condition, and possible scene hazards.

Scene Safety

Look for danger to yourself, bystanders, other rescuers, or the patient. As a first-aider, your top priority should be maintaining your own well-being and the well-being of any fellow first-aiders. A patient can be served only by healthy rescuers, not by other patients.

Driving cold rain may make constructing on-the-spot shelter an immediate priority to avoid hypothermia or other threats to the patient and first-aiders. Rockfall or avalanche may dictate a move out of the path of danger. Protect your patient by protecting yourself.

Mechanism of Injury or Illness

Assess the mechanism of injury or illness (MOI). Look around. Your observations of the scene can give clues about what happened. Ask eyewitnesses and the patient what happened. Is the patient ill or injured? If ill, gather a short history of the illness. If injured, what is the mechanism? If the patient fell, find out how far, and if he or she was wearing a helmet. Did the person land on soft ground, snow, or rocks? Did he or she fall free or tumble? Mechanism can give us critical information about the location and severity of injuries.

Find out if you have more than one patient. If so, a quick initial assessment may tell you who needs your immediate attention and how best to use your companions to organize the scene and care for the patients.

Body Substance Isolation and Universal Precautions

This is the time to protect yourself from communicable or infectious disease. Practice body substance isolation. Put on gloves to reduce contact with blood and other body fluids and substances.

Health care people practice body substance isolation or universal precautions to protect themselves against infectious disease. It's impossible to know for sure if the patient is germ free. All body fluids and tissues are considered infectious, and appropriate precautions are taken. Protect yourself by washing your hands; using gloves, eyewear, and face masks; properly disposing of soiled bandages, dressing, and clothing; and avoiding needle-stick injury.

Disposable latex, vinyl, or other synthetic or natural rubber gloves should be in your first aid kit. Wear them when there is a chance you may contact a patient's blood, other body fluids, mucous membranes, or broken skin, or if you handle bandages, clothing, or other items contaminated with blood or other body fluids. Hands should be thoroughly washed, ideally before and certainly after contact with a patient.

Long-sleeve shirts and pants and pocket masks for mouth-to-mask ventilation are recommended in situations in which splashes of blood and other body fluids are likely to occur. If there is splashing blood, vomit, or other fluids, wear a protective mask and glasses, or at least a bandanna over your nose and mouth. Wear your sunglasses or raingear if nothing else is available. Items such as gloves and bandages that are contaminated should be placed in sealed plastic bags and labeled as a biohazard or incinerated in a hot fire.

INITIAL ASSESSMENT

The initial assessment is a ritual performed on every patient. Its purpose is to find and treat life-threatening medical problems. Besides attending immediately to vital functions, it provides order during the first frantic minutes of an emergency. You check, stop, and fix problems in the vital respiratory and circulatory systems. You assume disability and protect the spine. You assess and treat for environmental hazards.

Establishing Responsiveness

As you approach the patient, introduce yourself and ask if you may help. You're both being polite and finding out if the patient is responsive. If there is no response, attempt to arouse the patient by saying hello loudly—the person may just be asleep. If this fails to arouse the patient, try a painful stimulus—pinch the shoulder or neck muscle or rub the breastbone.

At this point, if there is any mechanism of injury, control the cervical spine (neck). Place hands on the head to prevent unnecessary movement of the neck.

If the patient is awake and talking, the airway is not obstructed; the person is breathing and has a pulse. If the patient is quiet, you need to check the ABCs (airway, breathing, and circulation) immediately. In both conscious and unconscious patients, you proceed through the entire initial assessment and check for disability, environmental threats, and hidden major injury.

ABCDEs

The initial assessment checks the airway, breathing, and circulation, plus possible serious bleeding and shock. The airways are the mouth, nose and throat, and trachea. The trachea brings oxygen to the lungs and is also known as the windpipe. Oxygen is exchanged between the air and the blood in the lungs. Circulation is composed of the heart, the blood vessels, and the blood. It transports nutrients and waste products

---

The Initial Assessment

Assess for responsiveness
 Attempt to arouse the patient
A—Assess the airway
 Open the airway
 Look in the mouth and clear
  obvious obstructions
B—Assess for breathing
 Look, listen, feel
C—Assess for circulation
 Check pulse at the neck
 Look for severe bleeding
 Treat for shock

D—Assume disability
 Observe cervical spine
  precautions
 Avoid moving the patient
 Consider the jaw thrust to
  open the airway
E—Protect the patient from the
 environment
 Expose and examine major
  injuries

throughout the body. We use ABCDE (airway, breathing, circulation, disability, environment, expose, examine) as a memory aid for the correct sequence. ABC is also familiar as the initial phase of cardiopulmonary resuscitation (CPR).

Airway. The airway is the path air travels from the atmosphere into the lungs. An obstructed airway is a medical emergency because oxygen cannot reach the lungs. Assess the state of the airway by opening it with the head-tilt–chin-lift method or the jaw thrust and by looking, listening, and feeling for air movement. If you see an obvious obstruction—a piece of food, perhaps—take it out.

If you can see, hear, or feel air moving from the lungs to the outside, the airway is open. A patient making sounds is able to move air from the lungs to the outside and past the vocal cords. This indicates that the airway is at least partially open.

Signs of an obstructed airway are lack of air movement, labored breathing, use of neck and upper chest muscles to breathe, and pale gray or bluish skin. If you discover an airway obstruction, attempt to clear the airway before proceeding to assessment of breathing. The appropriate techniques are those used in CPR for treating a foreign body–obstructed airway.

Breathing. Assess breathing using the "look, listen, and feel" format taught in CPR. Look for the rise and fall of the chest as air enters and leaves the lungs. Listen for the sound of air passing through the upper airway. Feel the movement of air from the patient's mouth and nose on your cheek. If the patient is not breathing, give two slow, even breaths, then proceed with a check for a pulse.

Circulation. Check for the presence or absence of a pulse. Place the tips of your middle and index fingers over the carotid artery for at least 10 seconds. The carotid is a large central artery, accessible at the neck. Other possible sites are the femoral artery in the groin and the radial artery in the wrist (preferable for a conscious patient).

It may be difficult to feel a pulse if the patient has a weak pulse from shock, is cold, or is wearing bulky clothing or if the

The INITIAL ASSESSMENT

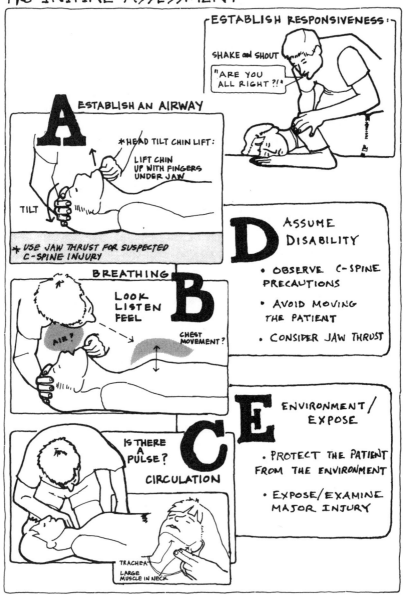

accident scene is confused by wind and water noise, blowing snow, or alarmed bystanders. Finding a pulse is not always easy. If you are unsure about the location or presence of the carotid pulse, try the femoral or the radial pulse.

If the patient is conscious or moaning, he or she must have a pulse. If there is no pulse, start CPR. If there is a pulse but no breathing, start rescue breathing.

Look for bleeding. Severe bleeding can be fatal within minutes. Look for obvious bleeding or wet places on the patient's clothing. Run your hands quickly over and under the patient's clothing, especially bulky sweaters or parkas, to find moist areas that may be caused by serious bleeding. Most external bleeding can be controlled with direct pressure and elevation of the wound. Chapter 3 ("Soft Tissue Injuries") addresses bleeding control in detail.

Disability. Initially assume a spinal injury in any accident victim. Since moving a spine-injured patient can cause paralysis, move the patient only if necessary and as little as possible. The airway opening technique for an unconscious victim or an accident victim is the jaw thrust. It does not require shifting the neck or spine. See chapter 6 ("Head, and Spinal Cord, and Eye Injuries").

Environment/Expose. Without moving the patient, expose and examine for major injuries, which may be hidden in bulky outdoor clothing. Quickly unzip zippers, open cuffs, look under parkas.

Assess and manage environmental hazards. It's not uncommon in wilderness medicine to protect the patient from extreme environments. You may need to move your patient off snow and onto an insulating pad, or out of a river onto dry ground.

THE FOCUSED EXAM AND HISTORY

Now pause a moment to look over the scene. The initial assessment is complete. Immediate threats to life have been addressed. Consider the patient's and the rescuers' needs. If the location of the incident is unstable—such as on or near rockfall, unstable scree, or a potential avalanche slope—move

FOCUSED ASSESSMENT and HISTORY

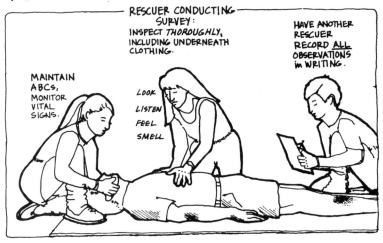

RESCUER CONDUCTING SURVEY:
INSPECT *THOROUGHLY*, INCLUDING UNDERNEATH CLOTHING.

HAVE ANOTHER RESCUER RECORD <u>ALL</u> OBSERVATIONS in WRITING.

MAINTAIN ABCs, MONITOR VITAL SIGNS.

LOOK
LISTEN
FEEL
SMELL

to a safer position. Provide insulation, adjust clothing, rig a shelter. Assign tasks: boil water for hot drinks, build a litter, set up camp, write down vital signs. Establishing clear delegation of tasks helps the rescuers by giving everyone something to do and helps the patient by creating an atmosphere

FOCUSED EXAM AND HISTORY

Complete this assessment after life-threatening problems have been treated.

Head-to-Toe	Vital Signs	Medical History
Look	LOC	SAMPLE
Listen	Heart rate	AEIOUTIPS
Feel	Skin	Chief complaint
Smell	Respiration	(OPQRST)
Ask	Temperature	
	Pupils	
	Blood pressure	

of order and leadership. See appendix C ("Emergency Procedures for Outdoor Groups").

The focused exam and history is a complete assessment of the patient done after life-threatening conditions have been stabilized. It consists of a complete physical exam, vital signs, and a thorough medical history.

Head-to-Toe Examination

The head-to-toe exam is a comprehensive physical examination. Begin the head-to-toe examination by first making the patient comfortable. Except in cases of imminent danger, avoid moving an injured patient until after the exam. Your hands should be clean, warm, and gloved. Ideally, the examiner should be of the same gender as the patient; otherwise, an observer of the same gender should be present during all phases of the exam. Designate a note taker to record the results of the focused exam and history.

As you examine the patient, explain what you are doing and why. Besides being a simple courtesy, this helps involve the patient in his or her care. This survey starts with the head and systematically checks the entire body down to the toes. One person should perform the survey in order to avoid confusion, provide consistent results, and minimize discomfort to the patient. Also, with a single examiner, the patient will be able to respond to one inquiry at a time.

The examination technique consists of looking, listening, feeling, smelling, and asking. If you are uncertain of what is abnormal, compare the injured extremity with the other side of the body or with a healthy person.

Head. Check the ears and nose for fluid and the mouth for injuries that may affect the airway. Check the face for symmetry; all features should be symmetrical down the midline from the forehead to the chin. The cheekbones are usually accurate references for facial symmetry. Feel the entire skull for depressions, tenderness, and irregularity. Run your fingers along the scalp to detect bleeding or cuts. Check the eyes for injuries, pupil abnormalities, and vision disturbances.

HEAD-TO-TOE EXAMINATION:

HEAD
NECK
SHOULDERS
ARMS
CHEST
ABDOMEN
BACK
PELVIS
LEGS
FEET

VITAL SIGNS:

LEVEL OF CONSCIOUSNESS
PUPILS
PULSE
SKIN SIGNS
BODY TEMPERATURE
RESPIRATIONS
RESPONSE TO STIMULUS (UNCONSCIOUS PATIENT)

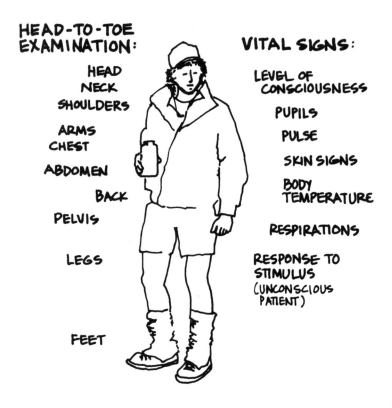

Neck. The trachea, or windpipe, should be in the middle of the neck. Feel the entire cervical spine from the base of the skull to the top of the shoulders for pain, tenderness, muscle rigidity, and deformity.

Shoulders. Examine the shoulders and the collarbone for deformity, tenderness, and pain.

Arms. Feel the arms from the armpit to the wrist. Check the pulse in each wrist; it should be equal on both sides. Ask the patient to move his or her fingers, then check grip strength by having the patient squeeze your hands. Check for sensation by gently pinching the fingers or scratching the palm of the hand and fingers. If no injury is apparent, ask the patient to move each arm through its full range of motion.

The Focused Exam and History:
Head-to-Toe Examination

Look for wounds, bleeding, unusual movements or shapes, deformities, penetrations, excretions, vomit

Listen for abnormal sounds, such as crepitus and airway noises

Feel for wounds, rigidity, hardness, softness, tenderness, deformity

Smell for unusual odors

Ask if anything hurts or feels odd or numb

Be alert for:

Head—airway, ears and nose for fluid or blood

Neck—airway, cervical spine

Shoulders—deformity

Arms—deformity, pulse, movement, sensation

Chest—deformity, painful or difficult breathing

Abdomen—tenderness, rigidity, distension, bruising

Back—pain, possible spine injury

Pelvis—pain, instability

Legs and feet—deformity, pulse, movement, sensation

Chest. Feel the entire chest for deformity or tenderness. Push down from the top and in from the sides. Ask the patient to breathe deeply as you compress the chest. Look for open chest wounds. Observe the rise and fall of the chest for symmetry.

Abdomen. Feel the abdomen for tenderness or muscle rigidity with light pressure. If there is tenderness, localize it into a quadrant. Look for distension, discoloration, and bruising.

Back. Feel the spine. Feel each vertebra from the shoulders to the pelvis. It may be difficult to accomplish this without moving the patient, but it is important to slide your hand as far as possible under the patient. There may be a hidden injury.

Pelvis. Press down on the front of the pelvis and in from the sides. Is there deformity or instability? Does the pressure cause pain?

Legs and Feet. Check the legs from the groin to the ankle. Check the pulse in each of the feet; they should be equal. Check for sensation and motor function in the feet by touching the patient's feet and by asking the patient to move his or her toes and to push his or her feet against your hands.

Vital Signs

Vital signs are objective indicators of respiration, circulation, heart function, blood volume, and body temperature. Checking the vital signs helps further evaluate the ABCs. Airway and breathing are checked by noting skin color, respiratory rate and depth, and level of consciousness (LOC). Circulation is evaluated by pulse, skin color, skin temperature, and level of consciousness.

Measure and record vital signs every 15 to 20 minutes. The initial set of vitals—LOC, pulse, respiration, skin signs, pupils, temperature, etc.—provides baseline data on the patient's condition. The changes that occur thereafter provide information on the progress of the patient.

Focused Exam and History: Vital Signs

Level of consciousness—
　Assess with AVPU
Heart rate—Assess pulse
　rate, rhythm, force
Skin signs—Assess skin
　color, temperature, and
　moisture
Respiration—Assess rate,
　rhythm, force

Temperature—Assess oral
　temperature with a
　thermometer
Pupils—Assess reactivity to
　light
Blood pressure—Unlikely to
　be recorded in the
　backcountry

Level of Consciousness.
LOC reflects brain function.
LOC may be affected by toxic
chemicals such as drugs or
alcohol, low blood sugar, abnormally high or low temperature,
diseases of the brain such as
stroke, circulatory or respiratory shock, or pressure from
bleeding or swelling caused by
a head injury.

> **A memory aid for assessing Level of Consciousness is AVPU:**
>
> ---
>
> **A**lert
> **V**erbal
> **P**ain
> **U**nresponsive

When you assess LOC, you
first determine the initial state. Begin by approaching the
patient, introducing yourself, saying "Hello," and asking if
you can help. You're being polite and finding out if the patient
is awake, asleep, or possibly unconscious.

Then describe the stimulus you used to arouse the
patient. If the patient opened his or her eyes and responded
after a simple "Hello," the person may have been asleep or
distracted. If you needed to shout loudly several times to
arouse the patient, the person would be described as not
awake but responsive to a verbal stimulus. If you needed to
use pain to arouse the patient, the person would be described
as not awake and responsive only to pain.

Alert. Normally, we are awake (or we wake quickly from
sleep), are alert, and know who we are, where we are, the date
or time, and recent events. This is described as A (awake), A
(alert), and O (oriented) times 0, 1, 2, 3, or 4, depending on
whether the patient knows who he or she is, where he or she
is, what date or time it is, and recent events.

AAO×4	The person knows person, place, time, and event
AAO×3	The person knows person, place, and time, but not event
AAO×2	The person knows person and place, but not time and event
AAO×1	The person knows person, but not place, time, and event
AAO×0	The person is awake and alert but is disoriented

A patient who is awake but not oriented to person, place, time, or event is described as disoriented. Any spoken response may be incoherent, confused, inappropriate, or incomprehensible.

Verbal. The patient is not awake but responds to a verbal stimulus, such as the rescuer saying, "Hello, how are you?" If the patient does not respond, repeat louder: "Hey! Sir (or Ma'am)! Wake up!" The patient's response may be opening the eyes, grunting, or moving. Higher levels of brain function respond to verbal input, lower levels to pain. Test for responsiveness to verbal stimuli first, painful stimuli second.

Pain. The patient is not awake, does not respond to verbal stimuli, but does respond to painful stimuli by moving, opening the eyes, or groaning. To stimulate for pain, pinch the muscle at the back of the shoulder or neck, or rub the sternum.

Unresponsive. The patient is not awake and does not respond to voice or painful stimuli.

Report the patient's initial state, the stimulus you gave, and the response. For example: "This patient is awake, alert, and oriented times four." Or, "This patient is not awake, but is arousable with a verbal stimulus. When awake, the patient knows his name but is otherwise disoriented."

Heart Rate. Every time the heart beats, a pressure wave is transmitted through the arteries. We feel this pressure wave as the pulse. The pulse rate indicates the number of heartbeats over a period of time. For an adult, the normal range is 60 to 90 beats per minute. An athlete may have a normal pulse rate of 50. Shock, exercise, altitude, illness, emotional stress, or fever can increase the heart rate.

The heart rate can be measured at the radial artery on the thumb side of the wrist or at the carotid artery in the neck. Place the tips of the middle and index fingers over the artery. Count the number of beats for 15 seconds and multiply by four.

In addition to rate, note the rhythm and strength of the pulse. The normal rhythm is regular. Irregular rhythms can be associated with heart disease and are frequently rapid.

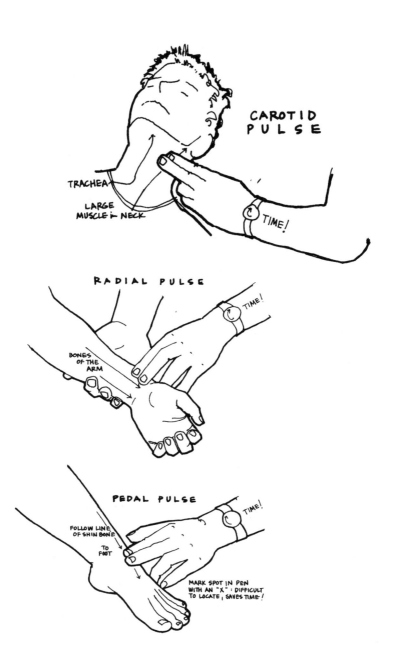

The strength of the pulse is the amount of pressure you feel against your fingertips. It may be weak or strong.

A standard pulse reading includes the rate, rhythm, and strength of the pulse. For example: "The pulse is 110, irregular, and weak." Or, "The pulse is 60, regular, and strong."

Skin Signs. Skin signs indicate the condition of the respiratory and cardiovascular systems. These include skin color, temperature, and moisture, often abbreviated SCTM.

Pinkness. In a light-colored person, normal skin color is pink. In darker-skinned individuals, skin color can be assessed at the nail beds, inside the mouth, palms of the hands, soles of the feet, or lips.

Redness. Redness indicates that the skin is unusually flushed with blood. It is a possible sign of recent exercise, heatstroke, carbon monoxide poisoning, fever, or allergic reaction.

Paleness. Pale skin indicates that blood has withdrawn from the skin. Paleness may be due to fright, shock, fainting, or cooling of the skin.

Cyanosis. Blue skin, or cyanosis, appears when circulation to the skin is reduced or the level of oxygen in the blood falls. Well-oxygenated blood is brighter red than poorly oxygenated blood. Cyanosis indicates that oxygen levels have fallen significantly, or that the patient may be cold.

Jaundice. Yellow skin combined with yellow whites of the eyes—jaundice—is a sign of liver or gallbladder disease. The condition results from excess bile pigments in the blood.

Temperature and Moisture. Quickly assess the temperature and moisture of the skin at several sites, including the forehead, hands, and trunk. In a healthy person, the skin is warm and relatively dry. Skin temperature rises when the body attempts to rid itself of excess heat, as in fever or environmental heat problems. Hot, dry skin can be a sign of fever or heatstroke. Hot, sweaty skin occurs when the body attempts to eliminate excess heat and can also be a sign of fever or heat illness.

Skin temperature falls when the body attempts to conserve heat by constricting blood flow to the skin; for example, during exposure to cold. Cool, moist (clammy) skin is an indicator of extreme stress and a sign of shock.

A report on skin condition should include color, temperature, and moisture. For example: "The patient's skin is pale, cool, and clammy."

Respiration. Respiratory rate is counted in the same manner as the pulse: Each rise of the chest is counted over 15 seconds and multiplied by four, or 30 seconds and multiplied by two. Watch the chest rise and fall, or observe the belly move with each breath. Normal respiration range is 12 to 20 breaths per minute.

The patient's depth and effort of breathing enable you to gauge his or her need for air and the presence or absence of chest injury. In a healthy individual, breathing is relatively effortless and unconscious.

A patient experiencing breathing difficulty may exhibit air hunger with deep, labored inhaling efforts. A patient with a chest injury may have shallow, rapid respirations accompanied by pain. Irregular respirations are a sign of a brain disorder. Noisy respirations indicate some type of airway obstruction. Assess and, if necessary, clear the airway.

Smell the breath. Fruity, acetone breath is a sign of diabetic coma. Foul, fecal-smelling breath may indicate a bowel obstruction.

Report respirations by their rate, rhythm, effort, depth, noises, and odors. For example, a patient in diabetic ketoacidosis may have respirations described as "20 per minute, regular, labored, deep. There is a fruity breath odor."

Body Temperature. Temperature measurement is an important component of a thorough patient assessment, but it is the vital sign that is least often recorded in the field. It can tell us of underlying infection or of abnormally high or low body temperatures. Although a normal temperature is 98.6°F (37°C), daily variation in body temperature is also normal, usually rising a degree during the day and decreasing through the night.

Temperature can be measured orally or rectally. Axillary readings—taken under the armpit—are the least reliable.

SHAKE THERMOMETER BULB END DOWN
TO PUSH MERCURY DOWN BELOW TEMPERATURE MARKINGS :

MERCURY
(SILVERY IN COLOR)

DEGREE MARKINGS
LINES SHOW .2° INCREMENTS

PLACE UNDER PATIENT'S TONGUE FOR 3 MINUTES.
REMOVE, ROTATE THERMOMETER UNTIL MERCURY CAN BE SEEN;
READ TEMPERATURE BY NOTING WHERE MERCURY STOPS: NORMAL TEMP. READING below:

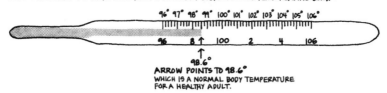

98.6°
ARROW POINTS TO 98.6°
WHICH IS A NORMAL BODY TEMPERATURE
FOR A HEALTHY ADULT.

Rectal temperatures are the most accurate indication of the core temperature available to first-aiders. Rectal temperature is sometimes considered necessary for suspected hypothermia but is rarely measured due to patient embarrassment and cold exposure. Diagnosis of hypothermia in the outdoors, discussed in chapter 9 ("Cold Injuries"), is often based on other factors, such as behavior, history, appearance, and LOC.

Before taking a temperature, shake down the thermometer to push the mercury below the degree markings. This is essential for an accurate reading. Place the thermometer under the patient's tongue for at least 3 minutes. The patient should refrain from talking or drinking during this time. A report on temperature should include the method, such as "100°F oral" or "37°C rectal."

Pupils. Pupils are clues to brain function. They can indicate head injury, stroke, drug abuse, or lack of oxygen to the brain. Both pupils should be round and equal in size. They should contract symmetrically when exposed to light and dilate when the light dims. Evaluate pupils by noting size, equality, and reaction to light.

PUPIL SIZE:

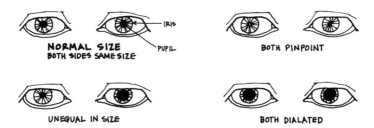

In the absence of a portable light source, such as a flashlight or headlamp, shield the patient's eyes for 15 seconds, then expose them to ambient light. Both pupils should contract equally. When in doubt, compare the patient's reactions to those of a healthy individual in the same light conditions.

A patient whose brain cells are deficient of oxygen may have equal but slow-to-react pupils. A wide, nonreactive pupil on one side and a small, reactive pupil on the other side indicates brain damage or disease on the side with the larger pupil. Very small, equal pupils may indicate drug intoxication.

Blood Pressure. The concept of blood pressure is discussed in chapter 2 ("Shock"). Although blood pressure is always measured when professional medical care is being administered, accurate measurement requires a stethoscope and a sphygmomanometer—equipment rarely carried on wilderness trips. Because evacuation decisions can be made without measuring blood pressure, this vital sign is not presented.

Medical History

The patient's medical history provides background that is often relevant to the present problem. Preparing the history is an ongoing process that you typically carry out while measur-

> **Focused Exam and History: Medical History**
>
> ---
>
> Chief complaint (OPQRST)
> SAMPLE
> AEIOUTIPS

ing vital signs and performing the head-to-toe exam. Obtaining an accurate history depends greatly on the quality of communication between you and the patient. This rapport begins as soon as you approach the scene. Communicating clearly, acting orderly, and appearing to be in control make it easier to obtain an accurate history.

Chief Complaint (OPQRST). Obtain the patient's chief complaint—the problem that caused him or her to solicit help. Pain is a common complaint—for example, abdominal pain or pain in the back after a fall. In lieu of pain, a chief complaint may be nausea or dizziness.

Onset. Did the chief complaint appear suddenly or gradually?

Provokes. What provoked the injury? If the problem is an illness, under what circumstances did it occur? What makes the problem worse, and what makes it better?

Quality. What qualities describe the pain? Adjectives may include stabbing, cramping, burning, sharp, dull, or aching.

Radiates. Where is the pain? Does it move, or radiate? What causes it to move? Chest pain from a heart attack can radiate from the chest into the neck and jaw. Pain from a spleen injury can be felt in the left shoulder.

> **A memory aid for pursuing questions about the chief complaint is OPQRST:**
>
> ---
>
> **O**nset
> **P**rovokes
> **Q**uality
> **R**adiates
> **S**everity
> **T**ime

Severity. On a scale of 1 to 10 (with 1 being no pain or discomfort and 10 being the worst pain or discomfort the patient has ever experienced), how does the patient rate this pain? This question can reveal the level of discomfort the patient is experiencing.

Time. When did the pain

start? How frequently does it occur? How long does it last? Correlate the patient's complaints with the vital signs.

Sample. The second step in taking the medical history can be considered a "history within the history" and can be remembered as SAMPLE.

Symptoms. What symptoms does the patient have? Nausea? Dizziness? Headache? Abdominal cramps? Ask the patient how he or she is feeling, or if anything is causing discomfort.

Allergies, Medications. Ask the patient questions about allergies and medications. This information may help prevent negative drug interactions during treatment.

Past History. The past history consists of a series of questions you ask the patient to discover any previous medical problems. First ask these general questions: Has the patient ever been in a hospital? Has the patient been treated by a physician? Is he or she seeing a physician currently?

> **A memory aid for taking the "history within the history" is SAMPLE:**
>
> Symptoms
> Allergies
> Medications
> Past history
> Last oral intake
> Events

Next, ask about specific body systems. Avoid medical jargon and leading questions. For example, asking the patient about any previous heart problems is less confusing than asking, "Do you have a cardiac history?"

Additional sources of information may include a medical alert tag or a medical information questionnaire. A medical alert tag is a necklace, bracelet, or wallet card that identifies the patient's medical concerns. It reports a history of diabetes, hemophilia, epilepsy, or other disorder; allergies to medication; and other pertinent information. Medical forms are common to many outdoor schools, camps, and guide services. The NOLS student medical history form is filled out by the student prior to the trip and is available for review by field staff.

Review all body systems for medical history:	
Cardiovascular (heart, blood pressure)	Urinary (kidney and bladder, infection, stones)
Respiratory (breathing, lungs, asthma)	Skin (rash, allergies)
Neurological (seizures, nerves, head injury)	Reproductive (menstrual, pregnancy)
Digestive (stomach, bowel function)	Endocrine (diabetes)
	Skeletal (accidents, broken bones, sprains)

Last Oral Intake. Ask the patient when he or she last ate and drank. This information is crucial should the patient require surgery. It may also tell you whether the patient is hydrated or give you important history if the patient is diabetic.

Recent Events. Recent events are unusual circumstances that have occurred within the past few days that may be relevant to the patient's present situation. Recent events might include symptoms of mountain sickness preceding pulmonary edema or changes in diet preceding stomach upset.

AEIOUTIPS:

Alcohol
Epilepsy
Insulin (diabetes)
Overdose
Underdose
Trauma (injury)
Infection
Psychology/Poison
Stroke

AEIOUTIPS. The final step in taking the medical history can be remembered as AEIOUTIPS. Particularly useful for investigating causes of unconsciousness, this list of reasons why a person might become unconscious is also useful in assessing a conscious patient. Investigate each possibility and look for clues that either rule out or confirm its presence. Since obtaining a history on an unconscious patient is impossible, carefully question bystanders for any background information they may be able to provide.

THE ASSESSMENT

The assessment is a review of the information gathered during the initial assessment and the focused exam and history. Examine the records of the head-to-toe examination, the vital signs, and the medical history. Think through the ABCDEs, OPQRST, SAMPLE, and AEIOUTIPS.

The Assessment
Review available information
Rule out other possibilities
Prioritize and treat
Review and repeat exam

Rule out possibilities as you assess. Many diagnoses are made by physicians on the basis of what a condition is not rather than what it could be. Is chest pain a muscle pull or a heart attack? Does the patient have the flu, mountain sickness, or early cerebral edema?

After thinking through all the available information, prioritize the patient's medical problems and begin to treat them.

The initial exam provides a baseline. Periodically repeat the exam to judge the patient's response to treatment and any changes for better or worse. If there is any change or deterioration in the patient, return to the beginning and repeat the initial assessment.

SOAP Notes

You may find it helpful to write down the results of your assessment. You may also need to use something written on a blank sheet of paper or a prepared form, such as the one illustrated here, to communicate with an evacuation or rescue party or the emergency room physician. Health care professionals commonly organize their medical notes into the SOAP format: subjective, objective, assessment, and plan.

Subjective information is told to you by the patient or bystanders. It includes age, sex, mechanism of injury, chief complaint, and OPQRST findings. Objective information is measurable or observable: vital signs and results from the SAMPLE history and the patient exam. Under assessment, categorize the patient's medical concerns in a problem list. For example, a problem list might be "sprained ankle, mild hypothermia," or "chest pain, possible heart attack." Describe under the plan section how you plan to treat these problems and any anticipated problems and changes in the patient's condition over time.

EXTENDED PATIENT CARE

Emergency medical care in the wilderness may be prolonged over hours or days in isolated locations. Splints, shelter, and litters may need to be improvised. In addition to first aid, basic nursing care is necessary to manage the physical and emotional needs of the patient.

Daily Needs

Keep the patient warm, clean, and comfortable. Remove soiled and wet clothing, and wash the patient at intervals. An individual immobilized on a litter may need extra insulation to keep warm. Hot water bottles, fires, or other expedition members may be needed as sources of warmth.

Drinking and eating are not appropriate in patients with an abnormal level of consciousness.

If the patient can drink, give water or clear soups and juices. Avoid hot chocolate, coffee, tea, or other beverages with high concentrations of sugar or caffeine. Excess sugar can delay fluid absorption; excess caffeine increases fluid loss.

Over a period of a few days, fluid intake is more important than solid food, as dehydration can complicate any existing medical condition. Dehydration is discussed in chapter 19 ("Hydration").

Arrange for the patient to urinate and defecate as comfortably as possible. These basic body functions are essential to overall well-being, despite embarrassment or temporary discomfort. The first-aider's sensitivity to and support for the patient are essential here.

For male patients, a water bottle usually works well as a urine receptacle. For female patients, a bedpan can be fash-

NATIONAL OUTDOOR LEADERSHIP SCHOOL
FIELD EVACUATION REPORT

Name of Evacuee _____ Course/Section _____

Course Leader_____ Date & Time of Incident _____

SUBJECTIVE: Age____ Sex ____ Location of Patient: Common name _____

Mechanism of Injury/Illness _____

_____

Chief Complaint (OPQRST*) _____

_____

OBJECTIVE: Vital Signs**

Date/Time	LOC	Pulse	RR	Skin	Pupils	T

Signs/Symptoms (patient exam)_____

_____

Allergies_____ Medications _____

Past Medical History _____

Last Oral Intake _____

Events (recent, relevant)_____

ASSESSMENT: Problem list (prioritize)_____

PLAN: Emergency Care Rendered/Changes in Patient's Condition _____

_____

_____

_____

Evacuation Plan (timetable, backup, pickup point)_____

_____

_____

_____

Instructor Signature _____ Date_____ Time _____

*OPQRST = onset, provocation, quality, region/radiation, severity, time sequence.

**LOC = alert×4 (person, place, time, event), verbal, pain, unresponsive; pulse = rate, strength, and rhythm; RR = respiratory rate, depth, and rhythm; skin = color, temperature, moisture; pupils = equality, roundness, reactivity to light; T = temperature.

ioned from a frying pan or a large-mouth water bottle, or an article of clothing can be used as a diaper. Bowel movements can be managed by assisting the patient with an improvised bedpan.

Emotional Support

An ill or injured patient experiences a variety of emotions, including fear about the quality of care and the outcome of the injury or illness, the length of evacuation, loss of control and independence, loss of self-esteem, and embarrassment. To help the patient cope with such roller-coaster feelings, maintain your calm, respond promptly and clearly to questions, and treat the patient with respect and sensitivity.

Respecting your patient means using manners as you would in an average social situation. Introduce yourself, call the patient by name, and ask permission to give treatment. In doing so, you also begin to involve the patient in his or her own care. As you examine and treat the patient, explain your actions. Warn the patient if you might cause pain. Involve the patient in evacuation decisions.

Reassurance, concern, and sympathy are appropriate. It's healthy to allow the patient to discuss the incident. Talking about an accident begins the process of emotional healing. Do not critique the incident or lay blame on any party involved. This will only increase the patient's anxiety and agitation.

Anticipate a lull in your enthusiasm and energy as the initial excitement wears off, fatigue sets in, and you realize the amount of work required to care for and evacuate the patient. These emotions are a reality of rescue. They should not be communicated to the patient as a lack of concern. See chapter 21 ("Stress and the Rescuer") for more on rescue stress.

FINAL THOUGHTS

An incomplete patient assessment—failure to measure vital signs or review history and physical findings—has been the source of unnecessary and needlessly rushed evacuations. Helicopters have flown into wilderness areas for simple knee sprains and for hyperventilation misdiagnosed as a head injury. Rescue teams have hiked through the night expecting to treat serious injuries, only to find a walking patient with minor injuries. Resources are wasted. The patient, rescuers, and expedition members are needlessly put at risk.

Likewise, the same mistake has delayed the evacuation of patients to a physician. Life-threatening fevers have been overlooked because a temperature was not measured. Diabetic complications have been missed because no one asked about the patient's medical history.

There are also many stories of outdoor leaders who, although they lacked medical experience, performed a simple and methodical assessment, checked the ABCs for life-threatening problems, then followed the focused history and exam protocols. They used a checklist, took their time, and made a written record of their findings. The information gathered was the foundation for quality first aid.

SUMMARY:
PATIENT ASSESSMENT

SCENE SIZE-UP: safety, mechanism of injury or illness, number of patients, body substance isolation, and universal precautions

INITIAL ASSESSMENT:
Establishing responsiveness
   Responsiveness: verbal, then pain stimulus
ABCDEs: assess for immediate threats to life
   Airway: open
   Breathing: look, listen, feel
   Circulation: pulse and bleeding
   Disability: cervical spine, jaw thrust, protect spine
   Environment/expose: protect the patient from cold and wet, check for major injury

FOCUSED EXAM AND HISTORY: Complete this assessment after life-threatening problems have been treated.

Head-to-Toe	*Vital Signs*	*Medical History*
Look	LOC	SAMPLE
Listen	Heart rate	AEIOUTIPS
Feel	Skin	Chief complaint
Smell	Respiration	(OPQRST)
Ask	Temperature	
	Pupils	
	Blood pressure	

THE ASSESSMENT:
Review available information
Rule out other possibilities
Prioritize and treat
Review and repeat exam

CHAPTER 2

SHOCK

INTRODUCTION
Shock is a simple name for a complex disorder of the circulatory system. Mid-nineteenth-century descriptions of shock as "a deadly downward spiral" and "a rude unhinging of the machinery of life" accurately portray a condition in which the circulatory system collapses in apparent disproportion to the initial injury. Shock is often the lethal component of burns, serious illness, fractures, injuries to the chest and abdomen, and severe bleeding and catastrophic injury. A first-aider must anticipate, recognize, and treat shock.

THE CIRCULATORY SYSTEM
The circulatory system is composed of the heart, the blood vessels, and the blood. Its primary function is to deliver a constant supply of oxygen to the tissues, and an interruption causes cells and tissues to malfunction and eventually die. The circulatory system also transports carbon dioxide from the cells to the lungs, keeps the electrolyte environment stable, delivers hormones from their source to their place of action, and mobilizes body defenses.

The heart is a two-sided pump that propels blood through a system of pipes (arteries, veins, and capillaries). The right side receives blood from the veins and pumps it through the lungs for oxygen replenishment. The left side pumps the oxygen-rich blood from the lungs to the rest of the body. Blood leaves the heart through arteries, which narrow into smaller vessels called arterioles and eventually become a vast network of microscopic vessels called capillaries.

Capillaries are woven throughout the tissues. The exchange

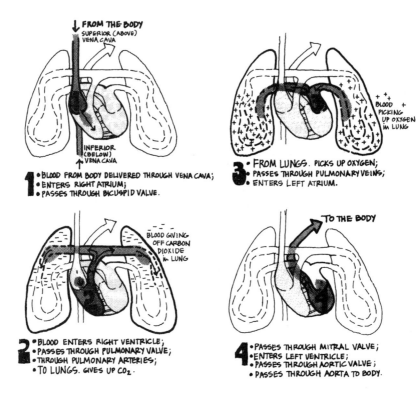

1. • BLOOD FROM BODY DELIVERED THROUGH VENA CAVA;
   • ENTERS RIGHT ATRIUM;
   • PASSES THROUGH BICUSPID VALVE.

2. • BLOOD ENTERS RIGHT VENTRICLE;
   • PASSES THROUGH PULMONARY VALVE;
   • THROUGH PULMONARY ARTERIES;
   • TO LUNGS. GIVES UP CO_2.

3. • FROM LUNGS. PICKS UP OXYGEN;
   • PASSES THROUGH PULMONARY VEINS;
   • ENTERS LEFT ATRIUM.

4. • PASSES THROUGH MITRAL VALVE;
   • ENTERS LEFT VENTRICLE;
   • PASSES THROUGH AORTIC VALVE;
   • PASSES THROUGH AORTA TO BODY.

of nutrients and waste products from the blood to the cells takes place across capillary walls only one cell thick. Blood vessels leaving the capillary beds widen into veins, conduits for blood returning to the heart. The venous blood returns to the right side of the heart and then to the lungs to be replenished with oxygen. The circuit is complete.

The circulatory system adjusts automatically to our energy demands, activity level, position, and temperature. The rate and force of pumping, the diameter of the vessels, and the amount of fluid in the system vary to meet the requirements of exercise, stress, sleep, and relaxation.

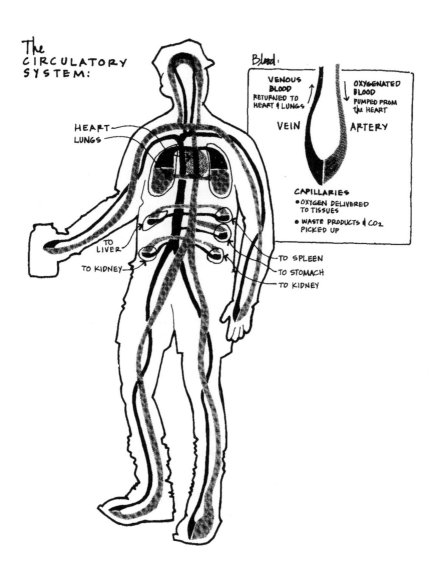

The
CIRCULATORY
SYSTEM:

Blood:

VENOUS
BLOOD
RETURNED TO
HEART & LUNGS

OXYGENATED
BLOOD
PUMPED FROM
the HEART

VEIN   ARTERY

CAPILLARIES
• OXYGEN DELIVERED
  TO TISSUES
• WASTE PRODUCTS & CO_2
  PICKED UP

HEART
LUNGS

TO
LIVER

TO KIDNEY

TO SPLEEN
TO STOMACH
TO KIDNEY

SHOCK

Cardiologist and wilderness medicine specialist Dr. Bruce Paton suggests the following analogy for shock: Imagine the body as a healthy wetland with a river running through lush vegetation. The vegetation depends on the river's flow of pure, unpolluted water and the nutrients it carries. If the river dries up or the water becomes poisoned, the plants shrivel and die. The maintenance of a healthy, well-oxygenated flow of blood through the tissues is called good perfusion.

Shock is the inadequate perfusion of tissue with oxygenated blood. It is a failure of any or all of three basic components of the circulatory system—heart, blood vessels, and blood—to deliver oxygenated blood to the tissues. Insufficient blood flow to the tissues causes inadequate oxygen and nutrient delivery and waste product removal. Shock is a state in which poor perfusion leads first to reversible then irreversible tissue damage. Bodily processes slow, and tissues begin to die.

Causes

Adequate blood pressure, like a healthy river flowing at a proper level into the wetland, is essential to maintaining perfusion of vital organs. Three factors influence blood pressure, and changes in any of them can have serious consequences. The three critical factors are blood volume, cardiac output (the volume of blood pumped per minute by the heart), and the state of constriction or dilation of the blood vessels (peripheral resistance).

CAUSES OF SHOCK

Fluid Loss	Decreased Cardiac Output	Blood Vessel Dilation
Bleeding	Heart attack	Severe infection
Severe infection	Heart injury	Spinal cord injury
Burns		Fainting
Serious diarrhea		

Fluid Loss. Fluid loss is a major cause of shock. The primary causes of fluid loss are bleeding, infections, extensive burns, and metabolic disorders. Massive bleeding results in a reduced blood volume; blood vessels are inadequately filled, and blood pressure falls. Shock can also develop from fluid loss during watery diarrhea, from illness such as diabetes, or from hidden bleeding into fractures of the femur and pelvis.

The average adult has 6 liters of blood. A 10 percent loss (.5 liter) is enough to affect blood pressure. A 25 percent blood volume loss (1.5 liters) can cause moderate shock. A 30 percent loss (2 liters) is considered serious shock.

Decreased Cardiac Output. The heart muscle may become so damaged by a heart attack that it cannot maintain adequate output (pump failure). Shock secondary to a heart attack is referred to as cardiogenic shock.

Blood Vessel Dilation. Dilated blood vessels cause blood pressure and perfusion to decrease despite the extra pumping of the heart in response to the shock. Fainting, a mild form of shock, results when momentary dilation of blood vessels occurs in a person's body as a response to a strong emotional stimulus. As the volume of blood returning to the heart diminishes, blood pressure falls and the person may faint. If a spinal cord injury damages nerves controlling vessel diameter, they may widen and cause shock. Changes in blood vessel diameter, however, are generally not an important cause of shock, except in overwhelming infection in which there is widespread dilation of small vessels.

Assessment

A patient in shock has a rapid pulse rate that may feel weak, irregular, and "thready." The skin is pale, cool, and clammy. These signs and symptoms are due to our "fight or flight" response—our body's response to danger—wherein release of adrenaline increases heart rate, causes the skin to pale and sweat, and causes nausea and restlessness. Blood is routed away from the digestive tract and concentrates around the muscles and essential organs. These changes pump the blood

Assessment for Shock

Rapid and/or weak pulse
Rapid and/or shallow respirations
Dilated pupils
Pale, cool, clammy skin
Anxiety or restlessness
Nausea
Thirst
Changes in level of consciousness

faster, reduce the size of the blood vessels, and route the blood to essential organs, possibly enabling the body to compensate for the shock.

Most people, when frightened, injured, or ill, have a "fight or flight" or acute stress response. Your heart beats strong and fast; you sweat, become pale, and feel nervous. If you're not seriously ill or injured and your circulatory system is healthy, this response should abate in a short time. The heart rate slows, you relax, and the skin returns to its normal color. When you measure a series of vital signs over time, you may see this initial acute stress diminish as you recover from the initial fright. If the circulatory system is unable to adjust, a downward spiral of deterioration may begin in which first tissues, then organs, and finally entire systems fail from lack of oxygen.

A progressively increasing pulse rate is a bad sign, indicating continuing blood loss or increasing shock. The skin becomes sweaty and pale, and the patient looks very ill. The patient may exhibit shallow, rapid breathing and be restless, anxious, irritable, and thirsty. Level of consciousness is variable. If shock prevents the brain from being perfused with oxygen-rich blood, the level of consciousness will deteriorate.

Treatment

Although shock is more likely with multiple injuries, serious illness, severe bleeding, dehydration, or a major fracture, initially you should treat every patient for shock. If the mechanism of injury is not serious and signs and symptoms stabilize or do not deteriorate, the patient is probably experiencing only a stress reaction.

Always assume that shock may occur, and begin treatment before signs and symptoms are manifested. Treatment begins with the triad of basic life support—airway, breathing, and circulation (ABC)—as well as control of bleeding and stabilization of fractures and other injuries. Thereafter, shock treatment moves to a second triad: temperature maintenance, position, and fluids.

Maintain Temperature. Protect the patient from excess heat and cold. Your goal is to maintain body temperature within normal limits. Insulate the patient from the cold ground, provide protection from wind and weather, and remove wet clothes and replace them with dry.

Elevate Legs. Unless the patient has a head injury, or injury to the legs or pelvis prevents it, position the patient with the legs elevated 8 to 10 inches to enhance blood return to the chest and head. Even with apparently minor injuries, this position can be used until you have assessed the problem and ruled out shock.

Treatment for Shock

Airway
Breathing
Circulation
Control bleeding, stabilize
    fractures
Maintain temperature
Elevate legs
Consider fluids

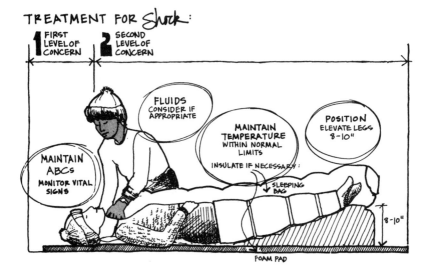

TREATMENT FOR Shock:

1 FIRST LEVEL OF CONCERN 2 SECOND LEVEL OF CONCERN

FLUIDS CONSIDER IF APPROPRIATE

MAINTAIN TEMPERATURE WITHIN NORMAL LIMITS
INSULATE IF NECESSARY: SLEEPING BAG

POSITION ELEVATE LEGS 8-10"

MAINTAIN ABCS MONITOR VITAL SIGNS

8-10"

FOAM PAD

Consider Fluids. If surgery will be necessary within 6 hours, don't give the patient fluids. Fluids may be given if surgery does not seem likely, the patient does not have an altered mental status, there is no abdominal injury, or you are more than 6 hours from the hospital.

When giving fluids by mouth, plain water is adequate. Using one teaspoon of salt per liter is acceptable, as are dilute bouillon drinks. Beware of strongly salty or sweet drinks. Sugar can interfere with the body's absorption of liquid; salt can be nauseating.

Some experts recommend the use of electrolyte drinks. If available, these may be used at half strength. Most electrolyte drinks, however, have a lot of sugar, which can delay absorption of the needed water. The goal is to give the patient fluids, not cause nausea and vomiting.

FINAL THOUGHTS

Shock, an insidious and complicated disturbance in the circulatory system, is difficult to treat in the backcountry. Paramedics, nurses, and physicians in urban medical systems are trained to quickly assess, transport, and use technical medical procedures to fight shock. None of this is available in the wilderness.

The basic treatments of bandages, splints, and physical and emotional support, reinforced by temperature maintenance, position, and fluids, are all assets in the wilderness management of shock. However, the definitive treatment of shock in the backcountry is evacuation.

SUMMARY: SHOCK

The main purpose of the circulatory system, which comprises the heart, blood vessels, and blood, is to supply oxygen to the cells. Shock is the failure of this system to perfuse tissues with oxygen-rich blood.

Causes

Fluid Loss	*Decreased Cardiac Output*	*Blood Vessel Dilation*
Bleeding	Heart attack	Severe infection
Severe infection	Heart injury	Spinal cord injury
Burns		Fainting
Serious diarrhea		

Signs and Symptoms
Rapid and/or weak pulse
Rapid and/or shallow respirations
Dilated pupils
Pale, cool, clammy skin
Anxiety or restlessness
Nausea
Thirst
Changes in level of consciousness

Treatment
ABCs: open and maintain airway
Control bleeding, stabilize fractures
Maintain temperature: insulate, dry, protect from wind
Elevate legs 8 to 10 inches to aid blood return to upper body
Consider fluids: plain water if no imminent surgery

CHAPTER 3

SOFT TISSUE INJURIES

INTRODUCTION

Outside the wilderness, we give little thought to the consequences of soft tissue injuries. Our lives are not disrupted by small wounds, and infection is an unusual aftermath. On NOLS courses, however, backcountry travelers take falls while carrying packs and experience lacerations while preparing meals or walking or swimming barefoot. On an expedition, even relatively minor injuries can have serious consequences. Cut or blistered feet can result in litter evacuations, and hand wounds can end climbing trips. Infection is a real and ever-present risk.

Responding with the proper first aid is essential to expedition members' health and safety. In addition to controlling bleeding, first aid for soft tissue injuries in the wilderness includes cleaning the wound, monitoring for signs of infection, and making decisions about when to evacuate.

SKIN ANATOMY

The skin is the single largest organ of the body. It protects the internal organs by providing a watertight shell that keeps fluids in and bacteria out. The skin helps regulate body temperature by providing a means of heat dissipation. Sweat glands produce sweat, which evaporates, cooling the body. Nerves near the skin's surface send messages to the brain about heat, cold, pressure, pain, and body position.

The skin is composed of three layers. The innermost layer is subcutaneous tissue, which consists mostly of fat. This layer is an insulator for the body and a reservoir for energy. Beneath the subcutaneous tissue lies muscle.

The second layer is the dermis, which contains sweat

glands, sebaceous glands, hair follicles, nerves, and blood vessels. Sweat glands are found on all body surfaces, with most on the palms of the hands and soles of the feet. Sweat glands secrete .5 to 1 liter of sweat per day and can produce up to 1 liter per hour during strenuous exercise. The sebaceous glands produce sebum (oil) and lie next to the hair follicles. Sebum waterproofs the skin and keeps the hair supple. Blood vessels in the dermis provide nutrients and oxygen to each cell and remove waste products such as carbon dioxide.

The outermost layer of the skin is the epidermis. The epidermis is made up primarily of dead cells held together by sebum. These dead cells continually slough off and are replaced by more dead cells.

Soft tissue injuries are classified as open or closed. With closed injuries, the skin remains intact; open injuries involve a break in the skin's surface.

LAYERS OF THE SKIN:

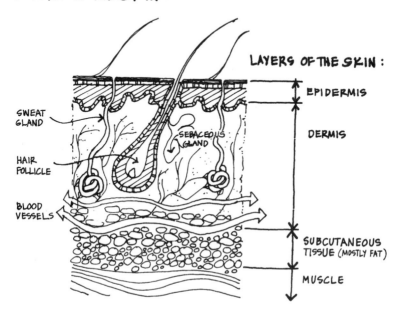

CLOSED INJURIES

Closed injuries include contusions (bruises) and hematomas. With both, the tissue and blood vessels beneath the epidermis are damaged. Swelling and discoloration occur because blood and plasma leak out of the damaged blood vessels. With contusions, blood is dispersed within the tissues. Hematomas contain a pool of blood—as much as a pint surrounding a major bone fracture. Depending on the amount of blood dispersed, reabsorption can take from 12 hours to several days. In some cases, the blood may have to be drained by a physician to enhance healing.

Treatment

A memory aid for treating closed injuries is RICE: rest, ice, compression, and elevation.

Rest. Rest decreases bleeding by allowing clots to form. In the event of a large or deep bruise, extremities can be splinted to decrease motion that may cause newly formed clots to break away and bleeding to continue. See chapter 5 ("Fractures and Dislocations").

Ice. Ice causes the blood vessels to constrict, decreasing bleeding. Never apply ice directly to bare skin, as this can cause frostbite. Instead, wrap the ice in fabric of a towel-like thickness before applying to the skin. Ice the wound for 20 to 40 minutes every 2 to 4 hours for the first 24 to 48 hours.

Compression. Apply manual pressure or a pressure dressing. When applying a pressure dressing, wrap it snugly enough to stop bleeding but not so tightly that the blood supply is shut off. Check by feeling for a pulse distal to the injured site. Check pressure dressings every 20 to 30 minutes for the first 2 hours then every 2 hours thereafter to

---

**Treatment for
Closed Injuries: RICE**

Rest to allow clots to form
Ice 20 to 40 minutes every 2 to 4 hours
Compression to reduce swelling and bleeding
Elevate above heart level

ensure that swelling has not turned the pressure dressing into a tourniquet.

Elevation. Elevate the injury above the level of the heart. Elevation reduces bleeding and swelling by decreasing the blood flow to the injury.

OPEN INJURIES

Open injuries include abrasions, lacerations, puncture wounds, and major traumatic injuries—avulsions, amputations, and crushing wounds.

Abrasions. Abrasions occur when the epidermis and part of the dermis are rubbed off. These injuries are commonly called "road rash" or "rug burns." They usually bleed very little but are painful and may be contaminated with debris.

Abrasions heal more quickly if treated with ointment and covered with a semiocclusive or occlusive dressing.

Lacerations. Lacerations are cuts produced by sharp objects. The cut may penetrate all the layers of the skin, and the edges may be straight or jagged. If long and deep enough to cause the skin to gap, lacerations may require sutures. Sutures are also indicated if the cut is on the face or hands or over a joint, or if it severs a tendon, ligament, or blood vessel. Tendons and ligaments must be sutured together to heal properly. Lacerations on the hands or over a joint may be sutured to prevent the wound from being continually pulled apart by movement. Lacerations on the face are usually sutured to decrease scarring.

Puncture Wounds. Puncture wounds are caused by pointed objects. Although the skin around a puncture wound remains closed and there is little external bleeding, the object may have penetrated an artery or organ, causing internal bleeding.

If an impaled object is through the cheek and causing an airway obstruction, it must be removed to allow the patient to breathe. Otherwise, leave impaled objects in place. Removing the object may cause more soft tissue injury and increase bleeding by releasing pressure on compressed blood vessels.

OPEN INJURIES

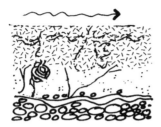

ABRASION
EPIDERMIS / DERMIS
RUBBED OFF.

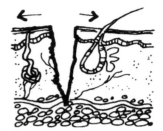

LACERATION
CUTS PRODUCED BY
SHARP OBJECTS.
EDGES CAN BE CLEAN
OR RAGGED.

AVULSION
THE TEARING OFF OF A
FLAP OF SKIN OR ENTIRE
LIMB.

PUNCTURE
POINTED OBJECT
PENETRATES SKIN AND
POSSIBLY AN UNDERLYING
ORGAN OR ARTERY.

Stablilize and prevent movement of impaled objects with protective padding. Some people argue for removal of impaled objects in situations of long or difficult transportation. This advice usually applies to objects in the extremities, not those in the chest, head, belly, or eye. Check with your physician adviser for guidance on this question.

Puncture wounds are difficult—sometimes impossible—to

clean. Depending on the size of the wound, high-pressure irrigation with a syringe of water or 1 percent povidone-iodine may clean some of the debris.

Tetanus is a rare but serious complication. Although tetanus is more likely to occur in a farm or ranch environment than on a "clean" mountainside, it is a good idea to make sure your tetanus booster is up-to-date before you take off into the backcountry. Tetanus boosters should be given at least every 10 years.

Major Traumatic Injuries. Major traumatic injuries include avulsions, amputations, and crushing injuries.

Avulsion. An avulsion is a "tearing off" that can range in severity from a small skin flap to the near amputation of an entire limb. Skin tends to separate along anatomical planes, such as between subcutaneous tissue and muscle.

To treat a small to moderate-sized avulsion, clean the skin flap and reposition it over the wound. Apply small strips of tape or butterfly bandages to the edges, leaving a space between each strip so the wound can drain. If the area avulsed is larger than 2 inches in diameter, a skin graft may be required for the wound to heal properly.

Amputation. Amputation is the complete severance of a part or extremity. Bleeding may be profuse or relatively light. If blood vessels are partially torn, they cannot constrict, and bleeding may be massive. In contrast, the stump of a cleanly severed extremity may not bleed profusely because the severed blood vessels respond by retracting and constricting. If elevation and direct pressure do not stop the stump from bleeding, a tourniquet may be necessary.

After treating the patient, rinse the amputated body part with clean water; wrap it in dry, sterile gauze; and place it in a plastic bag. Then place the bag in cold water or on ice. Do not bury the part in ice, as this may cause cold injury. Make certain that the wrapped part accompanies the patient to the hospital. Reattachment may be possible if you can get to a hospital quickly.

Crushing Injuries. Crushing injuries can cause extensive damage to underlying tissue and bones, and large areas may be lacerated and avulsed. Always consider what underlying body parts may be damaged, and always conduct a focused exam to find out if any bones have been fractured or if an internal organ has been crushed.

Treatment

To protect against any disease that an injured person may be carrying, the Centers for Disease Control and Prevention (CDC) recommend using rubber or latex gloves when touching blood, body fluid, mucous membranes, or any nonintact skin or when handling any items or surfaces that are soiled by blood or body fluid.

Control Bleeding. Controlling bleeding is the first priority when treating open wounds. Death can come quickly to a patient with a tear in a major blood vessel. There are four methods for controlling bleeding. The most effective—direct pressure and elevation—will stop most bleeding when used in combination. Pressure points and tourniquets are also used.

Direct Pressure. The best method for controlling bleeding is to apply pressure over the wound site. Using your hand and a piece of wadded fabric—preferably sterile gauze—apply direct pressure to the wound. Be sure to wear rubber or latex gloves or place your hand in a plastic bag. If the wound is large, you may need to pack the open area with gauze before applying pressure. Maintain pressure for 5 minutes, then slowly release. If the bleeding resumes, apply pressure for 15 minutes.

Elevation. As with closed injuries, the combination of splinting, a pressure dressing, and elevation will help decrease the bleeding. Direct pressure and elevation control almost all bleeding. In fact, it is unusual for a wound to require the first-aider to utilize pressure points or a tourniquet.

Controlling Bleeding

Direct pressure
Elevation
Pressure points
Tourniquets

Pressure Points. Pressure points are areas on the body where arteries lie close to the skin and over bones. Pressure applied to the artery at one of

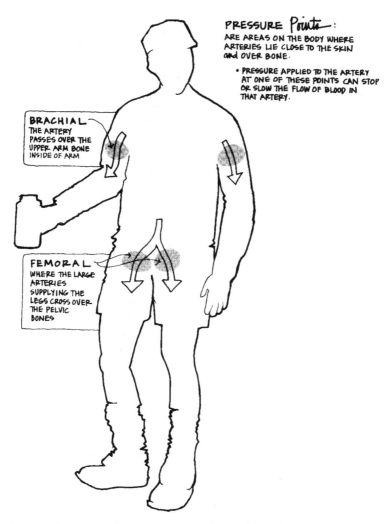

PRESSURE Points:
ARE AREAS ON THE BODY WHERE
ARTERIES LIE CLOSE TO THE SKIN
and OVER BONE.

• PRESSURE APPLIED TO THE ARTERY
AT ONE OF THESE POINTS CAN STOP
OR SLOW THE FLOW OF BLOOD IN
THAT ARTERY.

BRACHIAL
THE ARTERY
PASSES OVER THE
UPPER ARM BONE
INSIDE OF ARM

FEMORAL
WHERE THE LARGE
ARTERIES
SUPPLYING THE
LEGS CROSS OVER
THE PELVIC
BONES

these points can slow or stop the flow of blood in that artery, thereby reducing bleeding at the site of the injury. Pressure on these points is rarely effective by itself and is usually applied in conjunction with other techniques.

Tourniquets. Apply a tourniquet only as a last resort, when no other method will stop the bleeding. Tourniquets completely stop the blood flow, and if the tourniquet is left on

How to Apply a Tourniquet

1. Once you've determined that a tourniquet is necessary, apply it above the elbow or knee, as close to the injury as possible, between the wound and the heart. Use a bandage that is 3 to 4 inches wide and 6 to 8 layers thick. Never use wire, rope, or any material that will cut the skin.
2. Wrap the bandage snugly around the extremity several times, then tie an overhand knot.
3. Place a small stick or similar object on the knot, and tie another overhand knot over the stick.
4. Twist the stick until the bandage becomes tight enough to stop the bleeding. Tie the ends of the bandage around the extremity to keep the twists from unraveling.
5. Using a pen, write "TK" on the patient's forehead and the time the tourniquet was applied. Once it is in place, do not remove the tourniquet. It should remain in place until the patient arrives at the emergency room.
6. In wilderness situations some experts suggest slowly releasing the tourniquet after 45–60 minutes. If bleeding has stopped, the tourniquet many no longer be necessary. Check with your physician adviser about this issue.

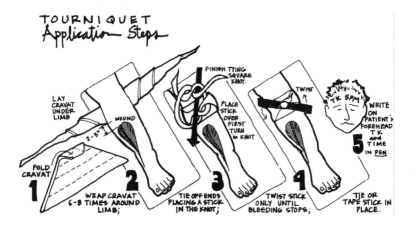

TOURNIQUET
Application Steps

for more than a few hours, there is a chance that the tissue distal to the tourniquet will die and the extremity may require amputation.

Clean the Wound. Consider any wound, even a minor finger cut or a blister, as potentially infected. On wilderness expeditions wound cleaning is a priority. When you clean a wound, you eliminate as much potentially infectious bacteria and debris as possible without further damaging the skin.

Wash Your Hands and Put on Gloves. Wash your hands. Use soap and water to prevent contamination of the wound. Put on rubber or latex gloves.

Scrub and Irrigate the Wound. Scrub the skin around the wound, being careful not to flush debris into the wound. Clip long hair, but don't shave the skin. Then scrub or irrigate an open wound for at least 3 minutes with water that has been disinfected with chlorination or iodination, water that has been boiled and cooled, or 1 percent povidone-iodine (usually one part 10 percent povidone-iodine diluted with 10 parts water to approximate the color of dark tea). Medical science tells us that the volume of water is the most important factor in cleaning the wound. At NOLS, we carry 35cc syringes in the first aid kit for pressure-irrigating wounds. Plastic bags or water bottles with pinholes can work as improvised irrigation syringes. Try to remove all debris even if this requires some

---

Cleaning Wounds

Wash your hands with soap and water	Rinse thoroughly with disinfected water
Put on rubber or latex gloves	Dress and bandage the wound
Scrub and irrigate the wound	Check circulation, sensation, and movement
Scrub the area around the wound	
Use sterilized tweezers to remove debris	
Use pressure irrigation	

painful scrubbing. Remove large pieces of debris with tweezers that have been boiled or cleaned with povidone-iodine.

Rinse with Disinfected Water. After cleaning the wound, rinse off the solution with liberal amounts of disinfected water. See chapter 17 ("Hygiene and Water Disinfection"). Check underneath the patient to make sure that he or she is not lying in a pool of solution, as prolonged exposure to the solution can cause burning. Also check for further bleeding— you may need to apply direct pressure again if blood clots were broken loose during the cleaning process.

Dress and Bandage the Wound. Dressings are sterile gauze placed directly over the wound; bandages hold the dressing in place. Both come in many shapes and sizes. Semi-occlusive (Telfa) or occlusive (Second Skin, Opsite, Tegaderm) dressings promote healing by keeping the area moist. Ointments (such as Polysporin or Bacitracin) serve the same purpose. Dry dressings that adhere to the wound impede the healing process.

Next, apply an antibiotic ointment. The ointment should be applied to the dressing rather than directly to the wound. This avoids contaminating the remaining antibiotic in the tube or bottle. Apply the bandage neatly and in such a way that blood flow distal to the injured area is not impaired. After applying the bandage, check the pulse distal to the injury.

Do not close wound edges until the wound has been thoroughly cleaned. Generally, the edges of a small wound will come together on their own. If the skin is stretched apart, butterfly bandages or Steri-strips can hold the edges together. If the injury is over a joint, the extremity may require splinting to prevent the edges from pulling apart. Highly contaminated wounds should be packed open.

Physicians don't agree on how long a wound can be kept open until it is stitched. A wound that will not close on its own or with a bandage can usually be stitched even a day or two later. The need to use sutures to close a wound does not, by itself, create an emergency. Reasons to expedite an evacuation for an open wound include obvious dirt or contamination; animal bites; wounds that open joint spaces; established infection; wounds from a crushing mechanism; any laceration to a cosmetic area, especially the face; wounds with a lot of dead tissue on the edges or in the wound itself; and wounds that obviously need surgical care, such as open fractures and very deep, gaping lacerations.

After the Bandage Is Applied. Check circulation, sensation, and movement of the body part distal to the injury. Can the patient tell you where you are touching? Can he or she flex and extend the extremity? Is the area distal to the injury pink and warm, indicating good blood perfusion? Any negative answers to these questions may indicate nerve, artery, or tendon damage that will require evacuating the patient.

If a dressing becomes soaked with blood, leave it in place and apply additional dressings. Removing the dressing disturbs the blood clots that are forming. After bleeding has been controlled, dressings should be changed daily and the injured area checked for signs of infection.

Infection. Redness, swelling, pus, heat, and pain at the site; faint red streaks radiating from the site; fever; chills;

Infection

Signs	Indications for Evacuation
Redness and swelling	Fever, chills, swollen lymph
Pus, heat, pain	nodes
Red streaks radiating from the	Red streaks radiating away from
wound	wound
Fever and chills	Wound cannot be opened to
Swollen lymph nodes	drain

Treatment for Infected Wounds

Pull wound edges apart and
clean wound
Soak in warm antiseptic solution

and swollen lymph nodes are all signs of infection. Drawing a circle around the red area with a pen will help you determine whether the infection is spreading or resolving.

An infection that is localized to the site of the injury can be treated in the field. If the edges of the wound are closed, pull them apart and soak the area in warm antiseptic solution or warm water for 20 to 30 minutes three to four times a day. If the infection starts to spread—as evidenced by fever, chills, swollen lymph nodes, or faint red streaks radiating from the site—or if the wound cannot be opened to drain, evacuate the patient.

Blisters. Blisters—a common backcountry occurrence— can be debilitating. Blisters are caused by friction and occur in areas where the epidermis is thick and tough enough to resist abrasion. At first there is a red, sore area called a "hot spot." If the friction continues, the epidermis separates and fluid enters the space, causing a blister.

The First Step: Prevention. Prevent blisters by making sure boots fit properly, wearing two pairs of socks to decrease friction on the skin, checking feet frequently at rest breaks, and stopping at the first sign of rubbing. Apply a solid piece of moleskin or athletic tape to areas that you suspect may cause problems.

Hot Spots. Cut a doughnut-shaped piece of moleskin and center it over the hot spot as a buffer against further rubbing.

Small Blisters. If a small blister has already developed, cut a doughnut-shaped piece of molefoam and center it over the blister. The doughnut "hole" prevents the adhesive from sticking to the tender blister and ripping it away when the molefoam is changed.

Larger Blisters. If the blister is nickel-sized or larger, drain it. Begin by carefully washing your hands and putting on rubber or latex gloves. Clean the area around the blister to decrease the risk of infection. Use a needle that has been soaked in an antiseptic solution such as povidone-iodine for 3 minutes or has been heated until it glows red, then cooled. Insert the needle at the base of the blister, allowing the fluid to drain from the pinprick. After draining the blister, apply an antibiotic ointment and cover the area with gauze. As with an intact blister, center a doughnut-shaped piece of molefoam over the drained blister and gauze. Follow up by checking the blister every day for signs of infection.

FINAL THOUGHTS
Most bleeding can be stopped by using pressure and elevation. Wounds should be aggressively cleaned with povidone-iodine and irrigated with copious amounts of disinfected water. Monitor wounds for signs and symptoms of infection.

**SUMMARY:
SOFT TISSUE INJURIES**

CONTROLLING BLEEDING
Direct pressure
Elevation
Pressure points
Tourniquets

TREATMENT OF SOFT TISSUE INJURIES
Closed Injuries: RICE
Rest to allow clots to form
Ice 20 to 40 minutes every 2 to 4 hours
Compression to reduce swelling and bleeding
Elevate above heart level

Open Injuries
Stop bleeding
Assess damage
Clean the wound
Dress and bandage
Monitor for signs of infection

• *CONTINUED* •

SUMMARY:
SOFT TISSUE INJURIES *(continued)*

Cleaning Wounds
Wash hands with soap and water
Put on rubber or latex gloves
Scrub and irrigate the wound
   Scrub the area around the wound
    Use sterilized tweezers to remove debris
    Use pressure irrigation
Rinse thoroughly with disinfected water
Cover with antibiotic ointment
Dress and bandage the wound
Check circulation, sensation, and movement

Signs of Infection
Redness and swelling
Pus, heat, pain
Red streaks radiating from the wound
Fever and chills
Swollen lymph nodes

Treatment of Infected Wounds
Pull wound edges apart and clean wound
Soak in warm antiseptic solution

Indications for evacuation
   Fever, chills, swollen lymph nodes
   Red streaks radiating from wound
   Wound cannot be opened to drain

CHAPTER 4

BURNS AND LIGHTNING INJURIES

INTRODUCTION

Burns are infrequent injuries on NOLS courses, but the potential for serious burns from the sun, fires, stoves, and lanterns is great. Improper stove use has caused stoves to flare or pressure caps to release and flame, burning unwary cooks. People have tripped and fallen into fires. The most serious burns experienced on NOLS courses have been caused by spilled hot water. Chemical burns may occur from spilled gas or carbide from carbide lamps.

Minor burns may be no more than a trivial nuisance, yet they represent a potential site of infection. Burns of joints, feet, hands, face, and genitalia, however, can impair these complex structures. A large burn causes significant loss of fluid and may rapidly cause shock. Severe burns of an entire limb are potentially lethal.

TYPES OF BURNS

There are four types of burns: thermal, chemical, radiation, and electrical.

Thermal Burns

Thermal burns are caused by flames, flashes of heat (as in explosions), hot liquids, or contact with hot objects. The degree of associated tissue death depends on the intensity of the heat and the length of exposure. Water at 140°F (59°C) will burn skin in 5 seconds; water at 120°F (48°C) in five minutes.

Chemical Burns

Chemical burns are caused by contact with alkalis, acids, or corrosive material. Backcountry chemical burns are rare, but burns from leaking batteries or spilled gas are a possibility.

Radiation and Electrical Burns

Electrical burns in the wilderness are caused by lightning. The most common burn in the wilderness is a radiation burn, or sunburn.

ASSESSING BURNS

The assessment of a burn includes the depth and extent of the injury.

Depth of the Burn

Burns are classified as superficial, or first-degree; partial-thickness, or second-degree; and full-thickness, or third-degree burns.

Superficial. First-degree burns injure only the epidermis. A first-degree burn is red and painful and blanches white with pressure. There are no blisters, and the wound can be painful. The area heals in 4 or 5 days with the epidermis peeling.

Partial-Thickness Burns. Second-degree burns injure both the epidermis and the dermis and can be extremely painful. The skin appears red, mottled, wet, and blistered and blanches white with pressure. Blisters can develop quickly after the injury or may take as long as 24 hours to form. The burn takes from 5 to 25 days to heal, and longer if it becomes infected.

Full-Thickness Burns. Third-degree burns injure the epidermis, dermis, and subcutaneous tissue. The skin appears leathery, charred, pearl gray, and dry. The area is sunken and has a burned odor. The skin does not blanch and is not painful because blood vessels and nerve ending are destroyed. Painful first- or second-degree burns may surround the third-degree area. Full-thickness burns destroy the dermis and, if large, require skin grafts to heal.

Extent of the Burn: The Rule of Palms

The extent of burns can be determined by the Rule of Palms. The patient's palm represents 1 percent of his or her body

ASSESSMENT of BURNS:

SUPERFICIAL
EPIDERMIS ONLY BURNED
- SKIN RED, PAINFUL

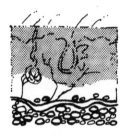

PARTIAL THICKNESS
EPIDERMIS AND DERMIS BURNED
- SKIN BLISTERED (MAY TAKE 24 HOURS+)
- RED, MOTTLED, WET, PAINFUL

FULL THICKNESS
EPIDERMIS, DERMIS <u>AND</u>
SUBCUTANEOUS TISSUE BURNED
- LEATHERY, DRY, CHARRED
- PEARLY GRAY in COLOR

The "RULE OF PALMS"

A PERSON'S PALM REPRESENTS
ROUGHLY 1% OF HIS BODY SURFACE.
USE THIS ESTIMATE TO DETERMINE
THE EXTENT AND SEVERITY OF BURNS.

surface area. Using the palm as a size indicator, estimate the percentage of body area involved.

TREATING BURNS

Thermal, electrical, radiational, and chemical burns are all treated essentially the same way. The source of the burn must be eliminated. If indicated, the airway should be checked. Then the burn itself is cooled, assessed, cleaned, and dressed. The guidelines presented in this chapter under final thoughts will help you determine whether the depth and extent of the burn call for evacuation and, if so, with how much urgency.

Thermal Burns

Put Out the Fire!. "Stop, drop, and roll" is the sequence to follow if someone catches on fire. Stop the person from running (which provides oxygen that keeps the fire burning). Make him or her drop to the ground and roll, or roll the person in a sleeping bag or jacket to put out the flames.

Quickly remove the patient's clothing and any jewelry. These retain heat and cause continued burning. Hot water spilled on legs clothed in polypropylene or wool can cause serious burns, as can water spilled into boots, because the boot and sock retain and concentrate the heat on the ankle.

Treatment for Burns	
Remove the source of the burn	Assess the airway
For thermal burns, stop, drop, roll	For inhalation burns, consider carbon monoxide poisoning
For dry chemical burns, brush off dry chemicals	Cool the burn
For wet chemical burns, flush with water for 20 minutes	Assess the depth and extent of the burn
Remove clothing and jewelry	Clean the burn
	Apply a cool, moist dressing

Check the Airway. If the patient is not breathing, begin artificial respiration. Check the pulse. If there is no pulse, start CPR.

Cool the Burn. After removing clothing, pour cool water (not ice-cold) or apply cool, wet cloths on the burned site. No more than 10 percent of the body should be cooled at one time, as cooling introduces the risk of hypothermia. Never put ice directly on the site, as it may cause frostbite. Ice also causes blood vessels to constrict, which deprives the burned area of blood and thus oxygen and nutrients.

Assess the Depth and Extent of the Burn. Most burns are combinations of partial- and full-thickness injuries. Assess the surface area of each burn type using the Rule of Palms.

Clean and Dress the Burn. Clean the burn with cool, clean water and apply antibiotic ointment. Embers or smoldering clothing on the surface should be removed; do not attempt to remove melted material from the skin. Dress it with a moist dressing. Keep the dressing moist with disinfected water, change the dressing once a day, and monitor the site for signs of infection. Blisters should be kept intact. If they do rupture, gently wash them with antiseptic soap and water, rinse well, pat dry, apply an antibiotic ointment, and cover with sterile gauze.

Inhalation Burns

Inhalation burns are caused by breathing hot air or gases and/or particles. The cilia (hairlike structures lining the upper airways) and mucous membranes lining the respiratory tract may be destroyed instantly. The mucous membranes swell, and fluid leaks into the lungs. The body is unable to expel mucus because the cilia are damaged. Mucus collects in the upper airway, decreasing carbon dioxide and oxygen exchange. Oxygenation is impaired when carbon monoxide from burning material competes with oxygen for binding sites on red blood cells.

If you suspect an inhalation burn, check the mouth, nose, and throat for signs of soot, redness, or swelling. Are the facial hairs or nasal hairs singed? Check for signs of respiratory distress, such as coughing or noisy, rapid breaths.

Other symptoms of inhalation burns include headache, weakness, nausea, vomiting, loss of manual dexterity, confusion, and lethargy. Carbon monoxide poisoning must be suspected in a patient with inhalation burns. A cherry red coloring to the skin is a very late sign of carbon monoxide poisoning and may not occur until after the person has died. Using stoves in tents or snow caves can cause carbon monoxide poisoning.

Inhalation burns always require that the patient be evacuated to a medical facility. Signs and symptoms of respiratory distress may not become apparent for 24 to 48 hours.

Chemical Burns

Flush chemical burns with any available water for a minimum of 20 minutes. Brush off any dry chemical before rinsing the burn. Remove clothing, jewelry, and contact lenses, as these may retain the chemical and continue to burn the victim.

Speed is important. The longer a chemical stays on the body, the more damage it causes. Looking for specific antidotes wastes time. Use plain water to flush, then wash the burn with mild soap and water.

Rinse a chemically burned eye with water for at least 20 minutes. After flushing the affected eye, cover it with a moist dressing. After 20 to 30 minutes, remove the dressing. If the patient complains of changes in vision, reapply the dressing and evacuate.

Radiation Burns

Most skin damage is caused by short wavelengths of ultraviolet radiation (UVA and UVB). UVB causes more sunburn than UVA, but both wavelengths damage skin. The only known beneficial effect of solar radiation on skin is in the metabolism of vitamin D. Long-term exposure to the sun increases your risk of skin cancer.

Two-thirds of ultraviolet radiation is received during the

hours of 10:00 A.M. to 2:00 P.M. At high altitude, the thin atmosphere filters out less ultraviolet radiation, and the skin is damaged more quickly. Snowfields reflect 70 to 85 percent of the ultraviolet radiation. Water reflects 2 percent when the sun is directly overhead, and more when the sun is lower. Finally, grass reflects 1 to 2 percent. Mountaineering at high altitudes, especially on snow, increases the risk of sun-related problems. Clouds filter out infrared heat radiation, and your skin feels cooler, but ultraviolet radiation still passes through and the risk of sun exposure still exists.

Sunburn. People with fair skin, usually blonds and redheads, are susceptible to burning. Darker skin contains more of the protective pigment melanin but does not eliminate the chance of sunburn or provide protection against the cumulative effects of sun exposure.

Unprotected skin can receive first- or second-degree burns from the sun. Fever blisters or cold sores often follow sunburn of the lips. These are herpes simplex (viral) infections and can be quite painful. A patient with extensive sunburn may complain of chills, fever, or headache.

Phototoxic Reactions. A phototoxic reaction is an abnormally severe sunburn related to the ingestion of a drug, plant, or chemical or the application of a drug, plant, or chemical to the skin. Certain drugs, such as sulfonamides (Bactrim, Septra), tetracyclines (Vibramycin), oral diabetic agents, and tranquilizers (Thorazine, Compazine, Phenergan, Sparine), increase the skin's sensitivity to sunlight.

Treatment of Sunburned Skin. Cold, wet dressings will relieve some of the pain. Aspirin, ibuprofen, or related nonsteroidal anti-inflammatory drugs are recommended. Anesthetic sprays and ointments may relieve the pain but increase the risk of a phototoxic reaction.

Sunscreens. Exposure to the sun in small doses promotes tanning, which protects the skin from burns. Unfortunately, degenerative changes still occur in the skin, so it is best to use sunscreens or sunblocks and to wear broad-brimmed hats, long-sleeve shirts, and long pants.

Tips for Preventing Sun-Related Injury: Don't Sunburn!

1. Apply sunscreen 30 minutes before going out, and reapply it frequently.
2. Apply sunblock to your lips, nose, and other sensitive areas.
3. Wear a hat with a brim.
4. Wear sunglasses with 100 percent UV protection, even on cloudy days.
5. Minimize sun exposure between 10 A.M. and 3 P.M.
6. Wear a long-sleeve shirt and pants.
7. Examine your skin, and see a physician if you notice a mole changing shape, color, or size or if you have a "sore" that won't heal.

Sunscreens are rated by their sun protection factor (SPF). The SPF number is a guideline for the length of time a person wearing the sunscreen can spend in the sun. SPF is based on the minimal "erythemal dose," or the length of time before the exposed skin becomes red. For example, a person without sunscreen may be able to spend 30 minutes safely in the sun. Applying a sunscreen with an SPF of 10 should allow the same person to spend 10 times as long in the sun, or 300 minutes, before the skin turns red. This system assumes that the sunscreen is not washed off by water or sweat and is used in adequate amounts.

Creams that completely block ultraviolet radiation (zinc oxide, A-Fil, red veterinarian petrolatum) are good for areas that are easily burned, such as the nose, ears, and lips. Use a sunscreen that guards against both UVB and UVA radiation—the label should explain the coverage of the sunscreen. Sunscreens should be applied on cloudy or overcast days as well as on sunny ones. The ultraviolet radiation that penetrates cloud cover is often great enough to burn the skin. Sunscreens work better if applied when the skin is warm and allowed to soak in half an hour before sun exposure. It's a good habit to apply sunscreen well before you are exposed.

Snow Blindness. Burning of the cornea and conjunctiva by the sun is called snow blindness. Affected people aren't actually blind, but they're reluctant to open their eyes because of the pain. The eyes feel dry, as if they are full of sand. Moving, blinking, or opening the eyes is painful. The eyes are red and tear excessively. This can happen with as little as an hour exposure to bright sunlight. Symptoms may not develop for 8 to 12 hours after the eyes have been exposed to the sun.

Treatment. Snow blindness heals spontaneously in several days. Cold compresses, pain medication, and a dark environment relieve the pain. Don't rub the eyes or put anesthetics in the eyes. These can damage the cornea.

Sunglasses, especially those with side blinders, decrease the ultraviolet radiation received by the eyes and prevent snow blindness. If you lose your sunglasses, make temporary ones from two pieces of cardboard with slits cut in them to see through. Wear sunglasses on cloudy or overcast days as well as sunny days.

LIGHTNING INJURIES
Lightning is the only significant cause of backcountry electrical burns. According to the Centers for Disease Control, there are 100 deaths per year in the United States and approximately 1,000 injuries.

Types of Injuries
Injuries can occur from the high voltage (200 to 300 million volts), secondary heat production, or the explosive force of the lightning. A person can be injured by lightning in five ways:
1. Direct hit: Actually being struck by lightning.
2. Lightning "splash": Lightning hits another object and splashes onto objects or people standing nearby.
3. Direct transmission: Being in contact with an object that has been hit directly.
4. Ground current: Receiving the ground current as it dissipates from the object that has been hit.
5. Blunt trauma from the explosive force of the shock wave.

Most victims are splashed by lightning or hit by ground current. Very few people actually sustain a direct hit. Although a direct hit can deliver 200 to 300 million volts, the duration is short (1 to 100 milliseconds), and severe burns are uncommon. More likely, a person will suffer internal injuries (cardiac arrest, damage to the brain and spinal cord) and fractures from shock waves.

Lightning burns form distinctive patterns. Linear burns follow areas of heavy sweat concentration. A linear burn may begin beneath the breasts, travel from the sternum to the abdomen, then split down both legs; or it may follow the midaxillary line (an imaginary line drawn through the middle of the armpit to the waist).

Lightning-caused punctate burns are circular, ranging in size from a few millimeters to a centimeter in diameter. Also, featherlike patterns may be caused by electron showers that leave imprints on the skin. Most lightning burns are first- or second-degree, with some of the punctate burns being third-degree.

Most lightning burns are superficial, but lightning strikes may throw victims a considerable distance, causing head and spinal injuries, dislocations, fractures, and blunt chest and abdominal trauma. The respiratory center in the brain may also be injured, causing respiratory and cardiac arrest.

Lightning knocks 72 percent of its victims unconscious. Of

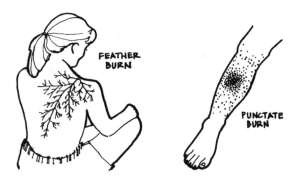

FEATHER BURN

PUNCTATE BURN

those, 66 percent suffer temporary lower extremity paralysis, 33 percent suffer upper extremity paralysis, and 50 percent have one or both eardrums ruptured. Other signs and symptoms are confusion, amnesia, temporary deafness or blindness, and mottling of the skin. Pulses may decrease or disappear in the lower extremities due to injury-induced spasms of the blood vessels.

Treat cardiac arrest with CPR. The heart may restart beating before respirations begin. Artificial respiration may need to be continued due to paralysis of the respiratory center in the brain.

How to Prevent Lightning Injuries

Remember: Lightning usually hits the tallest object in the area, and water conducts electricity, therefore:

Don't stand under the only tall object in the area. It is better to be in a large group of trees than under the only tree out in the open.

Don't stay at or near the top of peaks or ridges. Head down as quickly as possible.

Don't hide in shallow caves or stand at the entrance of a cave, as you may be in the path of the electrical current.

Avoid being the tallest object near a body of water.

Get out of water and off wet ground. Don't swim!

Get away from objects that conduct electricity (ice axes, tent poles).

Watch for hair standing on end and a blue ring around objects (Saint Elmo's fire). Listen for high-pitched "zinging" sounds. These indicate that a strike is imminent. Leave the area immediately.

Squat down with your feet facing downhill, keep your hands off the ground (to avoid ground current going through you), or sit on something dry and nonconducting (foamlite pad, rope, day pack).

Stay alert to local weather patterns and cloud buildup. In the Rocky Mountains, the afternoons are generally more dangerous than the mornings.

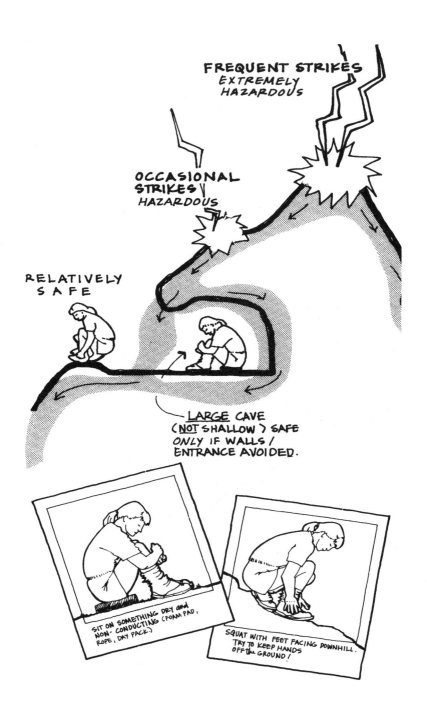

FREQUENT STRIKES
EXTREMELY
HAZARDOUS

OCCASIONAL
STRIKES
HAZARDOUS

RELATIVELY
SAFE

LARGE CAVE
(NOT SHALLOW) SAFE
ONLY IF WALLS /
ENTRANCE AVOIDED.

SIT ON SOMETHING DRY and
NON-CONDUCTING (FOAM PAD,
ROPE, DAY PACK.)

SQUAT WITH FEET FACING DOWNHILL.
TRY TO KEEP HANDS
OFF the GROUND!

LIGHTNING *Safety*

DANGER FROM GROUND CURRENTS
HAZARDOUS
GRAY SHADING & ARROWS SHOW
PROBABLE FLOW.

RELATIVELY
SAFE

FINAL THOUGHTS

The American Burn Association and the American College of Surgeons classify burns by depth and extent.

Minor burns:

Partial-thickness burns of less than 15 percent of the body

Full-thickness burns of less than 2 percent of the body and not involving the hands, feet, face, or groin

Moderate burns:

Partial-thickness burns of 15 to 25 percent of the body

Full-thickness burns of less than 10 percent of the body and not involving the hands, feet, face, or groin

Major burns:

Partial-thickness burns of more than 25 percent of the body

Full-thickness burns of more than 10 percent of the body

Partial- or full-thickness burns involving the hands, feet, face, or groin

These guidelines provide a useful reference for deciding whether a patient can be treated in the field or should be evacuated. Patients with moderate and major burns should be quickly evacuated to a physician for further evaluation. Minor burns should also be seen by a physician, but unless they are complicated by shock or infection, the evacuation need not be hurried. Infection is a risk when treating minor burns in the field. Burns, like other soft tissue wounds, must be kept clean to reduce the risk of infection.

A patient with burns of the face may also have inhalation burns. Partial- and full-thickness burns of the hands and feet may require special treatment to preserve function, and burns of the groin may produce enough swelling to prevent urination. Burns completely encircling a limb may cut off circulation.

Burns are serious injuries, more easily prevented than treated. Keep safety in mind at all times, especially when around fires and stoves and when lightning develops.

Clothing is portable shade and a simple sunburn prevention method. A brimmed hat shades the face and neck. Long-sleeve shirts and pants protect skin from the sun. Develop the habit of putting on sunscreen early and often.

BURNS AND LIGHTNING INJURIES

TYPES OF BURNS
Thermal: flames, flashes of heat, hot liquids
Electrical: lightning
Chemical: alkalis, acids, corrosives
Radiation: sunlight

ASSESSMENT OF BURNS
Assess Depth
Superficial or first-degree: affect only the epidermis; the skin is red and painful
Partial-thickness or second-degree: injures the epidermis and dermis; the skin is mottled, wet, blistered, and painful
Full-thickness or third-degree: affect the epidermis, dermis, and subcutaneous tissues; the skin is leathery, charred, pearl gray, and dry; the area is sunken, has a burned odor, and is often not painful
Assess Extent
Rules of Palms

TREATMENT OF BURNS
Remove the source of the burn
    For thermal burns, stop, drop, and roll
    For dry chemical burns, brush off the chemicals
    For wet chemical burns, flush with water for 20 minutes
    Remove clothing and jewelry
Assess the airway
Cool the burn
Assess the depth and extent of the burn
Clean and dress the burn
For Lightning Injuries
    Assess the ABCs
    Institute CPR and rescue breathing as necessary
    Assess for traumatic injury

CHAPTER 5

FRACTURES
AND DISLOCATIONS

INTRODUCTION

As recently as 90 years ago, a fractured femur was a deadly injury. First aid was nonexistent, and broken bone ends often did not heal. Open fractures frequently became infected, and amputation was a common unpleasant consequence. Modern emergency medicine, especially assessment and splinting in the field, has reduced these complications.

Fractures and dislocations are infrequent at NOLS, making up less than 3 percent of our field safety incidents. Among the general public, however, fractures and dislocations make up as much as 20 percent of reported wilderness injuries. NOLS instructors have cared for femur fractures in the remote backcountry of Yellowstone Park in the winter and at 16,000 feet on Denali. They've expertly splinted uncomplicated wrist fractures and walked patients as far as 20 miles out of the wilderness. They've accurately diagnosed a complicated elbow fracture requiring a helicopter evacuation.

THE SKELETAL SYSTEM

A bony skeleton shapes the body. From this scaffolding hang the soft tissues: the vital organs, blood vessels, muscles, fat, and skin. The skeleton is strong to support and protect internal organs, flexible to withstand stress, and jointed to allow for movement.

Bone is living tissue combined with nonliving intracellular components. The nonliving components contain calcium and make bone rigid. Bones are connected by ligaments and connective tissue. An adult has 206 bones, ranging in size from the femur, or thigh bone—the largest—to the tiny ossicles of the inner ear.

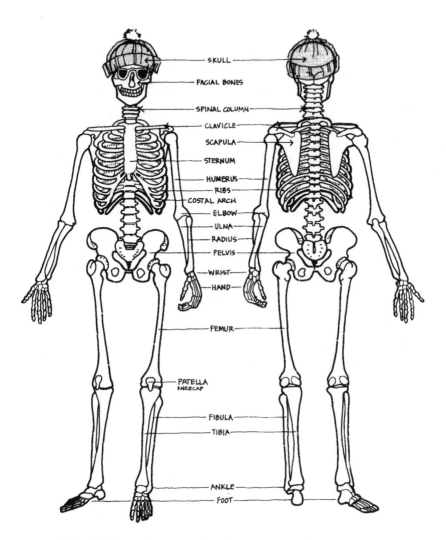

The skeleton has axial and appendicular components. The axial bones are the pelvis, spinal column, ribs, and skull. Injuries to these structures—except for pelvic fractures—are discussed in the chest and head injury chapters. This chapter covers injuries to the appendicular skeleton: the arms and legs.

The upper extremity consists of the scapula, or shoulder blade; the clavicle, or collarbone; the upper arm bone, or humerus; two bones in the forearm, the radius on the thumb side and the ulna on the little finger side; and 22 bones in the wrist and fingers.

The lower extremity consists of the pelvis; the thighbone, or femur; a small bone in front of the knee, the patella; two bones in the lower leg, the tibia and fibula; and 26 bones in the ankle and foot.

Bones connect at joints. Some joints are fixed; others allow movement. Joints are held together by ligaments, connective tissue, and muscle. Joint surfaces are covered with cartilage to reduce friction, and joint fluid lubricates them for smooth movement.

FRACTURES AND DISLOCATIONS

A fracture is a break in a bone. Fractures can be open or closed. With open fractures, the skin is broken, exposing the bone to contamination. Closed fractures are covered with intact muscle and skin.

Fractures can also be described as transverse, spiral, oblique, or crushed, referring to the type of fracture. This

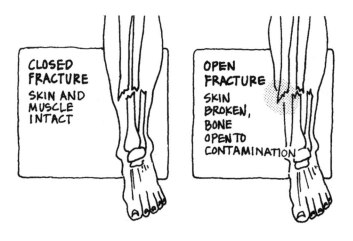

CLOSED FRACTURE SKIN AND MUSCLE INTACT

OPEN FRACTURE SKIN BROKEN, BONE OPEN TO CONTAMINATION

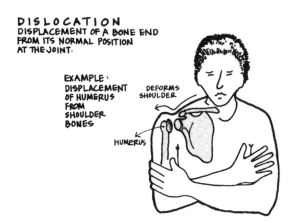

DISLOCATION
DISPLACEMENT OF A BONE END
FROM ITS NORMAL POSITION
AT THE JOINT.

EXAMPLE:
DISPLACEMENT
OF HUMERUS
FROM
SHOULDER
BONES

DEFORMS
SHOULDER

HUMERUS

information is usually obtained from an x ray and has little effect on first aid.

Fractures, in addition to causing pain, loss of function, and swelling, can be complicated by infection and damage to blood vessels and nerves. Fractured bone ends can pinch or sever blood vessels, blocking circulation or causing bleeding. Fractures of large, long bones, such as the femur, humerus, or pelvis, are often accompanied by blood loss that can cause life-threatening shock. Infection is a potentially severe complication of an open fracture.

A dislocation is the displacement of a bone end from its normal position at a joint. Dislocations damage the supporting structures at the joint. Blood vessels and nerves can be disrupted. The ball-and-socket joint of the shoulder is a common site for dislocation. Elbow, finger, and ankle dislocations are also possible. Less common are dislocations to the wrist, hip, and knee. Fractures and dislocations can occur together.

Signs and Symptoms
Signs and symptoms of fractures or dislocations include pain and tenderness; crepitus, a grating sound produced by bone ends rubbing together (also a sign of instability and unnatural movement at the fracture site); swelling and discoloration,

---

Signs and Symptoms of Fractures and Dislocations

Pain and tenderness	Loss of function or range of
Crepitus	motion at a joint (dislocation)
Swelling and discoloration	Loss of function at a bone
Deformity	(fracture)

---

indicating that fluids are pooling in the damaged tissue; deformity of a limb or joint; and loss of function. Dislocations cause loss of function at a joint; fractures cause loss of function to a limb.

Assessment

Humans are bilaterally symmetrical animals, meaning that one side is the mirror image of the other. Comparing an injured with an uninjured limb can reveal a subtle angulation or deformity. The mechanism of injury also provides a clue to the extent and location of the injury. Particularly violent inci-

---

Assessment of Fractures and Dislocations

Assess the bone or joint	Assess circulation, sensation,
Remove clothing, visualize	and movement (CSM)
the injury	Circulation
Look for deformity, swelling,	Check distal pulse in wrist
discoloration	or foot
Feel for tenderness,	Check temperature and
deformity, swelling	color in the hand or
	foot
	Sensation and movement
	Ask the patient to move
	fingers or toes
	Test for sensation to
	touch or pain

dents, such as falls from a height or direct blows to a joint, are common fracture mechanisms in the outdoors.

Remove clothing if at all possible and visualize the injury. Look at the limb for deformity, swelling, or discoloration. Feel the limb for localized tenderness, abnormal bumps or protrusions, and swelling.

Assess for circulation, sensation, and movement (CSM). Assess circulation by feeling the radial pulse at the wrist or the pedal pulse in the foot. Impaired circulation may also be evidenced by cold, gray, or cyanotic extremities.

Assess sensation and movement by asking the patient to move fingers or toes. Test for reaction to touch or pain. A blocked artery with loss of distal circulation is an emergency. After 6 to 8 hours, serious damage may result. Damage to a nerve is not as urgent, as the damage usually occurs immediately and may be irreparable.

Treatment
Treat fractures and dislocations by immobilizing the injury. Immobilization prevents movement of bones, reduces pain and swelling and the possibility of further injury, prevents a closed fracture from becoming an open fracture, and helps reduce disability.

Immobilize the Injury. Any time there is loss of function to a limb or joint, the injury should be immobilized in a splint. If it is not clear whether the injury is a sprain or a fracture, immobilize. It is better to splint a sprain than to fail to immobilize a fracture. Immobilize the bones above and below a dislocated joint, and immobilize the joints above and below a fractured bone.

Clean and Dress Wounds. Clean and dress all wounds before splinting. Treat open fractures as contaminated soft tissue injuries and clean them thoroughly. Clean exposed bone ends and keep them moist with a dressing soaked in disinfected water. An infected fracture is a serious problem that can result in long-term complications.

Splint Before Moving. Splint the injury before moving the patient. A quick splint fashioned from a foamlite sleeping pad can stabilize the injury if you must move the patient off

Treatment of Fractures and Dislocations

Immobilize the injury
  Bones above and below
    dislocations
  Joints above and below
    fractures
Clean and dress wounds
Splint before moving
Remove jewelry, watches, and
  tight clothing
	Elevate to reduce swelling
	RICE
	Assess circulation, temperature,
	  and sensation before and
	  after splinting
	Assess for other injuries
	Treat for shock

dangerous terrain or to drier, warmer conditions. Strap an injured arm to the body. Tie injured legs together.

Remove Jewelry, Watches, and Tight Clothing. Remove jewelry and watches and loosen clothing that might compromise circulation should swelling occur. If you are managing a splint in cold weather, hot water bottles or chemical heat packs tucked into the splint can provide warmth.

Elevate to Reduce Swelling. Elevate the injured limb 6 to 10 inches to reduce swelling. RICE treatment, which is discussed in the athletic injuries chapter, helps reduce pain and swelling and is appropriate for splinted fractures and immobilized dislocations. In warm environments where hypothermia and frostbite are not concerns, cold packs or ice or snow encased in a plastic bag and wrapped with a sock help reduce pain and swelling.

Assess Circulation, Sensation, and Movement. Before and after the splint is applied, assess circulation, sensation, and movement to fingers or toes. Repeat this assessment periodically during transport as well.

Assess for Other Injuries. A fracture or dislocation warrants a full patient assessment for other injuries as well.

Treat for Shock. A fracture in and of itself does not cause shock. Damage to nearby tissues, organs, and blood vessels, however, may be a life-threatening problem. Splinting is the basic treatment for shock because it reduces pain and continued injury. Be especially alert for shock with femur and pelvic fractures, multiple fractures, and open fractures.

Angulated Fractures, Dislocations, and Traction-in-Line

Years ago, in basic first aid we learned to splint fractures and dislocations in the position in which they were found. We were concerned that moving bones to straighten bent extremities would injure blood vessels and nerves. In practice, however, we found that gentle traction and straightening of any fracture reduces pain and makes splints more stable.

Medical opinion now favors straightening any obvious

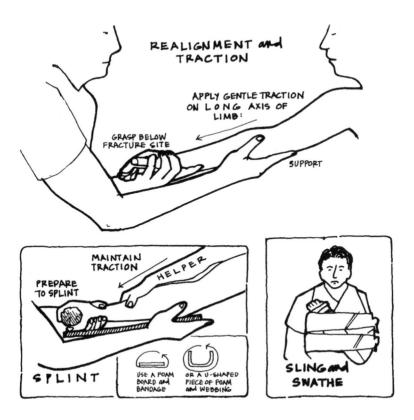

REALIGNMENT and TRACTION

APPLY GENTLE TRACTION ON LONG AXIS OF LIMB:

GRASP BELOW FRACTURE SITE

SUPPORT

MAINTAIN TRACTION

HELPER

PREPARE TO SPLINT

SPLINT

USE A FOAM BOARD and BANDAGE

OR A U-SHAPED PIECE OF FOAM and WEBBING

SLING and SWATHE

long bone fracture using gentle traction-in-line. The current wisdom is that the danger of muscle, nerve, or blood vessel injury from gentle traction-in-line is less than the damage, discomfort, and pain from an injury splinted in an awkward position for long periods.

To straighten a fracture, apply gentle traction-in-line and realign the bone ends. To do this, grasp the limb below the fracture site while another person supports the limb. Align the limb with a gentle pull applied on the long axis of the bone. If resistance or pain occurs, stop and splint in the deformed position.

Consensus opinion in wilderness medicine supports reducing dislocations in the field if prompt transport is not possible or if circulation is impaired. The first-aider should use judgment and discretion when transport to a medical facility is possible within a few hours. Early reduction reduces pain; is easier if done before swelling, stiffness, and muscle spasms develop; makes immobilization and transportation easier; and reduces risks of long-term circulation and nerve injury. Dislocations are relocated with a variety of traction-in-line techniques, depending on the location of the injury. We recommend that you contact a physician or a reputable wilderness medical program for advice and training on specific relocation techniques.

SPLINTING

In the wilderness, improvised splints are the rule, and they may remain in place for days. Splints should pad, support, and immobilize the limb and insulate the extremity from cold. They should be lightweight to make transporting the patient easier and allow access to feet or hands to check circulation. There are many commercial splints on the market, but in the backcountry, two commonly available items

---

Qualities of a Good Splint

Rigid; supports the injury
Pads the injury
Insulates from cold
Lightweight
Offers access to distal circulation

easily meet these specifications. They are the foamlite pad used for insulation under sleeping bags and the triangular bandage.

Basic Splinting Techniques

Two basic splinting techniques cover most first aid situations. One is to make a foamlite tube to splint an arm or leg. The other is to fashion a sling and swathe to immobilize injuries to the upper extremities. The one exception is the case of a fractured femur, which should be immobilized using a traction splint.

Foamlite Tube. To make a foamlite tube, roll the foam sleeping pad into a U-shaped tube and trim to fit the limb. Secure with cravats (triangular bandages), bandannas, sling webbing, or tape.

Sling and Swathe. The sling and swathe immobilizes arm, shoulder, and collarbone injuries using two triangular bandages, bandannas, or cravats.

First clean and dress any open wound. Then use soft material such as a pile jacket to pad the injury. Add a firm supporting layer outside the soft padding. Often this is a foamlite pad, Crazy Creek Chair, or Therm-A-Rest pad. Sticks, tent poles, or the stays in soft packs can provide additional support.

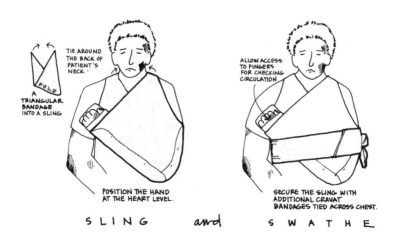

SLING and SWATHE

Secure with tape, webbing, or cord. Support the foot or hand, but provide access to fingers and toes to assess for CSM. Upper extremity injuries are often further supported with a sling and swathe.

Specific Splinting Techniques

Hand. The hand and fingers should be splinted in the "position of function," the position of the hand when holding a glass of water. Fingers can also be "buddy-taped" to each other to reduce range of motion yet still allow some degree of function. If the injury is confined to the fingers, the wrist need not be splinted. If the injury involves the bones at the base of the fingers, splint the wrist as well.

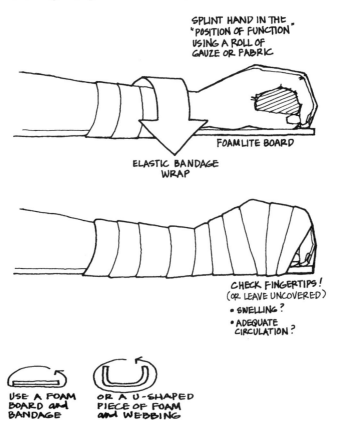

SPLINT HAND IN THE "POSITION OF FUNCTION" USING A ROLL OF GAUZE OR FABRIC

FOAMLITE BOARD

ELASTIC BANDAGE WRAP

CHECK FINGERTIPS! (OR LEAVE UNCOVERED)
• SWELLING?
• ADEQUATE CIRCULATION?

USE A FOAM BOARD and BANDAGE

OR A U-SHAPED PIECE OF FOAM and WEBBING

Wrist and Forearm. Splint injuries to the wrist and forearm with a foamlite stabilizer or a sling and swathe. Elevating the hand above the level of the heart helps reduce swelling and pain. The two bones of the forearm, the radius and ulna, are connected by a strong band of connective tissue. Forces applied to one bone can be transmitted to the other, and simultaneous fractures of both bones are common.

Elbow. An elbow dislocation is a serious injury that calls for rapid evacuation. Several nerves and arteries pass around the complex elbow joint and may be damaged by displaced bone ends. The simplest splint for the elbow is the sling and swathe. Splint this injury in the position in which you find it. If the elbow is at an awkward angle, a sling and swathe will not work well. Try a foamlite pad stabilized with a tent pole or the stay from a soft pack bent to the angle of the joint. If possible, bandage the whole arm to the trunk for greater stability.

Upper Arm. The radial nerve and brachial artery lie close to the humerus and can be injured by a fracture. Damage to the artery is most common with elbow dislocations. Damage to the nerve is most common with midshaft fractures. Check the pulse at the wrist. The ability to bend back the hand tests the radial nerve. The humerus can be splinted with a combination of a foamlite splint and sling and swathe. Wrap foamlite on the inside of the arm, over the elbow, and up the outside of the arm for added stability. The patient may be more comfortable if the sling and foamlite cup the elbow without putting pressure on the humerus.

Shoulder. The humerus fits into a shallow socket in the scapula, forming the shoulder joint and allowing for a wide range of motion (ROM). This ROM makes the joint susceptible to injury. Most dislocations are anterior, with the head of the humerus displaced out of the socket toward the chest.

The signs of dislocation are drooping shoulder, a depression on the front of the shoulder, and loss of function or ROM at the joint. The sling and swathes provide a simple and effective splint. If the shoulder is immobile at an awkward angle, padding may be necessary to support the arm away from the chest.

Collarbone. The clavicle acts as a strut, propping the back of the shoulder. It can be fractured by a direct blow to the shoulder or by a blow transmitted up an extended arm. A broken collarbone is a common mountain bike injury. Deformity and tenderness can often be found by feeling the entire clavicle from sternum to shoulder. Typically, a patient with an injured clavicle is unable to use the arm on the injured side. Splint with a sling and swathe, immobilizing the shoulder and arm.

Pelvis. The pelvis is a bowl-shaped structure consisting of three bones fused with the sacrum, the lower portion of the vertebral column. The upper part of the femur meets the pelvis at a shallow socket and forms the hip joint.

A broken pelvis is a serious injury. It takes considerable force to break a pelvis; such force can cause associated internal injuries, including rupture of the bladder and blood loss. Treat this patient as if he or she has a back injury, and immobilize the trunk and legs. A backboard, Stokes litter, or improvised litter is necessary to immobilize and carry the patient.

Femur and Hip. A dislocated hip is usually the result of a high-velocity mechanism such as a fall from height. A leg with a dislocated hip is generally shortened, with the foot and knee turned in. If the hip is dislocated for more than a few hours, the blood supply to the head of the femur can be compromised, and permanent damage to the bone can occur. Splint hip fractures or dislocations with a U-shaped foamlite tube, immobilizing the entire leg.

Muscles surrounding the fracture of long bones may contract, causing the bone ends to override. This increases pain and soft tissue damage, as well as increasing the possibility of artery and nerve injury. Spasm of the large thigh muscles is of special concern in fractures of the femur. A femur fracture can bleed as much as 2 liters into the surrounding tissues, causing life-threatening shock. The leg may appear shortened and the thigh swollen. The femur is best splinted with traction.

Traction Splints. Traction is the treatment of choice for a midshaft femur fracture. Traction splints place tension on the muscles surrounding a fracture, reducing pain and spasm and helping with realignment. Traction splints for femur fractures in the wilderness are a challenge to improvise, and the traction straps require constant attention to make sure they are not causing reduced blood flow to the foot.

How to Construct Traction Splint. Before you begin constructing the traction splint, splint the injury with a full-leg foamlite splint. The leg splint will provide support, insulation, and padding. Follow this by applying padding at the

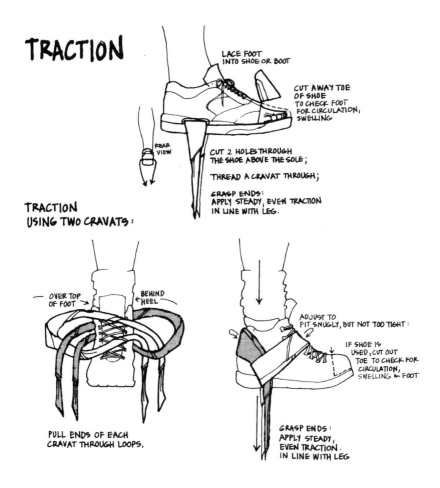

TRACTION

LACE FOOT
INTO SHOE OR BOOT

CUT AWAY TOE
OF SHOE
TO CHECK FOOT
FOR CIRCULATION,
SWELLING

REAR
VIEW

CUT 2 HOLES THROUGH
THE SHOE ABOVE THE SOLE;

THREAD A CRAVAT THROUGH;

GRASP ENDS:
APPLY STEADY, EVEN TRACTION
IN LINE WITH LEG.

TRACTION
USING TWO CRAVATS:

OVER TOP
OF FOOT

BEHIND
HEEL

ADJUST TO
FIT SNUGLY, BUT NOT TOO TIGHT:

IF SHOE IS
USED, CUT OUT
TOE TO CHECK FOR
CIRCULATION,
SWELLING & FOOT

PULL ENDS OF EACH
CRAVAT THROUGH LOOPS.

GRASP ENDS:
APPLY STEADY,
EVEN TRACTION.
IN LINE WITH LEG

ankle. Ideally, you can promptly provide traction-in-line for the thigh and hold it while you are preparing the traction splint. This is not always practical, however, and you may need to apply a fixation splint, construct your traction splint, then apply traction.

1. To prepare for applying traction, attach traction straps over the boot or padded ankle. Fold two cravats into long, narrow bandages. Fold lengthwise, and pass one over and one behind the ankle, making sure the ends of each bandage are facing in opposite directions. Now pull the ends of each bandage through the loop in the other bandage. The bandages should fit snugly and flat against the ankle. The toes should remain visible or at least accessible for assessing blood flow and nerve function.

2. To construct the traction splint, place a ski pole, tent pole, or any polelike object a foot longer than the leg against the outside of the leg. Anchor the pole using a well-padded strap over the thigh at the hip.

3. Apply traction on the thigh by pulling the traction straps. Maintain traction by securing the traction straps to the end of the pole. Tie the traction splint to the leg splint.

Knee. Most knee injuries can be wrapped with an Ace bandage, taped, or stabilized with a foamlite splint in such a way that the patient can walk out without further damage. A grossly unstable knee with major ligament rupture is accompanied by severe pain, inability to move the joint or bear weight, swelling, and obvious deformity. This injury requires a simple splint and a litter evacuation. In some cases, it may be difficult to tell if the femur, the tibia, or the knee is injured. Assume the worst and splint the femur.

Lower Leg. The lower ends of the tibia and fibula are the prominent knobs on the sides of the ankle. The thin layers of skin over the tibia make open fractures common. Splint both the knee and the ankle in a roll of foamlite.

Ankle. It can be difficult to differentiate between a fracture and a sprain to the ankle. The injury can be immobilized with a stirrup of foamlite and wrapped with clothing for

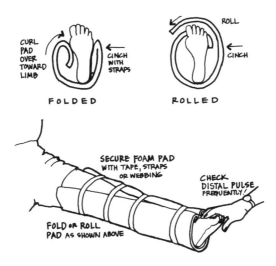

insulation and padding. Knee and ankle injuries are also addressed in chapter 15 ("Athletic Injuries").

FINAL THOUGHTS

In NOLS' experience, fractures and dislocations are not common in wilderness activities, but they do occur, and the first-aider should be prepared. A careful assessment, traction-in-line, immobilization, and RICE are the cornerstones of our treatment. Most of us, conscious of weight and bulk when we travel in the wilderness, don't carry prepared commercial splints. We know that we can create what we need from materials at hand such as clothing, sleeping pads, packs, stays, tent poles, bandannas, and natural materials such as sticks. Practice improvising splints from the material you commonly have with you in the wilderness.

SUMMARY:
FRACTURES AND DISLOCATIONS

Fracture: A break in a bone. Skin over an open fracture is broken, exposing bone to infection. Skin over a closed fracture remains intact.

Dislocation: The displacement of a bone from its normal position at a joint.

SIGNS AND SYMPTOMS
Pain and tenderness
Crepitus
Swelling and discoloration
Deformity
Loss of function and range of motion at a joint (dislocation)
Loss of function at a bone (fracture)

ASSESSMENT
Assess the bone or joint
   Remove clothing, visualize the injury
   Look for deformity, swelling, discoloration
   Feel for tenderness, deformity, swelling
Assess CSM
   Circulation
      Check distal pulse in wrist or foot
      Check temperature and color in the hand or foot
   Sensation and movement
      Ask the patient to move fingers or toes
      Test for sensation to touch or pain

TREATMENT
Immobilize the injury
   Bones above and below dislocations
   Joints above and below fractures

• CONTINUED •

SUMMARY:
FRACTURES AND DISLOCATIONS *(continued)*

Clean and dress wounds
Remove jewelry, watches, and tight clothing
Splint before moving
Elevate to reduce swelling (RICE)
Assess CSM before and after splinting
Assess for other injuries
Treat for shock
Consider relocation of a dislocation or angulated fracture with
gentle traction-in-line if:
    The femur is fractured
    The fracture cannot be splinted or transported in its
       current position
    Pulse or sensation is absent or impaired
Basic splints
    Upper extremity—sling and swathe
    Lower extremity—U-shaped foamlite tube

CHAPTER 6

HEAD, SPINAL CORD, AND EYE INJURIES

INTRODUCTION

Motor vehicle accidents are a prominent cause of brain and spinal cord injuries, but camping and traveling in the wilderness do not eliminate the risk. Wilderness travel and recreational activities such as climbing, skiing, and paddling carry a risk of death and disability from brain and spine injury. A rock fall while climbing can injure one's brain. Falls while climbing or skiing can break one's back or neck and may damage the spinal cord. Although these are rare events, you need to be prepared to assess and manage these situations in the backcountry.

CENTRAL NERVOUS SYSTEM ANATOMY

Together, the brain, spinal cord, and peripheral nerves monitor and control all body functions.

The brain governs thoughts, emotions, senses, memory, and movement, as well as basic physiological functions. The brain processes information from our senses, initiates motor responses, remembers, solves problems, and makes judgments.

The three main divisions of the brain are the cerebrum, the cerebellum, and the brain stem. The cerebrum is the largest part of the brain, the center for our "higher" cognitive functions: problem solving, memory, speech, hearing, sight, and so forth. The cerebellum, in the lower rear of the skull, regulates posture, coordination, and motor responses. The brain stem, at the base of the brain, maintains consciousness, heart rate, blood pressure, and breathing.

The skull houses and protects the brain. The brain is covered by three layers of tissue, known collectively as the meninges: the dura mater, the pia, and the arachnoid. Cerebrospinal fluid (CSF), nourishing and cushioning the brain,

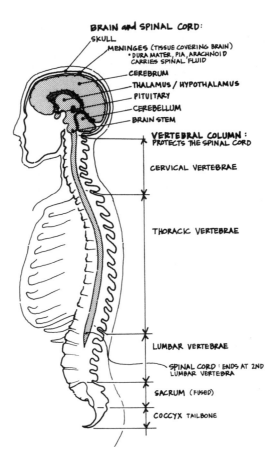

BRAIN and SPINAL CORD:
SKULL
MENINGES (TISSUE COVERING BRAIN)
• DURA MATER, PIA, ARACHNOID
  CARRIES SPINAL FLUID
CEREBRUM
THALAMUS / HYPOTHALAMUS
PITUITARY
CEREBELLUM
BRAIN STEM
VERTEBRAL COLUMN :
PROTECTS THE SPINAL CORD
CERVICAL VERTEBRAE
THORACIC VERTEBRAE
LUMBAR VERTEBRAE
SPINAL CORD : ENDS AT 2ND LUMBAR VERTEBRA
SACRUM (FUSED)
COCCYX TAILBONE

flows within these layers. Blood vessels are located within the brain and the meninges.

Central nervous system tissue is extremely sensitive to oxygen deficiency. Depriving the brain of oxygen for only a few minutes can result in permanent damage.

HEAD INJURIES
Head injuries include scalp, skull, and brain injuries. Scalp and skull injuries can be serious by themselves, but we're more concerned with possible injury to the brain.

A large blood supply feeds the scalp, causing it to bleed profusely when cut. A bruised or lacerated scalp can therefore mask underlying injury to the skull or brain. Examine scalp injuries carefully to see if bone or brain is exposed or if an indentation, which might be a depressed fracture, is present. Bleeding from the scalp can be controlled by applying gentle pressure on the edges of the wounds, being careful to avoid direct pressure on possibly unstable central areas.

The skull consists of 22 fused bones. The strongest are the bones forming the top and sides of the protective box encasing the brain. Fractures of the skull are not in themselves life-threatening except when associated with underlying brain injury or spinal cord injury, or when the fracture causes bleeding by tearing the blood vessels between the brain and the skull. Many serious brain injuries occur without skull fractures.

Skull fractures can be open or closed. Open skull fractures, in addition to indicating that the head has been hit hard, expose the brain to infection.

Brain injury can be fatal when it disrupts heartbeat and breathing. In the long term, a severe brain injury may leave the patient physically immobile or mentally incompetent, with severely impaired judgment and problem-solving ability or an inability to process or communicate information properly.

The brain can be injured by a direct blow to the head or by twisting forces, which cause deformation and shearing against the inside of the skull. Some movement between brain and skull is possible. A blow to the head can make the brain "rattle" within the skull, tearing blood vessels in the meninges or within the brain itself.

A concussion is temporary brain dysfunction or loss of consciousness following a blow to the head. There may be no or only mild brain injury with a concussion. Contusions (bruising of brain tissue) and hemorrhages or hematomas (bleeding within the brain) are more serious injuries that can lead to increased pressure in the skull. Encased in this rigid box, a swelling or bleeding brain presses against the skull; the body has no mechanism to avoid or release such an increase in pressure. As pressure rises, blood supply is shut off by compression of swollen vessels, and brain tissue is deprived of oxygen. The brain stem can be squashed by the pressure, affecting heart and lung function.

Signs and Symptoms

Signs and symptoms of brain injury depend on the degree and progression of injury. Some indications of brain injury appear immediately from the accident; others develop slowly over time.

Changes in Level of Consciousness (LOC). Loss of consciousness may be short or may persist for hours or days. The patient may alternate between periods of consciousness and unconsciousness or be conscious but disoriented, confused, and incoherent—exhibiting changes in behavior and personality or verbal or physical combativeness. The patient may be unconscious but responsive to commands, unconscious but responsive to pain, or totally unconscious and unresponsive.

Headache, Vision Disturbances, Loss of Balance, Nausea and Vomiting, Paralysis, Seizures. Headache, vision problems, loss of balance, nausea and vomiting, and paralysis may accompany brain injury. In serious cases, the

---

Signs and Symptoms of Brain Injury

Changes in level of consciousness	Seizures
	Combativeness
Unconsciousness	Blood or CSF from ears, mouth, or nose
Disorientation, confusion, incoherence, irrationality	Soft tissue injury to skull
Headache	Obvious skull fracture
Vision disturbances	Raccoon sign, Battle's sign
Loss of balance	Slow pulse, rising blood pressure, irregular respirations
Nausea and vomiting	
Paralysis	

patient may assume abnormal positions, with the legs and arms stiff and extended or the arms clutched across the chest. A brain-injured patient may have seizures.

Combativeness. A brain-injured patient may become combative, striking out randomly and with surprising strength at the nearest person. If the brain is oxygen-deprived, supplemental oxygen and airway maintenance may help alleviate such behavior. Restraint may be necessary to protect the patient and the rescuers.

Blood or CSF Leakage, Soft Tissue Injury to Skull, Obvious Skull Fracture, Raccoon Sign, Battle's Sign. Blood or clear fluid (CSF) leaking from the ears, mouth, or nose is a sign of a skull fracture, as are pain, tenderness, and swelling at the injury site or obvious penetrating wounds or depressed fractures. Two other signs of skull fracture—bruising around the eyes (called the raccoon sign) and bruising behind the ear (Battle's sign)—usually appear several hours after the injury.

Slow Pulse, Rising Blood Pressure, Irregular Respirations. Changes in vital signs that indicate a serious brain injury are a slow pulse, rising blood pressure, and irregular respiratory rate. These contrast with the rising pulse, falling blood pressure, and rapid, regular respirations seen with shock.

Assessment

Initial assessment of brain injury can be difficult. The symptoms of a concussion, which is the least severe of injuries, are similar to those seen in more serious injuries. The assessment may also be complicated when the patient's LOC is affected by drugs, alcohol, or other traumatic injuries.

Assessment of a brain injury begins by checking the airway, breathing, and circulation (ABC); bleeding; and cervical spine. A patient with a brain injury is at high risk for cervical spine injury. Avoid movement of the neck. If you suspect brain or neck injury, use the jaw thrust to open the airway.

After a thorough physical assessment, including vital

JAW THRUST AIRWAY OPENING FOR SUSPECTED C-SPINE PATIENTS :
- DO NOT MOVE NECK OR SPINE.
- DO NOT TILT HEAD BACK

PLACE FINGERS IN FRONT OF EARLOBE.
PUSH JAW FORWARD AND UP.

ONE HAND ON EACH SIDE OF HEAD :

JAW

EAR

signs, evaluate the nervous system. Note the level of consciousness and the patient's ability to feel and move extremities. Use the AVPU (*a*wake and *a*lert, not awake but responsive *v*erbally, not awake but responsive to *p*ain, or not awake and *u*nresponsive) system to assess LOC. Question the patient or bystanders as to a loss of consciousness. Was it immediate, or was there a delay before loss of consciousness? Has the patient been awake but drowsy, sleepy, confused, or disoriented? Has the patient been going in and out of consciousness?

Watch any brain-injured patient carefully, even if the injury does not at first appear serious. Let the patient rest, but wake him or her up every couple of hours and assess LOC. Consciousness may progress into disorientation, confusion, and eventually unconsciousness.

Treatment

An urgent evacuation is required for any patient who has become unconscious, even for a minute or two, or who exhibits vision or balance disturbances, irritability, lethargy, or nausea and vomiting after a blow to the head. A patient who experiences momentary loss of consciousness but who awakens without any other symptoms may be walked out of the mountains with a support party capable of quickly evacuating the patient if his or her condition worsens.

Treatment of Brain Injury

ABCs
Assume cervical spine injury
If patient is vomiting, position on side
Control scalp bleeding
Do not control internal bleeding or drainage
Elevate head
Record neurological assessment

ABCs. An injured brain needs oxygen. Ensuring an open airway is the first step in treatment.

If Vomiting, Position Patient on Side. Brain-injured patients have a tendency to vomit. Logrolling the patient onto his or her side while maintaining cervical spine stabilization helps drain vomit while maintaining the airway. Use the jaw thrust to open the airway.

Control Scalp Bleeding. Cover open wounds with sterile dressings as a barrier against infection. Although it is acceptable to clean scalp wounds, cleaning open skull injuries may introduce infection into the brain, so leave them as you find them. Stabilize impaled objects in place.

Do Not Control Internal Bleeding or Drainage. Do not attempt to prevent drainage of blood or clear CSF from the ears or nose. Blocking the flow could increase pressure within the skull.

Elevate Head. Keep the patient in a horizontal or slightly head-elevated position. Do not elevate the legs, as this might increase pressure within the skull.

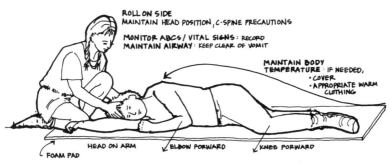

CARING FOR A BRAIN-INJURED PATIENT

Record Neurological Assessment. Watch the patient closely for any changes in LOC. These observations will be valuable to the receiving physician. Record changes in your patient report.

SPINAL CORD INJURIES
As with head injuries, spinal cord injuries primarily involve young people, with most cases occurring in men between the ages of 15 and 35. An estimated 10,000 new spinal cord injuries occur each year in the United States, and because central nervous tissue does not regenerate, victims are left permanently disabled—half as paraplegics and half as quadriplegics. Motor vehicle accidents account for the majority of spinal injury cases, followed by diving, motorcycle wrecks, and falls.

> **Signs and Symptoms of Spinal Cord Injury**
>
> Mechanism of injury
> Weakness in extremities
> Loss of strength or ability to move extremities
> Loss of sensation in extremities
> Tenderness in spine
> Numbness and tingling in hands and feet

The spinal cord is the extension of the brain outside the skull. A component of the central nervous system, the spinal cord is the nervous connection between the brain and the rest of the body.

The spinal cord is protected within the vertebrae, thirty-three of which form the backbone, or spine. A force driving the spine out of its normal alignment can fracture or dislocate the vertebrae, thereby injuring the spinal cord. However, there can be vertebral fractures or ligament and muscle damage to the backbone without damage to the spinal cord. Fractured or dislocated vertebrae can pinch, bruise, or cut the spinal cord, damaging the nervous connections.

The smallest vertebrae with the greatest range of motion are in the neck—the most vulnerable part of the spine. From there, the vertebrae become progressively larger as they support more weight. The location of damage to the spinal cord determines whether the patient may die or be left paralyzed from the neck down (quadriplegia) or the waist down (paraplegia).

Signs and Symptoms

Signs and symptoms of spinal cord injury include weakness, loss of sensation or ability to move, numbness and tingling in the hands and feet, soft tissue injury over or near the spine, and tenderness in the spine.

Assessment

Check for strength, sensation, ability to move, and weakness or numbness in the hands and feet. Ask the patient to wiggle fingers or toes, push his or her feet against your hands, or squeeze your hands with his or hers. Ask the patient to identify which toe or finger you are touching. If the patient is unconscious, check for sensation by applying a painful stimulus at the toes and fingers (a pinprick or pinch) and watching the patient's face for a grimace.

Treatment

Treatment for a spinal cord injury is to stabilize the spine to prevent further damage. Although it may be necessary to move a spine-injured patient, your first choice should be on-scene stabilization.

Stabilize the Spine. If spinal immobilization devices are not available, one person should always be at the head of the patient, controlling the head and maintaining stabilization of the neck. A clothing or blanket roll may be used as an improvised cervical or neck collar to aid in stabilization, freeing rescuers

---

**Treatment
of Spinal Cord Injury**

Stabilize spine
    Hands on patient's head
    Clothing or blanket roll
Move with logroll or four-person
    lift
Immobilize spine
    Cervical collar
    Backboard

IMPROVISED CERVICAL COLLAR

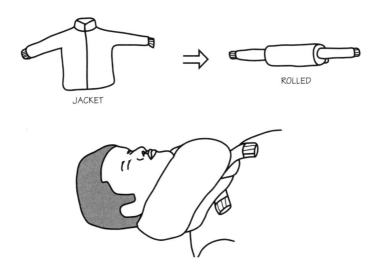

JACKET

ROLLED

for other tasks. A strap of cloth or bandage across the forehead secured with wrapped clothing stabilizes the head and neck.

STABILIZING THE HEAD:

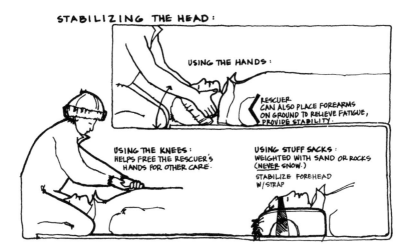

USING THE HANDS:

RESCUER CAN ALSO PLACE FOREARMS ON GROUND TO RELIEVE FATIGUE, PROVIDE STABILITY.

USING THE KNEES: HELPS FREE THE RESCUER'S HANDS FOR OTHER CARE.

USING STUFF SACKS: WEIGHTED WITH SAND OR ROCKS (NEVER SNOW.)

STABILIZE FOREHEAD W/STRAP

Move with Logroll or Four-Person Lift. Assume that the patient may have to be moved at least twice during the rescue—once to place insulation underneath the body to prevent hypothermia, and a second time to place the patient on a litter or backboard. Two common techniques for moving the patient are the logroll and the lift. Practice these under the guidance of an emergency care instructor.

A patient can be assessed and immobilized while lying facedown or on his or her back or side. Unless airway, breathing, or bleeding problems are present, you should take the time required to carry out the logroll or lift and explain your actions to the patient.

How to Perform a Four-Person Logroll

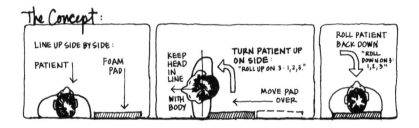

1. The rescuers take positions:
   Rescuer One maintains stabilization of the head throughout the procedure and gives the commands.
   Rescuer Two kneels beside the patient's chest and reaches across to the patient's shoulder and upper arm.
   Rescuer Three kneels beside the patient's waist and reaches across to the lower back and pelvis.
   Rescuer Four kneels beside the patient's thighs and reaches across to support the legs with one hand on the patient's upper thigh, the other behind the knee.
2. The rescuers roll the patient onto his or her side:
   Rescuer One, at the head, gives the command, "Roll on 3; 1, 2, 3," and the rescuers slowly roll the patient toward them, keeping the patient's body in align-

Techniques:

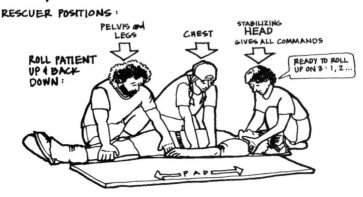

RESCUER POSITIONS:

PELVIS and LEGS

CHEST

STABILIZING HEAD
GIVES ALL COMMANDS

ROLL PATIENT UP & BACK DOWN:

READY TO ROLL UP ON 3 : 1, 2...

⟸ P A D ⟹

ment. Rescuer One supports the head and maintains alignment with the spine. Once the patient is on his or her side, a backboard or foamlite pad can be placed where the patient will be lying when the logroll is complete.

3. The rescuers roll the patient onto his or her back:
   When rescuer One gives the command, "Lower on 3; 1, 2, 3," the procedure is reversed, and the patient is slowly lowered onto the backboard or foamlite pad while the rescuers keep the spine in alignment.

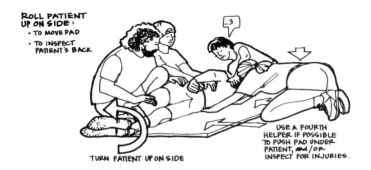

ROLL PATIENT UP ON SIDE:
- TO MOVE PAD
- TO INSPECT PATIENT'S BACK

..3

USE A FOURTH HELPER IF POSSIBLE TO PUSH PAD UNDER PATIENT, and/or INSPECT FOR INJURIES.

TURN PATIENT UP ON SIDE

Lifting Technique. The patient can be lifted by four people, enabling a fifth person to slide a backboard, foamlite pad, or litter underneath. The rescuer at the head again maintains stabilization during the entire procedure and gives commands. The other three rescuers position themselves at the patient's sides, one kneeling at chest level and another at pelvis level on the same side, while the third rescuer kneels at waist level on the opposite side. Before lifting, the rescuers place their hands over the patient to visualize their hands in position under the chest, lower back, pelvis, and thighs. They then slide their hands under the patient as far as they can without jostling the patient. On the command, "Lift on 3; 1, 2, 3," rescuers lift the patient 6 to 8 inches into the air, then lower him or her onto the pad or litter.

THE LIFT
The Concept:

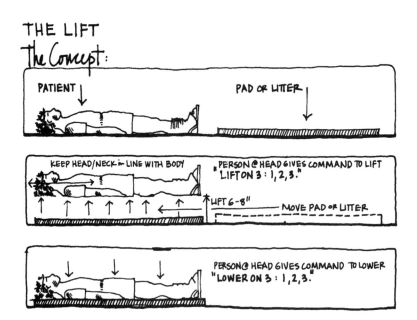

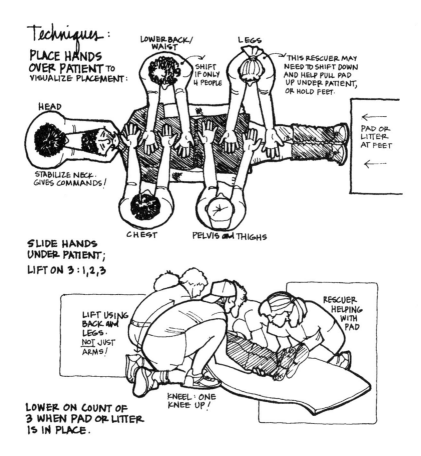

Techniques:
PLACE HANDS OVER PATIENT TO VISUALIZE PLACEMENT:

HEAD

LOWER BACK/ WAIST

LEGS

SHIFT IF ONLY 4 PEOPLE

THIS RESCUER MAY NEED TO SHIFT DOWN AND HELP PULL PAD UP UNDER PATIENT, OR HOLD FEET.

PAD OR LITTER AT FEET

STABILIZE NECK. GIVES COMMANDS!

SLIDE HANDS UNDER PATIENT; LIFT ON 3 : 1,2,3

CHEST

PELVIS and THIGHS

LIFT USING BACK AND LEGS. NOT JUST ARMS!

RESCUER HELPING WITH PAD

LOWER ON COUNT OF 3 WHEN PAD OR LITTER IS IN PLACE.

KNEEL : ONE KNEE UP!

Immobilize the Spine. Ideally, the patient should be moved as few times as possible, and preferably after immobilization on a backboard, Kendrick Extrication Device, SKED litter, or other spine-splinting device, and with a cervical collar and head immobilization. Until such equipment arrives, insulate and shelter the patient.

Wilderness treatment may require caring for a patient during prolonged immobilization. It's uncomfortable to lie still on a hard surface for hours. Current Advanced Trauma Life Support (ATLS) curriculum recommends that patients on

PATIENT PACKAGING POINTS

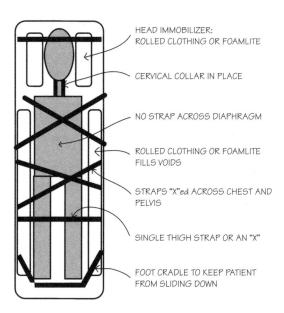

HEAD IMMOBILIZER:
ROLLED CLOTHING OR FOAMLITE

CERVICAL COLLAR IN PLACE

NO STRAP ACROSS DIAPHRAGM

ROLLED CLOTHING OR FOAMLITE
FILLS VOIDS

STRAPS "X"ed ACROSS CHEST AND
PELVIS

SINGLE THIGH STRAP OR AN "X"

FOOT CRADLE TO KEEP PATIENT
FROM SLIDING DOWN

FILL VOIDS WITH ROLLS OF FOAMLITE OR CLOTHING.

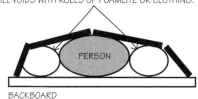

PERSON

BACKBOARD

INSERT PAD UNDER LOWER BACK AND KNEES.

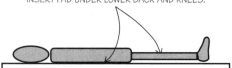

backboards be logrolled off the backboard approximately every 2 hours to prevent pressure sores on the back. Padding is important. A little bit under the lower back and behind the knees goes a long way to make the patient comfortable. Strapping over bony areas helps tie the patient down, but the straps should be padded and can be loosened when the patient is not being carried.

"Clear" the Spine. If a mechanism for a spinal cord injury has occurred, for example, from a fall from a height, a high-velocity skiing fall, a diving accident, or a blow to the head, initially assume the worst and control the head. After a thorough assessment, it is acceptable to consider "clearing" the spine of injury by using a method, approved by the Wilderness Medical Society, to rule out spine injury. Without this protocol, we would unnecessarily immobilize all patients with insignificant mechanisms for injury.

Clearing the spine begins with the assumption that there is a mechanism for spine injury. If there is no mechanism, there is no need to clear the spine. Start with a thorough patient assessment. Then proceed sequentially through this series of steps.

1. Is the mechanism of injury severe?
   If yes, immobilize the spine. If no, proceed to the next step.
2. Is the patient alert and sober?
   If no, immobilize the spine. If yes, proceed to the next step.
3. Is the patient free from distracting injuries?
   If no, immobilize the spine. If yes, proceed to the next step.
4. Is the patient free of pain, tenderness, tingling, or numbness in the neck and back?
   If no, immobilize the spine. If yes, proceed to the next step.
5. Is the patient free of unusual or abnormal sensations in the extremities, such as numbness or tingling?
   If no, immobilize the spine. If yes, clear the spine.

6. Can the patient gently move his or her head without causing pain?
   If no, immobilize the spine. If yes, clear the spine.

If the patient fails any step in this process, or you're uncertain about the results of your exam, immobilize the spine. If at any time you're uncomfortable with this process, you can choose a conservative plan and immobilize the patient.

EYE INJURIES
Foreign Body in the Eye

Usually the eyelashes, tears, and blinking defend the surface of the eye from foreign particles. If a foreign object, perhaps a speck of dust, dirt, or leaf, lands on the eye or inside the eyelid, it can be painful and irritating.

Examine the eye carefully. Don't rub it. Pull the lower lid down and have the patient look up. This allows you to see the lower part of the eye and inside the lower eyelid. Flip the upper lid over a small stick or cotton applicator and have the patient look down. This allows you to see the upper part of the eye and inside the upper eyelid.

Remove foreign material by irrigation with clean water or, if it's on the eyelid and not the eye itself, with gentle use of a piece of gauze. If the object is stuck, leave it in place. Never try to remove something from the eye with force. Close the

THE EYE

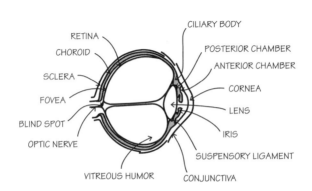

Evacuate Patients with These Eye Problems:

Hyphema (blood in the anterior chamber of the eye)

Any loss of vision, blurred or double vision

An object impaled in the eye

Acute, severe eye pain

A foreign body that you can't remove in the eye

Eye irritation that persists more than 24 hours

---

eye and bandage it shut with a folded gauze pad or sterile eye patch, and evacuate the patient.

The eye may feel irritated. This may be an abrasion to the surface of the cornea. Irrigate the eye. The patient may be more comfortable if you patch the eye shut. If the irritation is very painful or persists more than 24 hours, take the patient to a physician.

If the foreign object is impaled in the eye, do not remove it. The eye contains precious fluids that may leak out, and extracting the object can cause additional damage. Stabilize the object in place with gauze; cover and protect it against being banged. Because the eyes normally track together—when one moves, the other follows—bandage both eyes to prevent movement. Evacuate the patient.

Subconjunctival Hemorrhage

A subconjunctival hemorrhage is bleeding under the conjunctiva, the outer covering of the eye, and over the sclera, the white part of the eye. A subconjunctival hemorrhage may happen spontaneously after hard coughing or blood pressure increases or a direct blow to the eye. Most cases have no specific history and are noticed by someone else. Usually the hemorrhage is on only one side. By itself, it rarely indicates a significant problem and is not a reason for evacuation. If it is the result of a blow to the eye, examination by a physician is advised.

Hyphema is bleeding into the anterior chamber of the eye, often after a blow to the eye. Blood may be seen by looking at the iris or the colored part of the eye. A patient with hyphema should always be evacuated.

FINAL THOUGHTS

Airway maintenance, cervical spine precautions, and patient assessment are important treatments for patients with head and spine injuries, but they are only stopgap measures. A quarter of all brain and spine injuries result in death or permanent disability. The cost of treating a serious brain injury is staggering. In urban settings, first aid for brain or spine injuries includes rapid transport to neurological care—an impossibility in a wilderness setting.

Prevention is the best treatment: Wear a helmet!

SUMMARY:
HEAD, SPINAL CORD, AND EYE INJURIES

Signs and Symptoms of Brain Injury
Changes in level of consciousness
    Unconsciousness
    Disorientation, confusion, incoherence, irrationality
Headache
Vision disturbances
Loss of balance
Nausea and vomiting
Paralysis
Seizures
Combativeness
Blood or CSF from ears, mouth, or nose
Soft tissue injury to skull
Obvious skull fracture
Raccoon sign, Battle's sign
Slow pulse, rising blood pressure, irregular respirations

Treatment of Brain Injury
ABCs
Assume cervical spine injury
If patient is vomiting, position on side

• *CONTINUED* •

SUMMARY:
HEAD, SPINAL CORD, AND EYE INJURIES
(continued)

Control scalp bleeding
Do not control internal bleeding or drainage
Elevate head
Record neurological assessment

Signs and Symptoms of Spinal Cord Injury
Mechanism of injury
Weakness in extremities
Loss of strength or ability to move extremities
Loss of sensation in extremities
Tenderness in spine
Numbness and tingling in hands and feet

Treatment of Spinal Cord Injury
Stabilize the spine
    Hands on patient's head
    Clothing or blanket roll
Move with logroll or four-person lift
Immobilize the spine
    Cervical collar
    Backboard

Treatment of Eye Injury
Don't rub irritated eye
Don't manually remove stuck material
Irrigate eye to remove foreign material
Bandage shut the injured eye

Evacuate patients with these eye problems:
Hyphema (blood in the anterior chamber of the eye)
Any loss of vision, blurred or double vision
An object impaled in the eye
Acute, severe eye pain
A foreign body that you can't remove in the eye
Eye irritation that persists more than 24 hours

CHAPTER 7

CHEST INJURIES

INTRODUCTION

Accidents in North American Mountaineering has documented more than a few instances of mountaineers who've suffered serious chest and lung injuries from falls or punctured their chests with ice axes. Paddlers experience chest injuries from impact with rocks or from blows by the bows of kayaks. Horsepacking and backcountry skiing are other wilderness activities in which there are mechanisms—falls and collisions—for chest trauma. In the backcountry, our role is to recognize the injury, support the patient, and organize a rapid evacuation.

ANATOMY AND PHYSIOLOGY

Chest injuries can be serious if they compromise the respiratory or cardiovascular system. The respiratory system provides oxygen to and removes carbon dioxide from the body. The cardiovascular system transports these gases as well as nutrients and waste products to and from the cells. Contained within the chest cavity are some of the structures responsible for these processes: the airway passages, lungs, heart, and major vessels—the vena cava and aorta.

The clavicles, rib cage, and diaphragm form the boundaries of the chest cavity. The rib cage consists of twelve pairs of ribs. All the ribs are attached to the spine in the back. The upper seven pairs are attached to the sternum by cartilage; the next three pairs are attached to cartilage only; and the lowest two pairs ("floating ribs") are attached to the spine and not to anything in the front.

The Respiratory System

The components of the respiratory system are the nose, mouth, pharynx, larynx, epiglottis, trachea, bronchi, bronchioles, and alveoli. The diaphragm and muscles of the chest wall move air in and out of the lungs.

The average healthy adult breathes 12 to 20 times per minute, moving half a liter of air with each breath. Respiratory rate increases with exercise, altitude, illness, or injury. A person in good aerobic shape may breathe only 6 to 8 times a minute.

PARTS OF THE RESPIRATORY SYSTEM :

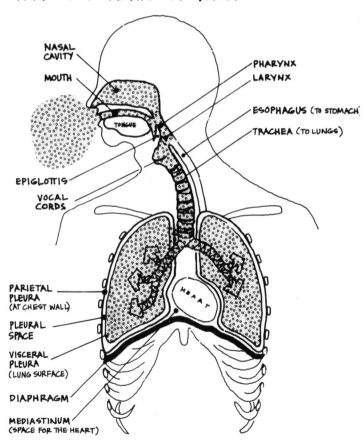

Nose, Mouth, Pharynx, Larynx. As air enters the nose or mouth, it is warmed and humidified by mucous membranes that line the respiratory tract. The mucus produced by the membranes and the cilia (hairlike structures) helps keep foreign material out of the lungs. Air passes from the nose or mouth into the pharynx, past the larynx, and into the trachea. The larynx consists of tiny bones, muscles, cartilage, and two vocal cords. Air forced past the vocal cords causes them to vibrate, producing sound.

Epiglottis. The epiglottis sits above the larynx and prevents food from entering the trachea by closing over the larynx during swallowing. If solids or liquids inadvertently enter the larynx, the vocal cords spasm, causing us to cough.

Trachea. The trachea is approximately 5 inches long and is composed of cartilage, which prevents the trachea from collapsing. At the bottom of the trachea, the tube divides into the right and left bronchi. After air enters the lungs via the bronchi, it follows smaller passageways called bronchioles until it enters the alveoli.

Alveoli. The alveoli are small air sacs surrounded by capillaries where red blood cells release carbon dioxide and pick up oxygen. Blood then flows into the pulmonary veins, which carry it to the heart and the rest of the body.

Lungs. The lungs occupy most of the chest cavity. Each lung is enclosed by a double-layered membrane called the pleura. The layer that attaches to the lung is called the visceral pleura, and the layer attached to the chest wall is called the parietal pleura.

Between the two layers is a thin film of fluid that lubricates the membranes and allows them to move freely. This area is called the pleural space, and under normal conditions, it is a potential space under negative pressure. If air enters the pleural space, as in a pneumothorax, the potential space, becomes an actual space, and the lung collapses.

Inspiration is the active motion of breathing. The diaphragm moves downward, and the intercostal muscles (muscles between the ribs) move the chest wall outward. As the ribs move outward, the negative pressure in the lungs increases, and air is sucked into the lung. When the pressure within the lungs and the atmospheric pressure are equal, air stops entering the lungs. At this point, the diaphragm and chest muscles relax, elastic recoil reduces lung size, and air is exhaled (expiration).

Diaphragm. The diaphragm is a specialized muscle that works both voluntarily and involuntarily. The level of carbon dioxide in the blood determines how fast and deeply we breathe. If the level of carbon dioxide in the blood increases, the respiratory center in the brain tells the diaphragm to increase the respiratory rate. If the level of carbon dioxide is too low, the brain tells the diaphragm to slow down. We can directly control the diaphragm by taking deep breaths or by holding our breath, but only for short periods of time, after which the involuntary control centers of the brain take over again.

The Heart

The heart lies under and to the left of the sternum in the mediastinum—the area between the lungs. The pericardial sac surrounds the heart and contains 20 to 60 milliliters of fluid. The fluid allows the heart to beat freely within the sac.

The heart is about the size of an adult fist. It has four chambers: two atria and two ventricles. Unoxygenated blood flows from the superior and inferior vena cava into the right atrium. It then enters the right ventricle and travels to the lungs via the pulmonary artery. After picking up oxygen in the lungs, the blood flows back into the left atrium via the pulmonary vein, then into the left ventricle, and leaves the heart via the aorta.

The myocardium (heart muscle) is an involuntary muscle under the control of the central nervous system. The heart increases or decreases its pumping rate according to signals from the brain. The heart also has an electrical conduction system of its own. The heart can continue to beat indefinitely if only the higher (thought) centers of the brain are damaged. If the respiratory and cardiac centers stop sending signals—for example, as in drowning—the heart may continue beating for only a few minutes.

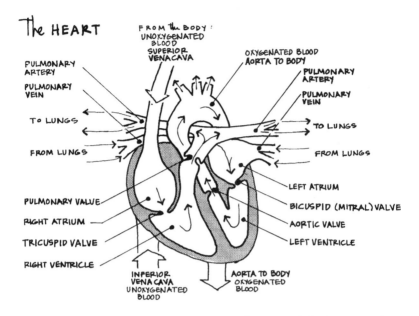

An average resting pulse rate for an adult is 60 to 80 beats per minute. A person in good aerobic shape will have a lower pulse rate; a person who is ill or injured may have a higher rate. Tachycardia occurs when the resting pulse rate is greater than 100 beats per minute; bradycardia, when the resting pulse rate is below 50.

INJURIES TO RIBS

With all chest injuries, coughing is painful and difficult. Nonetheless, you should encourage the patient to cough frequently to help move secretions out of the lung and prevent pneumonia. Splinting the chest with the hand or a sack filled with clothes will help ease the pain when coughing.

Evacuate the patient. If the patient is not in respiratory distress or in danger of further injuring the rib by falling, he or she can walk out. If the patient is in respiratory distress or suffering from a flail chest, he or she will need to be carried out.

Rib Fractures

The most commonly fractured ribs are ribs five through ten. Ribs one through four are protected by the shoulder girdle and are rarely fractured. The floating ribs—ribs eleven and twelve—are more flexible and will give before breaking.

Signs and Symptoms of Rib Fractures
Point tenderness over the fracture
Sharp, stabbing pain
Increased, shallow respiratory rate

Signs and Symptoms. Rib fractures cause deformity and/or discoloration over the injured area. The patient complains of tenderness over the fracture (point tenderness) when touched. Breathing or coughing causes sharp, stabbing pain at the site of the fracture. Respiratory rate increases as the patient breathes shallowly in an attempt to decrease the pain. The patient may clutch the chest on the fractured side in an attempt to splint it. Carefully observe rib fracture victims for other injuries.

Treatment. A single fractured rib that is not displaced (simple rib fracture) does not require splinting. Non-narcotic pain medication (acetaminophen or ibuprofen) may be all the treatment necessary. Avoid narcotics (such as codeine and Percodan), as they may depress respiration.

Tape the Fracture Site on One Side of Chest. If the pain is severe, tape the fractured side from sternum to spine with four or five pieces of 1- to 2-inch adhesive tape. This

Treatment of Rib Fractures
Tape the fracture site on one side of chest

decreases movement at the fracture site and diminishes pain. Tape should never be wrapped completely around the chest, as this can restrict breathing.

Flail Chest

A flail chest occurs when three or more adjacent ribs are broken in two or more places, loosening a segment of the chest wall. When the patient breathes in, the increased negative pressure pulls the flail segment inward, and the lung does not fill with air as it should. When the patient breathes out, the opposite occurs, and the flail segment may be pushed outward. The flail segment moves in a direction opposite of normal breathing, thus the term "paradoxical respirations."

Signs and Symptoms. A flail chest develops only with a massive chest injury, such as a heavy fall against a rock or a rockfall onto the chest. The patient may be in respiratory distress. Put

> ### Signs and Symptoms of Flail Chest
>
> Paradoxical chest movement
> Respiratory distress

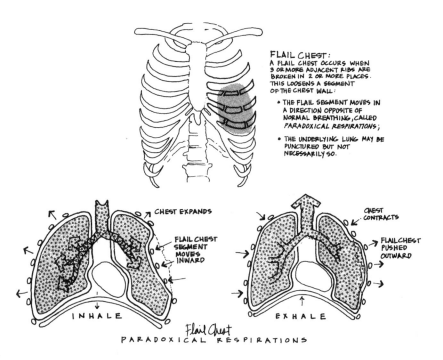

FLAIL CHEST:
A FLAIL CHEST OCCURS WHEN 3 OR MORE ADJACENT RIBS ARE BROKEN IN 2 OR MORE PLACES. THIS LOOSENS A SEGMENT OF THE CHEST WALL:

• THE FLAIL SEGMENT MOVES IN A DIRECTION OPPOSITE OF NORMAL BREATHING, CALLED PARADOXICAL RESPIRATIONS;

• THE UNDERLYING LUNG MAY BE PUNCTURED BUT NOT NECESSARILY SO.

CHEST EXPANDS

FLAIL CHEST SEGMENT MOVES INWARD

INHALE

CHEST CONTRACTS

FLAIL CHEST PUSHED OUTWARD

EXHALE

Flail Chest
PARADOXICAL RESPIRATIONS

your hands under the patient's shirt, and you will feel a part of the chest moving in while the opposite part of the chest is moving out. This is also clearly visible upon inspection.

Treatment. There are three ways to stabilize a flail segment so that normal respiratory function can continue:

1. Position the patient on the injured side with a rolled-up piece of clothing underneath the flailed segment.
2. Apply pressure with your hand to the flailed area. This works only as a temporary measure, as it is difficult to hold pressure while transporting the patient.
3. Tape a large pad firmly over the flail segment.

Treat the patient for shock and evacuate.

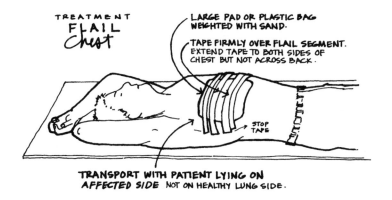

TREATMENT
FLAIL
Chest

LARGE PAD OR PLASTIC BAG WEIGHTED WITH SAND.

TAPE FIRMLY OVER FLAIL SEGMENT. EXTEND TAPE TO BOTH SIDES OF CHEST BUT NOT ACROSS BACK.

STOP TAPE

TRANSPORT WITH PATIENT LYING ON AFFECTED SIDE NOT ON HEALTHY LUNG SIDE.

INJURIES TO LUNGS

In addition to injuries to the ribs, the underlying lungs may be damaged. Blood vessels can be ruptured and torn, causing bleeding into the chest, and lungs can be punctured, causing air to leak into the chest.

Pneumothorax/Hemothorax

Pneumothorax occurs when air leaks into the pleural space, creating negative pressure that collapses the lung. Pneumo-

PNEUMOTHORAX

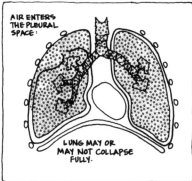

AIR ENTERS
THE PLEURAL
SPACE:

LUNG MAY OR
MAY NOT COLLAPSE
FULLY.

Tension
PNEUMOTHORAX:

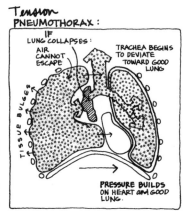

IF
LUNG COLLAPSES:
AIR
CANNOT
ESCAPE

TRACHEA BEGINS
TO DEVIATE
TOWARD GOOD
LUNG

TISSUE BULGES

PRESSURE BUILDS
ON HEART AND GOOD
LUNG.

thorax can be caused by a fractured rib that lacerates the lung (traumatic pneumothorax), a weak spot on the lung wall that gives way (spontaneous pneumothorax), or an open chest wound.

Hemothorax occurs when lacerated blood vessels cause blood to collect in the pleural space. The source can be a fractured rib or lacerated lung. If more than 1 liter of blood leaks into the pleural space, a hemothorax may compress the lung and compromise breathing. The loss of blood may also cause shock.

Spontaneous Pneumothorax. A congenital weak area of the lung may rupture, creating a spontaneous pneumothorax. The highest incidence occurs in tall, thin, healthy men between the ages of twenty and thirty. Eighty percent of spontaneous pneumothoraxes occur while the person is at rest. The patient complains of a sudden, sharp pain in the chest and increasing shortness of breath.

Tension Pneumothorax. If a hole opening into the pleural space serves as a one-way valve—allowing air to enter but not to escape—a tension pneumothorax develops. With each breath, air enters the pleural space, but it cannot escape with expiration. As pressure in the pleural space increases, the lung collapses into a ball 2 to 3 inches in diameter. Pressure in the pleural space eventually causes the mediastinum to shift to the unaffected side, putting pressure on the heart and good lung. If the pressure in the pleural space exceeds that in the veins, blood cannot return to the heart, and death occurs.

As pressure builds, you may see the trachea deviate toward the unaffected side, tissue between the ribs bulge, and the neck veins distend. Respirations become increasingly rapid. The pulse is weak and rapid; cyanosis occurs. Listening to both sides of the chest (with your ear on the chest wall) may indicate that air is entering only one side. Tapping on the injured side may produce a drumlike sound.

Open Chest Wounds

If a wound through the chest wall breaks into the pleural space, air enters, creating a pneumothorax. If the wound remains open, air moves in and out of the pleura, causing a sucking noise.

The goal of treatment is to limit the size of the pneumothorax. Quickly seal the hole with any nonporous material— a plastic bag or petroleum jelly–impregnated gauze, for example. Tape the bag or gauze down on all sides to complete the seal. If a tension pneumothorax develops, you can remove the bag or gauze long enough to allow air to exit the wound,

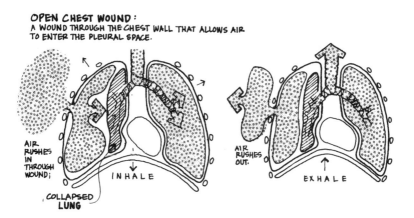

OPEN CHEST WOUND:
A WOUND THROUGH THE CHEST WALL THAT ALLOWS AIR TO ENTER THE PLEURAL SPACE.

AIR RUSHES IN THROUGH WOUND;

COLLAPSED LUNG

INHALE

AIR RUSHES OUT.

EXHALE

Injury to Lungs	
Assessment	**Treatment**
General	Maintain an open airway
Obvious chest trauma	Stop the bleeding
Shortness of breath	Quickly seal open chest wounds
Rapid, shallow respirations	Stabilize impaled objects
Cyanosis	Position patient for comfort
Shock	Evacuate
Coughing up blood	
Pneumothorax	
Sudden, sharp chest pain	
Tension pneumothorax	
Tracheal deviation	
Open chest wound	
Sucking noise	

then immediately reapply the dressing. You may need to repeat this process several times during the evacuation.

Pulmonary Contusion

A pulmonary contusion is a bruise of the lung. Fluid and blood collect at the site of the bruise, interfering with gas exchange. Large pulmonary contusions can cause severe respiratory distress.

Usually the patient has received a blow to the chest. The chest wall may be bruised. The patient is short of breath. Signs and symptoms of shock may be present with large contusions. The patient may cough up blood during the next few days after the injury. A severe contusion is almost always associated with several fractured ribs.

RESPIRATORY DISTRESS

Respiratory distress is an overall term that covers any situation in which a patient is having difficulty breathing. Respiratory distress can occur after an injury, during an illness such as pneumonia, during a heart attack or an asthma attack, or after inhalation of a poisonous gas.

Signs and symptoms of respiratory distress are anxiety and restlessness; shortness of breath; rapid respirations and pulse; signs of shock, including pale, cool, and clammy skin and cyanosis of the skin, lips, and fingernail beds; and labored breathing using accessory muscles of the neck, shoulder, and abdomen to achieve maximum effort. The patient is usually more comfortable sitting than lying.

Respiratory distress is a frightening experience for both the patient and the rescuer. If the underlying cause is emotional, as in hyperventilation syndrome (see chapter 18), a little reassurance may be all that's needed to alleviate the problem. If a chest injury with underlying lung damage or an illness such as pneumonia or a pulmonary embolus occurs, treatment in the field is difficult. Evacuation is the course of action. The airway can be maintained, the patient placed in the most comfortable position for breathing, the injury splinted or taped, wounds dressed, and the patient treated for shock.

INJURIES TO THE HEART
In addition to the lungs, the heart may also be damaged by blows to the chest. Contusions or bruises to the heart muscle, bleeding into the pericardial sac, and damage to the ventricles are grave injuries. Signs of shock and respiratory distress are evident. In the wilderness, treatment involves maintaining the airway, treating for shock, and evacuating.

FINAL THOUGHTS
Chest injuries range from painful but not life-threatening simple rib fractures to serious injuries of the chest wall, lungs, and heart. Chest injuries are often complicated by other injuries as well.

SUMMARY:
CHEST INJURIES

INJURY TO THE RIBS
Assessment
Rib fracture
   Point tenderness
   Sharp pain
   Increased, shallow breathing
Flail chest
   Paradoxical chest movement
   Respiratory distress

Treatment
Rib fracture
   Tape the fracture site
Flail chest
   Position patient on injured side with chest supported
   Tape a large pad over the flail chest

INJURY TO THE LUNGS
Assessment
General
   Obvious chest trauma
   Shortness of breath
   Rapid, shallow respirations
   Cyanosis
   Shock
   Coughing up blood
Pneumothorax/pulmonary embolism
   Sudden, sharp chest pain
Tension pneumothorax
   Tracheal deviation
Open chest wound
   Sucking noise

• CONTINUED •

**SUMMARY:
CHEST INJURIES *(continued)***

Treatment
Maintain an open airway
Stop the bleeding
Quickly seal open chest wounds
Stabilize impaled objects
Position the patient for comfort
Evacuate

CHAPTER 8

ABDOMINAL INJURIES

INTRODUCTION

The abdomen contains the major blood vessels supplying the lower extremities and the digestive, urinary, and reproductive systems. A lot can go wrong in the belly, and deciding how serious a problem is can be difficult, even for a physician. As first-aiders, our role is simple: to decide whether the problem is an "acute abdomen," and if so, to support and evacuate the patient. Knowledge of the location and function of the abdominal organs and some of the common abdominal problems can make this determination easier.

ABDOMINAL ANATOMY AND PHYSIOLOGY

The digestive tract processes food to nourish the cells of the body. Secretions within the digestive tract break down food into basic sugars, fatty acids, and amino acids. These products of digestion cross the wall of the intestine and travel to the liver via the veins for detoxification. From the liver, blood circulates nutrients to the individual cells of the body.

Abdominal and Pelvic Cavities. The abdominal cavity, like the chest, is lined by a slippery membrane, called the peritoneum, that covers the organs. The area behind the peritoneum between the abdominal organs and the muscles of the back is called the retroperitoneum. The diaphragm separates the chest from the abdomen.

The liver, gallbladder, stomach, spleen, pancreas, appendix, and large and small intestines lie in the abdominal cavity. The kidneys, ureters, adrenals, pancreas, aorta, and inferior vena cava are retroperitoneal. The female reproductive organs, bladder, lower end of the large intestine, and rectum are located in the pelvic cavity.

ORGANS OF THE
ABDOMINAL Cavity:

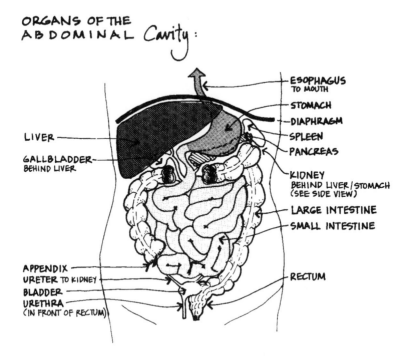

ESOPHAGUS
TO MOUTH
STOMACH
DIAPHRAGM
SPLEEN
PANCREAS
LIVER
GALLBLADDER-
BEHIND LIVER
KIDNEY
BEHIND LIVER/STOMACH
(SEE SIDE VIEW)
LARGE INTESTINE
SMALL INTESTINE
APPENDIX
URETER TO KIDNEY
BLADDER
URETHRA
(IN FRONT OF RECTUM)
RECTUM

Digestive Tract. The digestive tract starts at the mouth, where food mixes with saliva—a combination of mucus, water, salts, digestive enzymes, and organic compounds. As food is swallowed, it passes from the mouth into the pharynx. The pharynx divides into the trachea and esophagus. The trachea lies in front of the esophagus. Food could easily go into the trachea, but a thin flap of cartilage, the epiglottis, closes the entrance to the trachea with each swallow.

The esophagus is a 10-inch muscular tube extending from the larynx to the stomach. Contractions of the esophagus—peristalsis—propel food to the stomach.

Stomach. The stomach is a J-shaped organ approximately 10 inches long located in the upper left quadrant of the abdomen. The major function of the stomach is to intermittently store food and move it into the intestine in small amounts. Every 15 to 25 seconds, stomach contractions mix

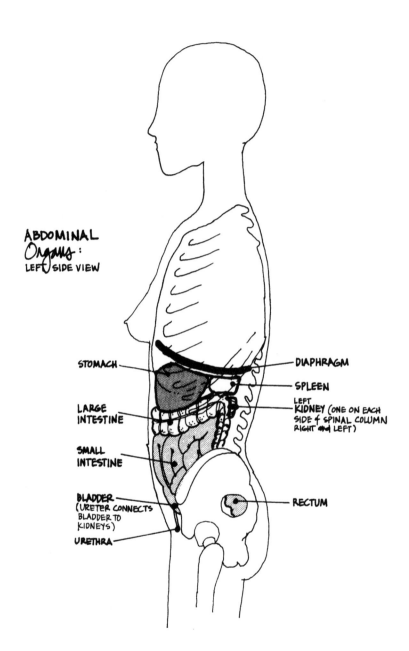

ABDOMINAL
Organs:
LEFT SIDE VIEW

STOMACH

DIAPHRAGM

SPLEEN

LEFT
KIDNEY (ONE ON EACH
SIDE OF SPINAL COLUMN
RIGHT and LEFT)

LARGE
INTESTINE

SMALL
INTESTINE

BLADDER
(URETER CONNECTS
BLADDER TO
KIDNEYS)

RECTUM

URETHRA

food with gastric juice, turning it into chyme, a thin liquid. Water, salts, alcohol, and certain drugs are absorbed directly by the stomach.

Small and Large Intestines. From the stomach, chyme passes into the small intestine, a tube 21 feet long and 1 inch in diameter. Within the first foot of the small intestine, food mixes with secretions from the pancreas and gallbladder. Ninety percent of the products of digestion (proteins, fats, carbohydrates, vitamins, and minerals) is absorbed in the lower end of the small intestine. Peristalsis moves food through the intestines.

Chyme passes from the small intestine to the large intestine, a tube 5 feet long and 2½ inches in diameter. The appendix is located just below the junction of the small and large intestines. The large intestine absorbs water, forming a solid stool.

The rectum is where feces are stored. The last 2 inches of the intestinal tract forms the anus, which consists of a series of sphincters that move the feces out of the body.

Liver. The liver lies beneath the diaphragm in the upper right quadrant. At four pounds in weight, it is the largest solid organ in the abdomen and the one most often injured. There are 500 functions of the liver, among them detoxifying the products of digestion; converting glycogen, fat, and proteins into glucose; storing vitamins; and producing bile.

Gallbladder. Bile, essential for fat digestion and absorption, is stored in the gallbladder, a pear-shaped organ ¾ inch long. The gallbladder responds to the presence of food (especially fats) in the small intestine by constricting and emptying bile into the intestine.

Pancreas. The pancreas is an oblong organ located in back of the liver. It contains two types of glands. One produces pancreatic juice, which aids in the digestion of fats, carbohydrates, starches, and proteins. The juice flows directly into the small intestine via the pancreatic duct. The other gland secretes chemicals, including insulin, that regulate sugar metabolism.

DIVIDING THE ABDOMEN INTO Quadrants:

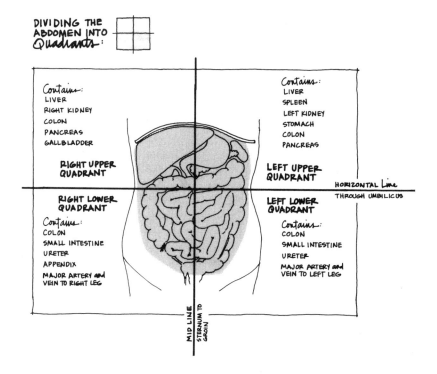

Contains:
LIVER
RIGHT KIDNEY
COLON
PANCREAS
GALLBLADDER

RIGHT UPPER QUADRANT

RIGHT LOWER QUADRANT

Contains:
COLON
SMALL INTESTINE
URETER
APPENDIX
MAJOR ARTERY and VEIN TO RIGHT LEG

Contains:
LIVER
SPLEEN
LEFT KIDNEY
STOMACH
COLON
PANCREAS

LEFT UPPER QUADRANT

HORIZONTAL Line
THROUGH UMBILICUS

LEFT LOWER QUADRANT

Contains:
COLON
SMALL INTESTINE
URETER
MAJOR ARTERY and VEIN TO LEFT LEG

MID LINE
STERNUM TO GROIN

Spleen. The spleen, located in the upper left quadrant beneath the diaphragm, is the only abdominal organ not involved in digestion. The spleen produces blood cells and destroys worn-out red blood cells.

Urinary System. The urinary system—kidneys, ureters, bladder, and urethra—discharges waste materials filtered from the blood. The two kidneys rid the blood of toxic wastes and control water and salt balance. If the kidneys fail to function, toxic waste will concentrate in the blood, causing death.

Urine flows from the kidneys to the bladder via the ureters. The bladder can hold up to 800 milliliters of urine. At 200 to 400 milliliters, we feel the urge to void. The bladder empties to the outside via the urethra. In women, the urethra is about 1½ inches long; in men, approximately 8 inches.

ABDOMINAL ILLNESS
Kidney Stones
Kidney stones occur when minerals precipitate from the urine in the kidney. Approximately three-quarters of kidney stones are crystalized calcium. Predisposing factors for kidney stones include urinary tract infections, dehydration, an increase in dietary calcium, too much vitamin D, and cancer.

Signs and Symptoms. As a stone passes down the ureter, the patient experiences excruciating pain that comes and goes with increasing intensity. The pain usually begins at the level of the lowest ribs on the back and radiates to the lower abdomen and/or groin. The patient is pale, sweaty, nauseated, and "writhing" in pain. There may be pain with urination and blood in the urine. Chills and fever are not present. The duration of the pain depends on the location of the stone. Pain is severe while a stone is passing from the kidney to the bladder and stops after the stone has dropped into the bladder. The pain may last as long as 24 hours, but the duration is usually shorter.

Treatment. Drinking copious amounts of water may help the patient pass the stone. Pain medication such as Tylenol with codeine or Percocet may relieve some of the pain. If pain continues for more than 48 hours or if the patient is unable to urinate, evacuate.

Appendicitis
Appendicitis is an inflammation of the appendix usually caused by a kinking of the appendix or by a hardened stool obstructing the opening. Due to the obstruction, mucus builds within the appendix, causing pressure, swelling, and infection. The highest incidence of appendicitis occurs in males between the ages of 10 and 30.

Signs and Symptoms. The classic symptoms of appendicitis are pain behind the umbilicus (the navel), anorexia, nausea, and vomiting. They usually develop gradually over 1 to 2 days. The pain then shifts to the lower right quadrant, halfway between the umbilicus and the right hipbone. The patient may have one or two bowel movements but usually does not have diarrhea. When you apply pressure with your hand over the appendix, the patient may complain of pain when you remove your hand. This is called rebound tenderness. A fever and elevated pulse may be present. Due to infection and pain, the patient may lie on his or her side or back with legs tucked onto the abdomen (fetal position).

Before the appendix ruptures, the skin over the appendix becomes hypersensitive. If you stroke the skin surface with a pin or grasp the skin between the thumb and forefinger and pull upward, the patient may complain of pain. If the appendix ruptures, the pain temporarily disappears but soon reappears as the abdominal cavity becomes infected (peritonitis). If the infection remains localized (abscess), the patient may only run a low fever and complain of not feeling well. The abscess may not rupture for a week or more.

Treatment. Appendicitis is a surgical emergency. The patient must be evacuated.

Peritonitis

Peritonitis is an inflammation of the peritoneum. Causes include penetrating abdominal wounds, abdominal bleeding, or ruptured internal organs that spill digestive juices into the abdominal cavity.

Signs and Symptoms. Signs and symptoms of peritonitis vary, depending on whether the infection is local or general. The patient lies very still, as movement increases the pain. He or she may complain of nausea, vomiting, anorexia, and/or fever. The abdomen is rigid and tender. The infection causes peristaltic activity of the bowel to stop, so the patient has no bowel movements. Shock may be present. The patient appears very sick.

Treatment. Peritonitis is a severe infection beyond our capability to treat in the wilderness; treat the patient for shock and evacuate.

Hemorrhoids

Hemorrhoids are varicose veins of the anal canal. They may be internal or external. Constipation, straining during elimination, diarrhea, and pregnancy can cause hemorrhoids. External hemorrhoids can be very painful. Internal hemorrhoids tend not to be painful but bleed during bowel movements. The stool may be streaked on the outside with blood. The patient may complain of itching around the anus.

   Treatment. Apply moist heat to the anal area. This can be done with a bandanna dipped in warm water. Rest, increased liquid and fruit intake to keep the stools soft, and/or anesthetic ointments (such as dibucaine, Preparation H, or Anusol) help decrease pain and bleeding.

Gastric and Duodenal Ulcers

Decreased resistance of the stomach lining to pepsin and hydrochloric acid, or an increase in the production of these chemicals, may result in ulcers. Stress, smoking, aspirin use, certain bacteria, caffeine or alcohol consumption, and heredity are possible causes.

   Signs and Symptoms. The patient complains of a gnawing, aching, or burning in the upper abdomen at the midline 1 to 2 hours after eating or at night, when gastric secretions are at their peak. The pain may radiate from the lowest ribs to the back and frequently disappears if the patient ingests food or antacids.

   Is it indigestion, or is it an ulcer? Indigestion symptoms tend to be associated with eating. The patient complains of fullness and heartburn and may belch or vomit small amounts of food. Indigestion worsens when more food is ingested. As time passes and the stomach empties, symptoms disappear. Indigestion tends to be related to a single meal.

   Treatment. The primary treatment for ulcers is to take antacids an hour after meals; eat small, frequent meals; and avoid coffee, alcohol, and spicy foods, which increase the secretions of the stomach. Long-term treatment includes rest and counseling to decrease stress. If the ulcer perforates the wall of the stomach, symptoms of peritonitis occur.

Gastroenteritis

Gastroenteritis, often called "traveler's diarrhea," is an inflammation of the stomach and intestines caused by bacteria, viruses, or protozoa. These organisms normally live in our intestines; we develop resistance to the particular strains from our home environment. When exposed to unfamiliar strains, we become sick. These organisms are most commonly transmitted through fecal contamination of water or food.

Signs and Symptoms. The patient experiences nausea, vomiting, diarrhea, headache, abdominal cramps, and/or generalized muscular aching. Fever and chills are not usually present. The illness usually lasts 2 to 5 days.

Treatment. The goal of treatment is to prevent dehydration and replace electrolytes that are lost in the stools. Diarrhea can cause the loss of large amounts of potassium and bicarbonate and varying amounts of sodium and chloride, causing an electrolyte imbalance.

The first solid foods the patient takes following an episode of diarrhea should be bland—plain rice, plain oatmeal, dry bread, or dry pancakes. See chapter 19 ("Hydration") for more information.

Prevention. Always wash your hands with soap and water before preparing meals and after urinating or defecating in order to decrease the risk of transmitting bacteria from the urine or stool to the mouth. See chapter 17 ("Hygiene and Water Disinfection") for further details on hygiene, foodborne illness, and proper food handling.

ABDOMINAL TRAUMA

Abdominal organs are either solid or hollow. When hollow organs are perforated, they spill their contents into the abdominal cavity. Solid organs tend to bleed when injured. Either bleeding or spillage of digestive juices causes peritonitis.

Blunt Trauma. Inspect the abdomen for bruises; consider how the injury occurred to diagnose what, if any, organs

Hollow Organs	Solid Organs
Stomach	Liver
Small and large intestines	Spleen
Gallbladder	Pancreas
Ureters	Kidneys
Urinary bladder	

may have been damaged. Pain, signs and symptoms of shock, and a significant mechanism of injury are reasons to initiate an evacuation.

Penetrating Wounds. Assume that any penetrating wound to the abdomen has entered the peritoneal lining. Treat the patient for shock and evacuate.

Impaled Objects. Leave any impaled object in place; removal will increase bleeding. Stabilize the object with dressings. If there is bleeding, apply pressure bandages around the wound. Evacuate the patient by the gentlest means to minimize movement of the impaled object.

Evisceration. An evisceration is a protrusion of abdominal organs through a laceration in the abdominal wall. Cover the eviscerated bowel with dressings that have been soaked in disinfected water. These should be moistened every 2 hours to prevent the loops of bowel from becoming dry. Several more layers of thick dressings should be applied to the wound to minimize heat loss. Change the dressings daily. Treat for shock, and evacuate the patient immediately.

Monitor vital signs hourly for the first 12 hours after treating a patient who has sustained a blow to the abdomen. Check the urine for blood. To do this, have the patient urinate into a water bottle and let the urine settle for at least 2 hours. Look for reddish fluid near the bottom of the bottle, which indicates the presence of blood in the urine. Report your findings to the physician when you evacuate the patient.

ABDOMINAL ASSESSMENT

The first-aider needs a few simple skills to be able to evaluate the condition of a patient with an abdominal problem.

1. Inspect the abdomen. Position the patient in a warm place, lying down. Remove the patient's clothing so that you can see the entire abdomen. A normal abdomen is slightly rounded and symmetrical. Look for old scars, areas of bruising, rashes, impaled objects, eviscerations, and distention. Check the lower back for the same. Look for any movement of the abdomen—wavelike contractions may indicate an abdominal obstruction.

2. Listen to the abdomen in all quadrants. Place your ear on the patient's abdomen and listen for bowel sounds (gurgling noises). An absence of noise indicates an injured or ill bowel. You must listen for at least 2 to 3 minutes in all quadrants before you can properly say that no bowel sounds are present.

3. Palpate the abdomen. With your palms down, apply gentle pressure with the pads of the fingers. Make sure your hands are warm and that you palpate in all the quadrants. Cold fingers or jabbing can cause the patient to tighten the abdominal muscles, thereby impeding the assessment. The abdomen should be soft and not tender. Abnormal signs include localized tenderness, diffuse tenderness, and stiff, rigid muscles ("boardlike abdomen").

4. Discuss the patient's condition with him or her. Ask about pain: Where is it located, where does it radiate to, and what is the severity and frequency? What aggravates or alleviates the pain? Are there patterns to the pain (at night, after meals, etc.)? Observe facial expressions. Do the patient's facial expressions conflict with his or her answers? Ask the patient about his or her past medical history. Any allergies, past surgery, diagnosis, treatment, or injuries? Have any relatives had abdominal problems? Any problems with swallowing, digestion, bowel, bladder, or reproductive organs? Any back or circulation problems?

FINAL THOUGHTS

There are many medical problems that cause acute abdominal pain. Determining the actual source of the pain and the urgency of the condition can be difficult, even for a physician. As the leader of a wilderness trip, your task is not to make a diagnosis; it is to decide whether the pain indicates an "acute abdomen," a possible surgical emergency requiring further evaluation.

Evacuation is recommended for anyone with abdominal pain that is localized, severe, or accompanied by a rigid abdomen or that persists or worsens over 12 to 24 hours. Evacuate a patient with abdominal pain and fever over 102°F (38°C); bloody diarrhea; or dehydration, persistent nausea, vomiting, and diarrhea for more than 24 hours. A female with abdominal pain not consistent with a simple urinary tract infection or gastroenteritis should be evacuated for assessment by a physician.

SUMMARY: ACUTE ABDOMINAL PAIN

Assessment (Indications for Evacuation)
Severe or prolonged abdominal pain
Blood in vomit, feces, urine
Tenderness or guarding of the abdominal wall
Fever above 102°F (88°C)
Persistent nausea, vomiting, or diarrhea for more than 24 hours

Treatment
Treat for shock
Allow no food or fluids by mouth
Evacuate

CHAPTER 9

COLD INJURIES

INTRODUCTION

On a snowy subzero morning in early November, after 2 days of searching, a lost hunter was found in the Wind River Mountains south of Lander, Wyoming. His nose, hands, feet, and stomach were severely frostbitten, and he showed limited signs of life. After several hours of evacuation by snow litter and four-wheel drive, rescuers delivered him to the emergency room with a rectal temperature of 74°F (23°C).

His ordeal was not over yet. The hypothermia caused his heart to stop, and only after 3 hours of warming and CPR did he begin to recover. His story was presented by the media as one of "miraculous" survival. He was lucky, and he knows it. Today, this man is a strong advocate of prevention.

Knowledge of the causes, assessment, and treatment of cold injuries is an essential component of wilderness medicine. Hypothermia is usually associated with cold climates, but hypothermia can occur even in warm climates, as it has on NOLS sea kayaking courses in Mexico. If you spend enough time outdoors, you will gain firsthand experience with cold injuries such as hypothermia, frostbite, and immersion foot.

THE PHYSIOLOGY OF
TEMPERATURE REGULATION

Humans are warm-blooded animals that maintain a relatively constant internal temperature regardless of the environmental temperature. We do this by producing heat through exercise and metabolism of food and by adjusting the amount of heat we lose to the environment.

Human cells, tissues, and organs operate efficiently only within narrow temperature limits. If your temperature rises

2°F above the normal of 98.6°F (37°C), you become ill. If it rises 7°F, you become critically ill. If your temperature decreases 2°F, you feel cold. A 7°F decrease puts your life in jeopardy.

Humans are designed to live in tropical climates; our heat loss mechanisms are highly developed. Our insulation mechanisms, however, are less efficient. To adapt structurally to cold, our bodies would have to grow thick insulating hair all over and develop greater reserves of fat. Rather than remaining angular and cylindrical, which promotes heat loss, our body shape would become rounder and shorter to prevent heat loss. This would especially affect our ability to tolerate lower body temperatures and near-freezing temperatures in our fingers and toes.

As it is, human beings can live in the cold because our intellectual responses enable us to deal effectively with environmental stress. Much of what students learn on NOLS courses is how to live comfortably in extreme environmental conditions by employing skill, disciplined habits, and quality equipment. We compensate for our physical deficiencies with behavioral responses such as eating, drinking, and creating microclimates through the use of clothing, fire, and shelter. The diminished intellectual response evident in early stages of hypothermia, as well as in altitude sickness, heat illness, and dehydration, dangerously impairs our ability to react to the environment.

Mechanisms of Heat Production

The three main physiological means for producing heat are metabolic rate, exercise, and shivering.

Resting Metabolism. The basal metabolic rate is like a constant internal furnace, liberating heat as a by-product of the biochemical reactions that keep us alive. Metabolic rate increases slightly when we are exposed to cold for long periods, but not enough to satisfy the body's entire heat requirements in winter conditions. Food is the fuel for metabolism. Nutritionally sound rations and good cooking skills are critical to health on wilderness expeditions.

**Mechanisms of Heat
Production**

Resting metabolism
Exercise
Shivering

An important heat source for infants and hibernating mammals is the oxidation of brown fat from deposits on the abdomen, in the armpits, and behind the shoulders. Oxidizing or burning brown fat produces considerable heat. This is of particular significance for infants, who, because of their small size, have a large surface area for heat loss. Brown fat cells are almost completely absent in adult humans.

Exercise. Exercise is an important method of heat production. Muscles, which make up 50 percent of our body weight, produce 73 percent of the heat generated during work. Short bursts of hard physical effort can generate tremendous amounts of heat, while moderate levels of exercise can be sustained for long periods. This valuable source of heat does have its limitations. Physical conditioning, strength, stamina, and fuel in the form of food and water are necessary to sustain activity.

Shivering. Shivering—a random quivering of muscles—produces heat at a rate five times greater than the basal metabolic rate. It is our first defense against cold. Shivering occurs when temperature receptors in the skin and brain sense a decrease in body temperature and trigger the shivering response.

As with all forms of work, the price of shivering is fuel. How long and how effectively we shiver is limited by the amount of carbohydrates stored in muscles and by the amount of water and oxygen available. In order to shiver, we have to pump blood into the muscles. Warm blood flowing close to the surface reduces our natural insulation and increases heat loss.

Shivering also hinders our ability to perform the behavioral tasks necessary to reduce heat loss and increase heat production. It is difficult to zip up your parka, start your stove, or ski to camp during violent shivering. Vigorous physical activity, however, can override the shivering response. If we don't capture the heat produced by vigorous exercise in insulating clothing, we can cool past the point of shivering without experiencing the response.

Mechanisms of Heat Loss

The core of the body contains the organs necessary for survival: the heart, brain, lungs, liver, and kidneys. The shell consists of the muscles, skin, and superficial tissues. The ebb and flow of blood from core to superficial tissues is a constant process. As our temperature rises, blood volume shifts and carries heat to the outer layers of the skin. As we cool, less blood flows to the periphery, preserving heat for the vital organs.

Our mechanisms for heat loss are so well developed that we lose heat in all but the hottest and most humid conditions. On a warm day, if we did not lose most of the heat our bodies produced, our body temperature would rise. The primary means of heat loss is through the skin. Warm, flushed skin can dispose of heat through conduction, convection, radiation, or evaporation.

The circulatory system controls heat by regulating the volume of blood flowing to the skin and superficial muscles. When we are resting comfortably, only a small percentage of blood flows directly to the skin. During heat stress, however, the blood vessels open up and blood flow to the skin may increase a hundredfold. During cold stress, blood is shunted from the periphery to the core, reducing the heat lost to the environment. Constricted blood vessels can reduce blood flow to the skin by 99 percent.

Conduction. Conduction is the transfer of heat through direct contact between a hot and a cold object. Heat moves from the warmer to the colder object. We lose heat when we lie on the cold, wet ground. We gain heat when we lie on a hot

Mechanisms of Heat Loss
Conduction
Convection
Radiation
Evaporation

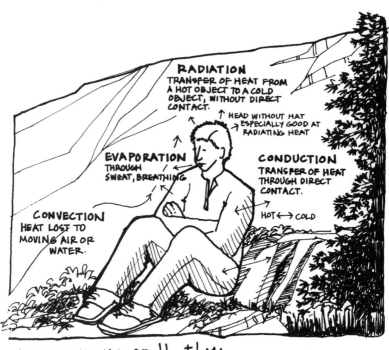

MECHANISMS OF Heat Loss

beach or rock. The rate of heat transfer is determined by the temperature difference between the two objects, the surface area exposed to the cold surface, and the effectiveness of the insulation between the body and the cold surface. The more efficient the insulation, the less heat is transferred. Warm, still air trapped in clothing is an effective insulator. Water, metal, and snow are good conductors.

We reduce conductive heat loss every night by sleeping with a foam pad between ourselves and the ground. If we wake up cold, we add insulation between ourselves and the ground or snow before we put on more clothing. Damp cotton conducts heat, so if we're cold and wearing a damp cotton shirt, we'll take that off. On winter expeditions we place extra insoles in

our boots, and in camp we stand on foam pads to reduce conduction between our feet and the snow.

Convection. Convective heat transfer occurs when the
medium of transfer moves. Whether through moving air or
water, heat escapes from the surface of the body by convection.
Moving air (wind chill), besides cooling us directly, strips away
the microclimate of air heated by the body. The loss of this
insulating layer next to the body further accelerates heat loss.

Moving water carries heat directly from the surface of the
body. To discover the cooling power of moving water, place your
fingers in a bowl of cold water. Slowly swirl your fingers. The
increase in heat loss is immediately perceptible. Immersion in
cold water is a profound threat to temperature balance.

Heat is transferred by convection through the body by the
blood. As we cool and the body shunts blood away from the
skin, the superficial tissues—especially in our fingers and
toes—no longer gain heat from the blood, which increases the
likelihood of frostbite.

We reduce convective heat loss by wearing wind-resistant
clothes, tight-weave nylon jackets and pants, and hoods to
protect the vulnerable head and neck.

Radiation. Radiation is the transfer of infrared, or heat,
radiation from a hot object to a cold object. With a normal
body temperature of 98°F (37°C), humans are often one of the
warmer objects in the environment, and we lose heat through
radiation. We receive radiative heat input from fires, from the
sun, or from reflection off snow, water, or rocks.

Radiative heat loss makes clear winter nights colder than
cloudy nights. Cloud cover reflects much of the earth's radiative heat back to the ground, reducing the severity of the
nighttime temperature drop. Reflected, radiated heat waves
bouncing off the walls and snowfields of a cirque during bright
sunshine increase warmth—and the possibility of sunburn.

When exposed to the environment, the skin acts as a
radiator. Unlike in the rest of the body, the blood vessels in
the head do not constrict and reduce the blood supply flowing
to the scalp. The head is therefore an excellent radiator of

heat, eliminating from 35 to 50 percent of our total heat production. Dry clothing, especially on the head, reduces radiative heat loss as well as providing insulation.

Evaporation. When perspiration evaporates from the skin's surface, we lose heat as the liquid water is converted to a gaseous state. Evaporative heat loss accounts for 20 percent of the body's total heat loss in normal conditions—much more when we are under heat stress or working hard. We use this to our advantage to cool ourselves in hot environments.

Sweating accounts for roughly two-thirds of evaporative heat loss. The remaining one-third is lost through breathing. Inhalation humidifies air and warms it to body temperature. During exhalation, evaporation of moisture from the surface of the lungs and airways uses heat and cools the body. The rate and depth of breathing and the humidity of the air determine the amount of heat and moisture lost. The colder and drier the air and the faster the breathing rate, the greater the heat loss.

We reduce evaporative heat loss by controlling our work rate, by using techniques such as the rest step (walking with flat feet, transferring weight slowly and smoothly from one leg to the other) when backpacking, and by avoiding hard breathing and sweating. Sweating in cold environments is to be avoided. It wets insulation and cools the body.

A constant balance of heat gain and loss is required to maintain a stable body temperature. The adjustments the body makes are designed to keep our vital organs—heart, brain, lungs, kidneys, and liver—within a temperature range in which they operate effectively. If core temperature rises above normal, potentially life-threatening conditions—heatstroke or high fever—develop. When core temperature drops below normal, hypothermia may be the result.

HYPOTHERMIA

Hypothermia occurs when body temperature drops to 95°F (34.5°C) or lower, a condition that is not exclusive to the winter environment. Hypothermia can develop whenever heat loss exceeds heat gain and is as common during the wind, rain, and hail of summer as it is during winter. Immersion in cold water can cause hypothermia. If body temperature drops as low as 80°F (26.4°C), death is likely.

Signs and Symptoms

The signs and symptoms of hypothermia change as body temperature falls. Mental functions tend to go first, and the patient loses the ability to respond appropriately to the environment. Muscular functions deteriorate until the patient is too clumsy to walk or stand. Biochemical processes become slow and deficient as the body cools.

Hypothermia in which body temperatures remain above 90°F (32°C) is classified on a scale of mild to moderate. Hypothermia below 90°F (32°C) is severe. A healthy adult with a body temperature of 93°F (33.5°C) is dangerously cold, but chances are good that warming will be successful. If the same person has a temperature of 90°F (32°C) or less, warming in the backcountry can be difficult, and the patient's life is in grave danger.

Early signs and symptoms of hypothermia can be difficult to recognize and may easily go undiagnosed. The patient

---

Signs and Symptoms of Hypothermia

Mental deterioration in decision-making ability	Shivering
Slow and improper response to cold	Loss of fine motor ability progressing to stumbling, clumsiness, and falling
Apathy, lethargy	Muscle stiffness and inability to move (in severe cases)
Increased complaints, decreased group cooperation	
Slurred speech, disorientation progressing to incoherence and irrationality and possible unconsciousness	

does not feel well. You may assume that he or she is tired, not hypothermic. Yet this is the stage at which successful warming in the wilderness is possible if we catch the problem.

Hypothermia in its later stages may be more obvious. The patient collapses, slurs words, is semiconscious, and is grossly uncoordinated with a clearly altered mental status. This stage of hypothermia is easier to recognize but much harder to treat in the wilderness.

Mild Hypothermia. In the early stages of hypothermia, the patient feels chilled and may shiver. The skin may be numb with goose bumps. Minor impairment of muscular performance is evident in stiff and clumsy fingers. Mental deterioration begins. Responses are slow and/or improper, such as not changing into dry clothes or failing to wear a rain jacket, wind garments, or hat.

An increase in muscle tension, followed by shivering, is the first response to cold. Shivering reaches its maximum when body temperature has fallen from 95°F (34.5°C) to 93°F (33.5°C). Shivering stops when the temperature falls into the low 90s. During the fast cooling phase, the heart rate increases to as high as 150 beats per minute.

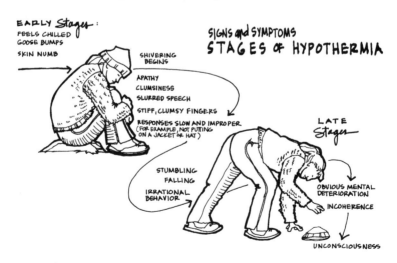

EARLY Stages:
FEELS CHILLED
GOOSE BUMPS
SKIN NUMB

SIGNS and SYMPTOMS
STAGES OF HYPOTHERMIA

SHIVERING BEGINS
APATHY
CLUMSINESS
SLURRED SPEECH
STIFF, CLUMSY FINGERS
RESPONSES SLOW AND IMPROPER (FOR EXAMPLE, NOT PUTTING ON A JACKET OR HAT)

STUMBLING
FALLING
IRRATIONAL BEHAVIOR

LATE Stages

OBVIOUS MENTAL DETERIORATION
INCOHERENCE
UNCONSCIOUSNESS

Moderate Hypothermia. As body temperature drops into the mid-90s (34°–36°C), muscular coordination deteriorates. The patient may stumble, walk slowly, lack energy, and become apathetic and lethargic. He or she talks less and may become uncooperative and complaining. Responses to questions may be inappropriate; the patient may exhibit slurred speech and confusion about time or place.

As body temperature approaches the low 90s, gross muscular incoordination becomes obvious: stumbling, falling, and inability to use the hands. The patient may become cantankerous or forgetful and display inappropriate behavior.

Severe Hypothermia. When body temperature drops below 90°F (32°C), shivering stops. Energy reserves are depleted, and obvious mental deterioration is present. The patient may be incoherent, disoriented, irrational, or unresponsive. Exposed skin is very cold and may be blue.

As the body becomes cooler, heart rate and blood pressure fall. Respirations slow and may finally cease around 78°F (26°C). In the mid to low 80s (28°–29°C), severe muscular rigidity may occur. The patient may become unconscious and exhibit dilated pupils. The pulse may be undetectable, and the patient may appear to have stopped breathing or to have died.

Recognizing Hypothermia (Assessment)

Hypothermia is easily overlooked. In cities, it has been mistaken for alcohol intoxication, stroke, and drug overdose. It may be associated with illnesses such as diabetes and other metabolic disturbances or with the elderly and the homeless. In the wilderness, hypothermia has been confused with fatigue, irritability, dehydration, and mountain sickness.

You can measure the patient's temperature to detect hypothermia. Choose a low-reading hypothermia thermometer for your medical kit; conventional thermometers read only to 94°F (34°C). A rectal temperature is ideal in the field; oral or axillary (armpit) temperatures may not reflect the status of the core organs. However, obtaining a rectal temperature on a cold and confused patient can be awkward. Also, undressing

Assessment of Hypothermia	
Mild to Moderate *Above 90°F (32°C)* Conscious Shivering Able to walk Alert (altered mental status possible)	**Severe** *Below 90°F (32°C)* Altered mental status No shivering Unable to walk

the patient to obtain a rectal reading may cause further cooling, is not practical, and is rarely done in wilderness.

The most important diagnostic tool in the backcountry is the first-aider's awareness of the possibility of hypothermia and attention to the patient's mental state. Anyone in a cool or cold environment is at risk for hypothermia. Persons with altered mental status (confused, slurred speech, disoriented) in the outdoors may be hypothermic. Any ill or injured person may have difficulty maintaining proper body temperature. Whether you can obtain a temperature or not, if you suspect hypothermia, treat it immediately and aggressively.

Treatment
Prevention of hypothermia is simple. Treatment is not. Warming can be a long and complex process that takes hours, and it may be impossible in the backcountry.

Mild to Moderate Hypothermia. A mildly hypothermic patient may be warmed in the field using backcountry warming techniques. In the absence of a serious underlying medical condition, the chances for successful warming are good. The patient in early hypothermia may respond well to removal of the cold stress. Although you cannot change the air temperature, you can replace wet clothing with dry, protect the patient from the wind, add layers of insulation, hydrate and feed the patient, and apply heat.

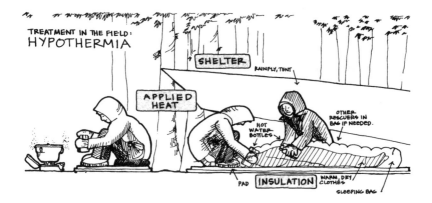

Most warmings of hypothermic people are simple. You dry them, dress them in warm clothes, get them to move, give them hot drinks, and everything works out fine. If a patient is more seriously cold, you place him or her in a sleeping bag "hypothermia wrap" with hot water bottles, build a fire, and take other aggressive actions as necessary.

Prevent Further Heat Loss. Remove the patient from the cold environment and make sure that he or she is dry. Dress the patient in dry clothing, especially a hat to reduce heat loss from the head and neck. For mild hypothermia, this and a hot drink are often all the treatment that's needed.

Feed and Hydrate the Patient. Hot drinks are a good source of heat, fluid, and sugar. But be careful not to burn the patient. The patient must be alert enough to hold the drink and consume it under his or her own power. Hot drinks and simple foods, such as candy bars, can be followed by a good meal after the patient is warmed. A warmed patient should not return to the cold until energy and fluid reserves have been replenished. A fatigued or dehydrated patient is a strong candidate for another episode of hypothermia. In our experience, it's best to keep the warmed patient in the sleeping bag for a good night's sleep and to give him or her a hot meal and several liters of water.

Place the Patient in a Sleeping Bag. A sleeping bag in a "hypothermia wrap" is the backcountry's most tried and true warming tool. The patient is placed into a sleeping bag with a second bag and a foam pad underneath and a third bag on top. Heat packs or hot water bottles close to the patient may be helpful sources of heat. This whole package is wrapped "burrito style" in a tarp or plastic sheet to insulate from wind and moisture loss. Mild or moderately hypothermic patients who can shiver and still produce heat often warm themselves if their body's heat is captured by warm, dry, windproof insulation.

Colder patients with depleted energy reserves may have lost the ability to produce heat. If left alone in a sleeping bag, they may only be insulated at their current temperature or may cool further. Heat packs or hot water bottles within the hypothermia wrap may provide enough heat to stabilize the patient's temperature.

The traditional recommendation is to place the patient in one or more bags with at least one other person as a heat source. In our experience, the hypothermia wrap with hot water bottles is a more effective practice. The insulation of the sleeping bags suffers as people get in and out, and the warmers are not available for other tasks such as setting up camp and preparing food. If one person in the group has become hypothermic, others are at risk. The warmers can quickly become cold and fatigued. Experts disagree on the amount of heat transferred body to body—some think it's low. The value of a warm person in the sleeping bag may be to heat the insulation, not to transfer heat directly to the patient. If this method is used, we recommend that the warmers wear at least a thin layer of clothing. Feed the warmers to keep their energy levels up. Clothing placed over the opening of zipped-together sleeping bags helps reduce heat loss. Placing several sleeping bags over the patient and the warmers also helps. A humid environment inside the sleeping bag reduces respiratory heat loss, as does loosely wrapping a scarf or other article of clothing across the patient's mouth and nose.

Place Hot Water Bottles on Torso, Hands, and Feet. Hot water bottles applied to the neck and groin—areas close to the core and containing large blood vessels—are an excellent

---

Backcountry Warming Techniques

Remove the patient from the cold environment

Dry the patient and dress him or her in dry clothing

Insulate the head and neck

Feed and hydrate the patient

Place the patient in sleeping bags

Place insulated hot water bottles on the torso, hands, and feet

Use fires as heat sources

Feed, hydrate, and rotate the warmers

Be persistent; warming takes time

---

source of heat. Research indicates that heat is also transferred well from the palms of the hands and soles of the feet. Be careful not to burn the patient. Apply the hot water bottles to yourself before applying them to your patient. Wrap them in socks to insulate them from direct contact with the patient.

Use Fires as Heat Sources. Fires are an excellent source of heat. Position the patient in the sleeping bag next to or between two fires. Use a space blanket as a reflector. If you are without a sleeping bag, dress the patient in dry clothes for insulation.

Be Persistent: Warming Takes Time. Individuals such as the hunter described in the introduction have recovered from prolonged, profound hypothermia. Newspaper headlines occasionally describe "frozen" and "dead" people who were successfully warmed. The adage to remember about hypothermia treatment is that "the victim is never dead until he is warm and dead."

Severe Hypothermia. A severely hypothermic patient produces little or no heat and, in the absence of external heat sources, may cool further. A cold heart is susceptible to abnormal rhythms such as ventricular fibrillation, a random quivering of the heart that fails to pump blood. Jarring or bouncing, almost inevitable in transport from the backcountry, can trigger this rhythm.

Treatment of Hypothermia	

Mild to Moderate
Above 90°F (32°C)
Prevent further heat loss
  Remove from cold
  Dry
  Insulate
Actively warm
  Sleeping bags
  Heat sources
  Hydrate, hot drinks
  Food for fuel; feed the
    shivering
	Severe
	Below 90°F (32°C)
	Evacuate to hospital for warming
	  Dry, insulate
	  Prevent further heat loss
	    (apply heat)
	  ABCs
	  Handle gently

There may be complications from an underlying medical condition or trauma and complex disturbances in the body's biochemical balance. For these reasons, a patient with severe hypothermia ideally is warmed in a hospital.

Evacuation of a severely hypothermic patient must occur simultaneously with attempts to prevent further cooling. If you do not apply heat to the patient during transport, further cooling is almost certain. Monitor ABCs and vitals, and carry the patient as gently as possible.

It may be difficult to find the pulse or respiration rate of a severely hypothermic patient. The heart rate may be 20 to 30 beats per minute, and the breathing rate only 3 to 4 times a minute. Take your time during assessment. Check the heartbeat and breathing for at least 1 minute, carefully watching for the rise and fall of the chest, listening for any breath sounds, and feeling for the pulse at the neck.

The Wilderness Medical Society advises not to start CPR on a hypothermia victim if there are any signs of life or if the chest wall is frozen. If you do start CPR on a hypothermic patient, you are committed to continuing it until the patient is warm. Check with your local physician to see if protocols for CPR and hypothermia have been established in your area.

FROSTBITE

Frostbite acts locally on areas such as fingers, toes, and ears. It is not life-threatening, but tissue damage from frostbite can result in loss of function or, in serious cases, gangrene and amputation.

Frostbite occurs when tissue is frozen. As blood flow declines, the fluid between cells can freeze. The formation of ice crystals draws water out of the cells, dehydrating them. Mechanical cell damage also occurs as the crystals rub together. Blood clots form in small vessels and circulation stops, further damaging cells.

A second phase of injury occurs during warming. Damaged cells release substances that promote constriction and clotting in small blood vessels, impairing blood flow to the tissues.

Low temperatures, contact with moisture, and wind chill accelerate heat loss and increase the likelihood of frostbite. Metal and petroleum products can cool well below the point of freezing. Skin contact with metal or supercooled gasoline causes immediate freezing. Constriction of an extremity, caused by tight boots, gaiters, or watchbands, or confinement

Causes of Frostbite	
Cold stress	Interference with circulation of
Low temperatures	blood
Wind chill	Cramped position
Moisture	Tight clothing (gaiters, wrist-
Poor insulation	watches, etc.)
Contact with supercooled metal	Local pressure
or gasoline	Tight fitting or laced boots
	Dehydration

in a cramped position may reduce blood flow and increase the likelihood of frostbite.

Blood brings oxygen and nutrients to the tissue, as well as heat. Dehydration and hypothermia impair circulation to the extremities by reducing the available fluid and by promoting constriction of blood vessels to preserve heat in the core.

Simple classification of frostbite includes first degree or superficial frostbite, also known as frostnip; second degree or partial-thickness frostbite; and third degree, deep, or full-thickness frostbite. Many experts classify frostbite only after it has thawed and the extent of the damage is apparent.

Frostnip or Superficial Frostbite

With frostnip or superficial frostbite, only the outer layer of skin is frozen. It appears white and waxy or possibly gray or mottled. Frostnip may occur from contact with a cold metal or a supercooled liquid or from exposure to severe wind chill. High winds together with cold temperatures create conditions for frostnip on exposed areas of the face, nose, ears, and cheeks.

Frostnip is similar in physiology to a first-degree burn and is sometimes called first-degree frostbite. After the nipped area is warm, the layer of frozen skin becomes red. Over a period of several days, the dead skin peels. As it heals, the appearance of the injury is similar to that of sunburn, a first-degree burn.

Warm frostnip immediately. Placing a warm hand on a frozen cheek or placing cold fingers into an armpit or warm (100° to 108°F, [38° to 42°C]) water will thaw the frozen area. Covering up from the wind and cold, thereby reducing the exposure, should prevent further injury.

Partial-Thickness Frostbite

Partial-thickness frostbite is similar to a second-degree burn. This injury has progressed from frostnip into the underlying tissues. Externally, it appears as a white, mottled, or gray area. It may feel hard on the surface, soft and resilient below. Blisters usually appear within 24 hours after warming.

Treatment for partial-thickness frostbite is rapid warming by immersion in warm (100° to 108°F [38° to 42°C]) water. Unlike frostnip, this injury should not be warmed by simple application of heat. Proper warming is crucial to healing.

Deep Frostbite

The most serious form of frostbite is deep, full-thickness, or third-degree frostbite. The injury extends from the skin into the underlying tissues and muscles. The external appearance is the same as frostnip and partial-thickness frostbite, but the frozen area feels hard. After thawing, the area may not blister or may blister only where deep frostbite borders on more superficial damage.

Differentiating partial-thickness from deep frostbite before thawing is difficult. Blisters containing clear fluid, extending to the tips of the digits, and forming within 48 hours of warming suggest partial-thickness frostbite. Blood-filled blisters that don't reach the tips of the digits, delayed blisters, or the lack of blisters indicates deep frostbite. Like partial-thickness frostbite, deep frostbite is warmed by immersion in warm water.

Treatment

Dangerous folk remedies for frostbite include rubbing the frozen part with snow, flogging the area to restore circulation, and exposing it to an open flame. The treatment of choice is rapid warming in warm water.

Delay Warming. Try to keep the injury frozen until warming can be carried out correctly. Many people, including one of these authors, have traveled long distances with frozen feet in order to reach a place where warming could be done once and done well. How long the area can be kept frozen without increasing the damage is a matter of controversy. Tissue damage seems to be related to the length of time the tissue stays frozen.

There are several problems with keeping a frostbitten extremity frozen while evacuation takes place. If the injury occurred from exposure to extreme cold, lack of proper clothing, or in conjunction with hypothermia, the frostbitten area

Treatment of Frostbite

Delay warming until it can be done once and done well	Post-thaw care
Rapidly warm in warm water	Protect the thawed tissue from trauma
Water should be between 100° and 108°F (38° and 42°C)	Elevate to reduce swelling
Completely immerse the frozen tissue	Place pads between toes and fingers
Use a large basin	Avoid constricting the extremity
Thaw completely	Prevent a second freezing
Ibuprofen is helpful for pain	

may warm as the problem that caused it is corrected. The activity of traveling may generate enough heat to begin thawing, thus increasing the possibility of further injury from freezing a second time or bruising. Unintentional slow warming is common.

If the injury is confined to a small area of the body, such as tips of toes or fingers, slow thawing is likely, and field warming should be started. If the injury is extensive, thawing will be difficult. Try to prevent frozen areas from thawing. Adjustments in clothing and work rate will be necessary.

Rapidly Warm in Warm Water. Treatment for frostbite, best done in a hospital, is rapid warming in water between 100° and 108°F (38° and 42°C). Use a thermometer to ensure that the water is the proper temperature. For a rough estimate, 105°F (40°C) is hot tap water. Water colder than 100°F (38°C) will not thaw frostbite rapidly. Water hotter than 108°F (42°C) may burn the patient.

Water temperature should remain constant throughout the procedure. This requires a source of hot water and several containers large enough to contain the entire frozen part. Do not pour hot water over the frozen tissue. Rather, immerse the frozen area, being careful not to let it touch the sides or bottom of the container. When the water cools, remove the frostbitten part, quickly warm the water, and reimmerse the part.

Thawing frozen fingers generally takes 45 minutes. There is no danger of overthawing, but underthawing can leave tissue permanently damaged. A flush of pink indicates blood returning to the affected site. Warming frostbite is generally very painful. Aspirin or ibuprofen is appropriate for pain relief. If hypothermia is present, it takes priority in treatment.

Post-Thaw Care. Air dry the extremity carefully; don't rub. Swelling will occur, along with blister formation. Inserting gauze between the fingers or toes keeps these areas dry as swelling occurs. Blisters should be kept intact. Once the tissue is thawed, it is extremely delicate, and seemingly minor trauma can damage it. Ibuprofen may be helpful for pain and inflammation.

Prevent freezing a second time after thawing. The freeze-thaw-freeze sequence will produce permanent tissue damage. The seriousness of frostbite injury is increased if freeze-thaw-freeze has occurred or if it is accompanied by fracture or soft tissue injury.

IMMERSION FOOT

Immersion foot results from exposure to continued wet, cold conditions—conditions that many outdoor recreationists avoid. Military operations, like NOLS expeditions, rarely have the luxury of choosing their weather conditions and may spend days in weather conducive to the development of immersion injury. Understandably, much of what we know about non-freezing cold injury—immersion foot or trench foot—comes from the military. In World War I, when the term trench foot was coined, the British Army experienced 29,000 immersion foot casualties in the winter of 1915–16; frostbite and immersion foot casualties for U.S. forces in Europe in World War II totaled 90,000.

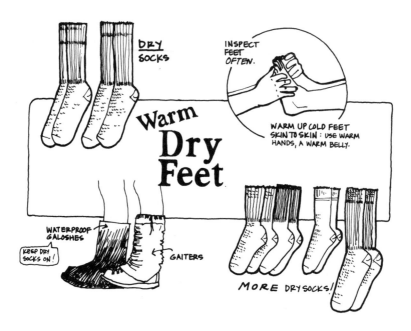

What is immersion foot? Immersion foot is a local, non-freezing injury that occurs in cold, wet conditions. The injury occurs when blood vessels constrict in response to heat loss, reducing blood flow to the extremity and depriving cells of oxygen and nutrients. The ensuing injury may range from a few weeks of sore feet to permanent muscle and nerve damage. In some cases, victims experience months of pain, disability, and even amputation.

It is common to hear that at least 12 hours' exposure to cold, wet conditions is necessary to produce the injury. Our experience, however, tells us that it can happen much quicker, over a long, wet, cold hiking day, for example, or in a multi-hour river crossing. Murray Hamlet, DVM, an expert on non-freezing cold injury, says that the minimum exposure is as little as 3 hours, although he thinks it takes 12 hours to sustain a serious injury. These episodes of short-onset immersion foot could be due to individual susceptibility or could be the culminating event of long-term exposure. There are times when our diligence prevents immersion foot, although we have chronically cool and constricted feet. Sadly, as little as an afternoon's lapsed attention can undo our best efforts.

Classic and Common Signs and Symptoms

Immersion foot is usually described in a worst-case scenario. The extremity appears cold, swollen, shiny, and mottled. Tactile sensitivity is reduced, as is capillary refill time. To check capillary refill time, press the patient's nail beds to blanch a spot. In a healthy individual, the blood returns and the white skin at the blanch site becomes pink within 2 seconds (the time it takes to say "capillary refill time").

The patient may describe the foot as feeling wooden. When the extremity warms, the skin becomes warm, dry, and red. The pulse is bounding. The injury is painful. The injured area may itch, tingle, and exhibit increased sensitivity to cold. The recovery period can last weeks. Nerve damage may be permanent. The development of blisters, ulcers, permanent numbness, and gangrene is possible.

All these classic signs and symptoms are true. However, you must be alert to subtle forms of nonfreezing cold injury that do not necessarily look mottled, gray, or waxy, nor do you always see poor capillary refill or altered skin color and temperature. All you may see is cool, pale extremities, numbness or tingling, and mild swelling. Pain is unusual in the field, becoming more common after blood flow has returned to the extremity.

Be suspicious about any numbness, tingling, or pain in your feet in cool conditions. Nerves are most susceptible to injury from reduced blood flow. Many of the long-term effects of immersion foot are due to damaged nerves in the feet: pain, numbness, chronic tingling, and itching.

The patient may not notice the constricted condition of the feet until after the trip. We've learned to advise people returning from prolonged wet and cold conditions to avoid long, hot showers or baths. The rapid warming can surprise the unwary with swollen, painful, and red feet.

Treatment
Warm immersion foot slowly at room temperature. In serious cases, swelling, pain, and blister formation prevent walking. Elevate the feet to reduce the swelling. Bed rest, to avoid trauma, is often necessary until the injury heals. Ibuprofen is recommended because of its anti-inflammatory properties. Aspirin and acetaminophen may also help.

Prevention
Our experience is that in prolonged cold, wet conditions, some degree of immersion foot is inevitable. The best footwear-gaiter system is of little help. Prevention is based on the consistent daily interaction among equipment, outdoor skills, and habits of vigilance and assessment.

There is no new thing under the sun. In World War I, the British significantly reduced immersion foot casualties by using techniques (without making major footwear changes) that we still follow today: wearing well-fitting boots with heavy wool socks; keeping the body warm; removing wet socks and drying and massaging the feet twice a day; not sleeping in wet footwear; drying wet socks against the skin; keeping feet out of water or mud as much as possible; watching carefully and reacting promptly to any numbness or tingling; and keeping footwear loose to allow for circulation.

What follows are suggestions from NOLS instructors that we have accumulated over the years.

Dry Your Socks. Drying socks is a continual activity on wilderness trips. During the day, we stick wet socks under our shirts to dry them against the skin, and at night, we drape them over our chests and bellies in our sleeping bags. We'll hang them in the sun and dry them over a fire. Keep one pair of dry socks in a dry place, such as in a sleeping bag or a small plastic bag.

Sleep with Warm, Dry Feet. Sleeping with dry feet is very helpful, but there is a false impression that this offers complete protection. People coping with prolonged wet, cold conditions have developed immersion foot by hiking for a single day in wet socks. A single night of sleeping in cool, wet socks has undone weeks of vigilant attention. Go to bed with warm, dry feet and keep them that way all night long.

Use the Environment to Your Advantage. Travel early. Stop before nightfall, leaving time to care for your feet. In spring and summer, use the overnight snowpack hardening to stay on top of the snow. Stop when the snowpack becomes wet and soft and dry your feet and socks in the afternoon sun. Choose campsites with good sun exposure and campfire possibilities.

Look at Your Feet. Warming cool feet on a companion's belly or stopping to change socks in the middle of the day should be routine tasks, not impositions. When the conditions are ideal for trench foot to occur, you may need to check susceptible people frequently; twice daily visual checks are often suggested. Visual checking must be part of the routine. Messages sent to the brain from the feet may be faulty due to nerve damage.

Give Your Feet Top Priority. In some places where people hike and ski, it is impossible to have dry feet all day. The best footwear won't keep you dry in soaking wet tundra or through multiple river crossings. On these days, if your socks are damp and your feet cool, stop, warm your feet, and, if possible, change into dry socks.

When you get to camp, get out of your wet boots immediately. Change into a pair of dry socks and begin to actively dry your wet or damp socks. Warm your feet promptly. Don't wait until bedtime.

Use Foot Powder. Foot powder does not seem to be helpful in preventing immersion injury, other than as a discipline in conjunction with changing socks. People with a tendency toward athlete's foot (a fungal infection) have found medicated foot powders helpful.

Display Good Habits. For outdoor leaders, role modeling good foot care on the trail and in camp is essential. To many outdoor enthusiasts, frostbite is the cold injury that is most well known. People are not well informed on the subtleties of

---

Immersion Foot

Signs and Symptoms	**Treatment**
Cold, mottled extremity	Remove feet from the cold, wet
Foot feels wooden, numb; pins	environment
and needles	Air dry
When warmed, foot becomes	Avoid constricting the extremity
red, dry, and painful with	Protect feet from trauma
bounding pulses	Elevate feet to reduce the
	swelling
Prevention	
Rotate socks as needed to keep	
feet dry	
Check feet daily	
Sleep with feet warm and dry	

nonfreezing cold injuries. Novices often assume that some degree of cooling is unavoidable and acceptable and inadvertently cross a line from extremity cooling to a cold injury.

Keep Your Core Warm. Poor nutrition, dehydration, wet socks, inadequate clothing, and constriction of blood flow by shoes, socks, gaiters, or tight clothing are all predisposing factors.

Use Proper Equipment. Plastic boots and supergaiters are improvements over leather boots but are not a panacea. Rubber galoshes, though unfashionable, are inexpensive, simple, and helpful in keeping footwear dry. Bring multiple pairs of socks; wear two pair on your feet and have at least two spare pairs.

FINAL THOUGHTS

The possibility of cold injury is our constant companion on wilderness trips. The most successful and easiest treatment for hypothermia is prevention by choosing effective insulating material such as wool and synthetics and water- and windproof parkas and pants, using these items properly, eating and staying hydrated, and honing your camping and navigation skills to live comfortably as you travel through the wilderness.

A common thread in many immersion foot and frostbite scenarios is people who tolerate cold feet, wait too long before intervening, and are surprised when they discover that they have been injured. If your feet are not definitely warm, you're doing something wrong. Novices may believe that they have to tolerate some level of cold extremities as an unavoidable consequence of camping. Although there is some truth to this, a novice lacks the experience to know how much one can tolerate before an injury occurs, and even an expert can be fooled. Don't be one of those people who rationalize not taking care of their feet by saying, "My feet are cold, but not that cold."

SUMMARY:
COLD INJURIES

HYPOTHERMIA: a lowering of the core body temperature that occurs when heat loss exceeds heat production. It is a dangerous disturbance of body function. Mild to moderate hypothermia (temperature above 90°F (32°C), patient conscious, shivering, able to walk) is treatable in the field. Severe hypothermia (below 90°F (32°C), patient unconscious, not shivering, unable to walk) requires warming in a hospital.

Signs and Symptoms of Hypothermia
Mental
Deterioration in decision-making ability
Slow and improper response to cold
Apathy, lethargy
Increased complaints, decreased group cooperation
Slurred speech, disorientation progressing to incoherence and
    irrationality and possible unconsciousness

Muscular
Shivering
Loss of fine motor ability progressing to stumbling, clumsiness,
    and falling
Muscle stiffness and inability to move (in severe cases)

Treatment of Hypothermia
Mild Hypothermia
Prevent further heat loss
    Dry
    Remove from cold
    Insulate
Actively warm
    Hydration with hot drinks
    Food
    Sleeping bags

Severe Hypothermia
Evacuate to hospital for warming
    Dry, insulate

• *CONTINUED* •

SUMMARY:
COLD INJURIES *(continued)*

Severe Hypothermia (cont'd)
Prevent further heat loss (apply heat)
ABCs
Handle gently

FROSTBITE: a local freezing injury classified as frostnip or superficial, partial-thickness, or deep. Frostbitten tissue is cold, gray, white, or mottled. Frostnip affects only the skin and is easily treated with immediate warming. Partial-thickness and deep frostbite affect underlying tissue layers and should be warmed rapidly in warm water.

Treatment of Frostbite
Delay warming until it can be done once and done well
Rapidly warm in warm water
    Water should be between 100° and 108°F (38° and 42°C)
    Completely immerse the frozen tissue
    Use a large basin
    Thaw completely
Post-thaw care
    Protect the thawed tissue from trauma
    Elevate to reduce swelling
    Place pads between toes and fingers
    Avoid constricting the extremity
    Prevent freezing a second time

IMMERSION FOOT: a local, nonfreezing injury. Signs and symptoms are swollen, pale, numb, or tingly feet.

Treatment of Immersion Foot
Remove feet from the cold, wet environment
Air dry
Do not constrict the extremity
Protect feet from trauma
Elevate feet to reduce swelling

CHAPTER 10

HEAT ILLNESS

INTRODUCTION

Our bodies produce heat constantly. When heat production exceeds heat loss, body temperature rises. Factors that reduce heat loss include high ambient air temperature, excessive clothing, and inability to sweat. To survive in a hot environment, human beings must eliminate enough heat to keep the body temperature within acceptable limits—97° to 100°F (35° to 37°C). Vital organs are irreversibly damaged when the body temperature stays at or above 107°F (41.5°C) for any length of time.

Heat illness is unusual on NOLS courses because we are diligent and aggressive about prevention. Outdoor leaders should be knowledgeable about the causes, recognition, and treatment of heat illness. Preventing heat illness, like preventing hypothermia, frostbite, altitude illness, and dehydration, is a 24-hour-a-day task.

PHYSIOLOGY

The body generates 2,000 to 5,000 kilocalories (kcal) of heat per day. Every metabolic function, blink of the eye, and beat of the heart produces heat. Basal metabolism alone would raise the body temperature 1.5°F per hour if heat were not dissipated.

Organs responsible for heat loss are the skin, cardiovascular system, and respiratory system. As discussed in chapter 9 ("Cold Injuries"), the four main mechanisms by which the body loses heat are radiation, evaporation, convection, and conduction. Of these, radiation and evaporation are the body's primary avenues of heat loss.

Radiation. Under heat stress, the body dilates superficial blood vessels, increases heart rate and cardiac output, and directs more blood to the skin. Normally, one-third to one-half a liter of blood per minute is shunted to the skin and superficial tissues. The body can increase skin blood flow to 4 liters per minute when it is heat stressed.

Radiation accounts for 65 percent of the heat lost when the air temperature is lower than body temperature. In hot environments, radiation is a major source of heat gain. The body can gain up to 300 kcal per hour when exposed to the sun.

Evaporation. Sweating by itself does not cool the body. Evaporation of perspiration cools the body because heat is necessary to change water from liquid to vapor. A heat-acclimatized person can sweat as much as 2 liters per hour for a total loss of 1 million kcal of heat.

ACCLIMATIZATION

Acclimatizing to heat entails increasing the rate of sweating, decreasing the sweating threshold, improving vasodilation, and decreasing electrolyte loss in the sweat. When acclimatized, we sweat faster and sooner and lose fewer electrolytes in the sweat.

To become acclimatized to a hot environment, the body requires 1½ to 2 hours of exercise in the heat daily for approximately 10 days to 2 weeks. To remain acclimatized requires 1½ to 2 hours of exercise per week.

PREDISPOSING FACTORS IN HEAT ILLNESS

Increased heat production, decreased heat dissipation, and a lack of salt and water are the basic factors that produce heat illness.

Other factors in the development of heat illness are age, general health, use of medications or alcohol, fatigue, and a prior history of heat illness. Patients with underlying problems (illness or injury) may not be able to tolerate heat. Underdeveloped physical mechanisms contribute to the incidence of heat illness in children. Individuals with compromised heart function are less able to adjust when stressed by heat. A study conducted by the U.S. Army demonstrated a correlation between lack of sleep, or fatigue, and the development of heat illness.

Antihistamines, antipsychotic agents, thyroid hormone medications, amphetamines, and alcohol are among the drugs that have been implicated in the development of heat illness. Some interfere with thermoregulation; others increase metabolic activity or interfere with sweating.

HEAT ILLNESS
A continuum of signs and symptoms provides evidence of heat illnesses that range from heat syncope and cramps to heat exhaustion and heatstroke. Symptoms of heat illness, like those of hypothermia and altitude illness, may be subtle and remain unrecognized until a sudden collapse occurs.

Heat Syncope
Heat syncope is fainting due to heat stress. Shunting of blood to the periphery decreases blood flow to the brain through vasodilation and pooling of blood in the large leg veins. Standing for long periods of time (soldier on parade syndrome) is a common cause of heat syncope.

Heat Syncope	
Sudden fainting episode in the heat	**Signs and Symptoms**
Usually self-limited	Tunnel vision, vertigo, nausea, sweating, weakness
Aggravated by dehydration	Sudden fainting
Aggravated by standing for long periods	
	Treatment
	Lie flat, elevate legs
	Hydrate

Assessment and Treatment. Prior to fainting, the person may complain of tunnel vision, vertigo, nausea, sweating, or feeling weak.

Heat syncope is self-limited; leave the patient lying flat, and the fainting will usually promptly resolve. Make sure the patient is hydrated. Conduct an initial assessment and focused exam to check for any injuries that may have occurred as a result of the fall.

Heat Cramps

Heat cramps are painful muscle contractions that follow exercise in hot conditions. We don't know for sure what causes the cramps. They are probably caused by a lack of salt and occur in muscles fatigued by exercise. People who sweat profusely and drink only water to replace lost fluids are more susceptible to heat cramps.

Heat Cramps
Usually occur after exercise
Affect fatigued muscle groups
Treatment
Rest, lie flat, elevate legs
Hydrate

Assessment and Treatment. Calf, abdominal, and thigh muscles can be affected, and muscle spasms in the abdomen can be severe. Treat by moving the patient to a cool spot and replenishing the lost salt. Mix one-quarter to one-half teaspoon of salt in a liter of fluid and have the patient drink it slowly. Avoid salt tablets, which tend to make people nauseous.

Heat Exhaustion and Heatstroke

The distinction between heat exhaustion and heatstroke is not completely clear. Some authorities consider heat exhaustion an early stage of heatstroke. Sweating, body temperature, and other symptoms may not be distinct between the two illnesses. The prevailing thought is that a patient with altered brain function—bizarre behavior, confusion, delirium, ataxia, seizure, or unconsciousness—should be considered to have heatstroke.

Risk Factors for Exertional Heatstroke

Overweight	Exertion
Overdressing	High humidity
Fatigue	High temperature
Dehydration	Not acclimatized
Alcohol use	Young athlete
Medications	

Heatstroke is caused by a failure of the body to dissipate heat. There are two broad classifications of heatstroke: classic and exertional. Classic heatstroke affects the chronically ill, the elderly, and infants. It develops slowly and is common during heat waves. Exertional heatstroke is more likely to affect healthy, fit individuals and to develop rapidly during exercise or hard, physical work.

Assessment. The signs and symptoms of heat exhaustion are caused by a lack of salt and water. The patient complains of weakness, fatigue, frontal headache, vertigo, thirst, nausea,

---

Assessment of Heat Exhaustion and Heatstroke

Heat Exhaustion	*Heatstroke*
Weakness	Delirious
Fatigue	Comatose
Headache	Rapid pulse
Vertigo	Rapid respiratory rate
Thirst	Temperature above 104°F
Nausea, vomiting	(39.5°C)
Elevated temperature	
(102° to 104°F/38.5° to	
39.5°C)	
Faintness	

vomiting, muscle cramps, and faintness. The body temperature is between 102° and 104°F (38.5° and 39.5°C). The patient may or may not be sweaty. Pulse and respiratory rate are elevated. Urine output is decreased due to dehydration.

In contrast to heat exhaustion, the onset of heatstroke is usually rapid. The patient becomes delirious or comatose. The pulse and respiratory rate are elevated. Only 20 percent of patients with heatstroke demonstrate any signs and symptoms prior to becoming delirious or unconscious. Prodromal signs and symptoms are confusion, drowsiness, disorientation, irritability, anxiety, and ataxia, as well as the signs and symptoms of heat exhaustion. Heatstroke victims usually have a rectal temperature above 104°F (39.5°C).

Treatment. Treatment of heat exhaustion and heatstroke is rapid cooling. Both the temperature reached and the length of time it is sustained can affect the long-term outcome of the disease.

Provide a Cool Environment, Lay the Patient Flat, Remove the Patient's Clothing, Cool with Water and Fanning. Shade the patient or move him or her from direct heat. Lay the patient flat and remove his or her clothing. Immersing the patient in cold water is controversial. If cold water constricts blood vessels, it interferes with heat loss. If it triggers shivering, it increases heat production. Spray the patient with water and fan the body to enhance evaporation. Apply cool cloths to the patient's trunk, armpits, abdomen, and groin, where large blood vessels lie near the skin surface.

Monitor Temperature. Hypothermia becomes possible with such precipitate cooling, so monitor the patient's temperature for hypothermia as well as rebound hyperthermia. Document how long the temperature was elevated, how

---

**Treatment
of Heat Exhaustion
and Heatstroke**

Cool environment
Remove clothing
Rest, lie flat
Cool water and fan
Hydrate
Monitor temperature
Evacuate (for heatstroke)

high it was, and how long it took to cool the patient. Body temperature may remain unstable even after cooling. Evacuate a heatstroke patient, keeping a close watch on temperature.

Hydrate. Do not give fluids by mouth until the patient is mentally alert enough to hold the glass and drink. If the patient is unconscious, make sure the airway is open and the patient is breathing. If the patient is seizing, do not restrain the patient, but remove objects that may cause harm.

Aspirin and acetaminophen will not lower the body temperature in heat illness and should not be given. High body temperatures decrease the ability of blood to clot, and aspirin further exacerbates this problem.

Evacuate (for Heatstroke). Any patient you suspect of having heatstroke should be evacuated immediately for further evaluation. Internal organ damage may not present itself for several days following the episode of heatstroke.

FINAL THOUGHTS
Prevention of heat-related illness is, of course, the best treatment. Leaders need to be alert for signs of developing heat illness in their groups. Environmental risk factors of high heat and humidity, coupled with dehydration, exertion, and overdressing, should raise caution flags. The vague symptoms of fatigue, headache, weakness, irritability, and malaise should be recognized as indicators of dehydration and heat illness.

Tips for Preventing Heat Illness
1. Shade the head and back of the neck to decrease heat gain from the sun.
2. Drink lots of fluids: ½ liter prior to strenuous exercise and ¼ liter every 20 minutes during exertion. It has been shown that a person voluntarily replaces only two-thirds of lost fluids; therefore, fluids must be forced on a regular basis. The best way to tell if you're hydrated is by the color of your urine. The urine should be clear to pale yellow. Dark urine indicates dehydration.
3. Make sure your diet contains an adequate amount of salt. The average American diet contains 10 to 12 grams

of salt per day, which should be adequate for exercising in hot environments. One study found that men working in the heat averaged 7 liters of sweat lost per day and adapted successfully on a diet that contained 6 grams of salt per day.

4. Wear loose-fitting, light-colored clothes. This maximizes heat loss by allowing convection and evaporation to take place.
5. Exercise cautiously in conditions of high heat and humidity. Air temperatures exceeding 90°F (32°C) and humidity levels above 70 percent severely impair the body's ability to lose heat through radiation and evaporation.
6. Recognize the diseases and drugs that impair heat dissipation.
7. Know the warning signs of impending heat illness—dark-colored urine, dizziness, headache, and fatigue.
8. Acclimatize. It takes 10 days to 2 weeks to acclimatize to a hot environment.

SUMMARY:
HEAT ILLNESS

HEAT SYNCOPE: characterized by a sudden fainting episode in the heat. It is aggravated by dehydration and by standing for long periods. It is usually self-limited.

Signs and Symptoms of Heat Syncope
Tunnel vision, vertigo, nausea, sweating, weakness
Sudden fainting

Treatment of Heat Syncope
Lie flat, elevate legs
Hydrate

HEAT CRAMPS: usually occur after exercise and affect fatigued muscle groups.

Treatment of Heat Cramps
Rest, lie flat, elevate legs
Hydrate

HEAT EXHAUSTION AND HEATSTROKE
Assessment of Heat Exhaustion and Heatstroke

Heat Exhaustion	*Heatstroke*
Weakness	Delirious
Fatigue	Comatose
Headache	Rapid pulse
Vertigo	Rapid respiratory rate
Thirst	Temperature above
Nausea, vomiting	104°F (39.5°C)
Elevated temperature	
(102° to 104°F/38.5° to 39.5°C)	
Faintness	

Treatment of Heat Exhaustion and Heatstroke
Cool environment
Remove clothing
Rest, lie flat
Cool water and fan
Hydrate
Monitor temperature
Evacuate (for heatstroke)

CHAPTER 11

POISONS, STINGS, AND BITES

INTRODUCTION

A poison is any substance—solid, liquid, or gas—that impairs health when it comes into contact with the body. Poisoning ranks fifth in causes of accidental death in the United States, and is responsible for approximately 5,000 deaths a year. Approximately 1 million cases of nonfatal poisoning from substances such as industrial chemicals, cleaning agents, medications, and insect sprays occur each year.

Virtually any substance can be poisonous if consumed in sufficient quantity. For example, vitamins can be highly toxic in overdose. A snakebite that kills a child may only produce illness in an adult. Accidental overdoses of aspirin kill more children each year than substances we commonly consider poisons.

A venom is a poison excreted by certain animals. Venomous animals have specialized glands that produce toxic substances for injection into adversaries and prey. All venoms are poisons, but not all poisons are venoms. Most animal venoms are complex mixtures of toxic and carrier (nontoxic) substances. The toxins in various venoms vary in potency, effect, and chemical makeup. They may impair nerve function, destroy cells, or affect the heart or blood.

Much information has been disseminated about the treatment of serpent, spider, and scorpion bites—much of it inaccurate. Outside the United States, there are snakes, spiders, and insects that carry deadly venoms. In the United States, however, snakes and spiders cause relatively few deaths each year. This is not to undersell the potency of these poisons, but rather to emphasize that ill-informed and misguided treatment can be as harmful to the patient as the venom.

POISONS

Poisons enter the body through ingestion, inhalation, absorption, and injection. In general, treat ingested poisoning in the backcountry by dilution and vomiting. Treat absorbed poisons, if dry, by brushing off the skin and, if wet, by flushing with water. Move the victim of an inhaled poison to fresh air and maintain the airway. As systemic symptoms of poisoning appear, provide the basics of care, including ABCs, continuous evaluation, and evacuation to a medical facility.

Ingested Poisons

Examples of ingested poisons include drugs, toxic plants, and bacterial toxins on contaminated food. The use of poorly labeled fuel bottles as water bottles has led to accidental ingestion of gasoline. Drugs, including nonprescription medications, can be accidentally or intentionally ingested in harmful amounts. Poisons absorbed from the stomach into the general circulation can affect several body systems.

Treatment of Ingested Poisons. If you suspect an ingested poison, induce vomiting—but only if the patient is fully conscious. Do not induce vomiting if the patient has a seizure disorder. If the patient is stuporous, unconscious, or having seizures, the airway may become obstructed with vomit.

Do not induce vomiting for ingested corrosive chemicals or petroleum products. Vomiting can increase the corrosive damage, as these chemicals burn both on the way down and on the way back up the esophagus. These substances are also extremely harmful if they enter the lungs and can cause a chemical pneumonia.

When syrup of ipecac or activated charcoal is available. Syrup of ipecac stimulates vomiting, and activated charcoal is a potent dilutent and absorbent. If available, give an adult 2 tablespoons (15 to 30 milliliters) of ipecac with half a liter of water. If vomiting does not occur within 20 minutes, the dose of ipecac and water may be repeated once. After vomiting has ceased, give 5 tablespoons of activated charcoal in a water slurry. The charcoal absorbs residual stomach contents.

Treatment of Ingested Poisons

Induce vomiting:
If ipecac or activated charcoal is available:
> Give 2 tbs syrup of ipecac with half a liter of water
> Repeat dose if no vomiting occurs after 20 minutes
> After vomiting ceases, give 5 tbs activated charcoal

or
Administer premixed activated charcoal (usually packaged in plastic bottles or tubes)
Usual adult dosage is 50 to 100 grams

If ipecac or activated charcoal is unavailable:
> 2 tbs mild soap or mustard
> Tickle back of throat

Do not induce vomiting if:
Corrosive or petroleum products
Altered level of consciousness
Seizures

Activated charcoal isn't the charcoal from a fire. It's a special preparation, usually packaged in 4-ounce plastic bottles or tubes. The patient drinks the slurry, which binds the poison and allows it to be excreted without being absorbed into the body.

When syrup of ipecac or activated charcoal is not available. Ingested poisoning is an infrequent wilderness medical problem, and most smaller first aid kits do not contain ipecac or activated charcoal. These may be available on larger expeditions, on well-stocked boats, or in base camps. The wilderness backpacker commonly has to rely on tickling the back of the throat to stimulate the gag reflex. You may find that 2 tablespoons of mild soap, such as Campsuds, or a teaspoonful of dried mustard swallowed with half a liter of water also induces vomiting.

Common Poisonous Plants in Western United States

Name	Genus	Name	Genus
Arnica	Arnica	Iris	Iris
Bleeding heart	Dicentra	Jimson weed	Datura
Buttercup	Ranunculus	Lily of the valley	Guaiacum
Clematis	Clematis	Monkshood	Aconitum
Coyotillo	Karwinskia	Mountain laurel	Kalmia
Nightshade	Atropa	Poison hemlock	Conium
Larkspur	Delphinium	Groundsel	Senecio
Camas	Zigadenus	Sweet pea	Lathyrus
Desert potato	Jatropha	Locoweed	Oyxtropus
False hellebore	Veratrum	Water hemlock	Cicuta
Foxglove	Digitalis		

In the backcountry, vomiting should be induced even if considerable time has passed, provided the patient remains conscious and has not ingested corrosive or petroleum products. After the patient has vomited, he or she should drink at least half a liter of water to dilute the poison. Save a sample of the poison and a sample of the vomit for later analysis.

In the backcountry, people have died after mistakenly eating poisonous plants and mushrooms. An expert should identify any vegetation you intend to eat. If you suspect ingested plant poisoning, treat by dilution and induced vomiting. Save samples for later identification.

Inhaled Poisons

Two climbers on Denali (Mount McKinley) died from carbon monoxide poisoning caused by using a stove in a poorly ventilated tent. Carbon monoxide is an odorless and colorless gas produced from incomplete combustion and is the most frequently encountered inhaled poison in the United States. Automobiles, portable stoves, lanterns, and heaters are all sources of carbon monoxide.

Carbon Monoxide Poisoning

Signs and symptoms	Treatment
Lightheadedness, dizziness, throbbing headache	Move patient to fresh air
Nausea and vomiting	Maintain airway
Irritability, impaired judgment	If possible, administer oxygen
Altered level of consciousness	
Seizures, respiratory failure, coma	

Carbon monoxide combines with hemoglobin in the blood, displacing oxygen and reducing the oxygen-carrying capacity of the blood. This can happen rapidly and without warning. At high altitudes, where less oxygen is available, the potential for poisoning increases. Signs and symptoms of carbon monoxide poisoning range from light-headedness and headache to coma, seizures, and death.

Treatment of Inhaled Poisons. The immediate treatment for any inhaled poisoning is to remove the patient from the source of the poison. Maintain the airway and move the patient to fresh air. Although not readily available in the wilderness, administration of oxygen is standard treatment. A patient who experiences a notable disturbance in alertness or coordination, complains of breathing difficulty, or loses consciousness should be evacuated to a physician for evaluation.

Prevent inhaled poisoning by keeping tents or snow shelters well ventilated during cooking or, better yet, by cooking outside.

Absorbed Poisons

Poisons can enter the body through the skin or mucous membranes. Pesticide sprays absorbed through the skin are a common source of poisoning. Toxins secreted into the skin by sea cucumbers and some species of exotic reptiles can cause serious reactions.

Treatment of Absorbed Poisons

Dry poisons: brush off, then rinse with water

Wet poisons: rinse thoroughly with water

Treatment of Absorbed Poisons. If the poison is dry, brush it off, then flush the area with large volumes of water. If the poison is wet, flush the site thoroughly with water, then wash with soap and water. Exceptions are lye and dry lime, which react with water to produce heat and further corrosion. Do not rinse lye or dry lime, but brush the powder off the skin.

Injected Poisons

The poisons that enter the body via the injected venoms of stinging insects and reptiles are often complex systemic poisons with multiple toxins. The injected poisons that most concern us in the wilderness are the venoms of snakes, bees, wasps, spiders, and scorpions.

Bees and wasps cause more deaths in the United States than snakes—approximately 100 deaths a year, usually from the acute allergic reaction known as anaphylactic shock.

Venomous Snakes. Imagine yourself trying to catch a small mammal for dinner, equipped only with a long, limbless body. You might develop the ability to leap quickly to your victim. You might also develop a venom to immobilize the victim. This is how a rattlesnake makes its living: striking quickly and accurately and immobilizing or killing its victims with venom.

Approximately 45,000 snakebites occur in the United States. each year, 8,000 of them from venomous snakes. Twelve to fifteen people a year die from these bites, mostly the young, elderly, and infirm. Bites commonly occur on the arms below the elbow and on the legs below the knee. In most cases, the snake is provoked by being handled, antagonized, or inadvertently stepped on.

Prevent snakebite by watching closely where you step. Never reach into concealed areas. Shake out sleeping bags and clothing before use. One NOLS student was bitten on the hand when he attempted to pick up a rattlesnake. Never handle snakes, even if you think they are dead.

There are two families of venomous snakes in the United States: Elapidae, represented by the coral snake, and Crotalidae, represented by the rattlesnake, copperhead, and cottonmouth, or water moccasin. Elapidae venom primarily affects the nervous system, causing death by paralysis and respiratory failure. Crotalidae venom is a complex mix of substances affecting the nerves, the heart, blood clotting, and other functions.

Coral Snake. The coral snake averages 23 to 32 inches in length and is thin and brightly colored, with adjacent red and yellow bands. It is the creature referred to in the old saying "red and yellow kill a fellow, red and black, venom lack." Coral snakes live in the southern and southwestern states, inhabiting dry, open, brushy ground near water sources. They are docile and bite only when provoked. Their short fangs generally limit their bites to fingers, toes, and loose skin folds.

The signs of systemic poisoning by the neurotoxic venom, which may occur several hours after the bite, include drowsi-

CORAL SNAKE

THIN, BRIGHTLY COLORED
23-32" LONG
└ ADJACENT RED/YELLOW BANDS

SYMPTOMS:

• LITTLE PAIN OR SWELLING

• NEUROTOXIC VENOM POISONING MAY LEAD TO DROWSINESS, WEAKNESS AND OTHER SYMPTOMS and PROGRESS TO POSSIBLE RESPIRATORY FAILURE.

ness, weakness, nausea, rapid pulse, and rapid respiration progressing to respiratory failure. Treatment is the same as for rattlesnake bites with one exception—the placing of a wide elastic bandage over the bite site. This technique is described later for non–North American snakebite.

Rattlesnake. Rattlesnakes have triangular heads, thick bodies, and pits between the eyes and nostrils. Coloring and length vary with the species. Most are blotched and colored in earthy browns, grays, or reds. Four feet is an average length, although large eastern diamondback rattlesnakes have reached 6½ feet in length. The number of rattles varies with the snake's age and stage of molt. Often the rattles do not rattle before a strike. Rattles are thought to have evolved as a warning device to prevent hoofed mammals from stepping on the snake.

Rattlesnake fangs retract when the mouth is closed and extend during a strike. Rattlesnakes periodically shed their fangs. At times, two fangs are present on each side. One is potent, the other not. Venom release is under the snake's control. A rattler can apparently adjust the volume of venom injected to match its victim's size. The age, size, and health of the snake affect venom toxicity. The same factors affect the victim's response to the venom.

Multiple strikes are possible, and depth of the bite varies, as does the amount of venom injected. Fang marks are not a reliable sign of envenomization, as 20 to 30 percent of bites do not envenom. Pain at the site with rapid swelling and bruising is a better sign that venom has been injected.

Signs and symptoms of venomous poisoning include swelling, pain, and tingling at the bite site; tingling and a metallic taste in the mouth; fever; chills; nausea and vomiting; blurred vision; and muscle tremors.

Gently clean the wound with an antiseptic soap and apply a sterile dressing. The goal of treatment is safe and rapid transport to a hospital for evaluation. Keep the affected limb at heart level or below. Keep the patient quiet, hydrated, and comfortable during evacuation. Activity and anxiety accelerate the absorption of the venom. Ideally, immobilize and carry the victim. Walking is acceptable if the patient feels up to it

RATTLESNAKES

GENERAL CHARACTERISTICS:

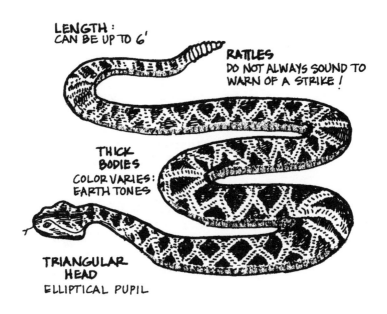

LENGTH:
CAN BE UP TO 6'

RATTLES
DO NOT ALWAYS SOUND TO
WARN OF A STRIKE!

**THICK
BODIES**
COLOR VARIES:
EARTH TONES

**TRIANGULAR
HEAD**
ELLIPTICAL PUPIL

MECHANISMS OF A RATTLESNAKE BITE:

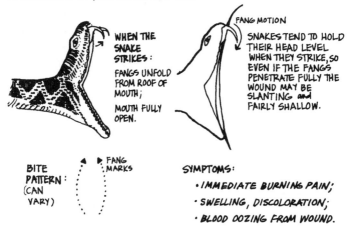

**WHEN THE
SNAKE
STRIKES:**

FANGS UNFOLD
FROM ROOF OF
MOUTH;

MOUTH FULLY
OPEN.

FANG MOTION

SNAKES TEND TO HOLD
THEIR HEAD LEVEL
WHEN THEY STRIKE, SO
EVEN IF THE FANGS
PENETRATE FULLY THE
WOUND MAY BE
SLANTING and
FAIRLY SHALLOW.

**BITE
PATTERN:**
(CAN
VARY)

FANG
MARKS

SYMPTOMS:
• IMMEDIATE BURNING PAIN;
• SWELLING, DISCOLORATION;
• BLOOD OOZING FROM WOUND.

Treatment
of Rattlesnake Bites

Clean wound with antiseptic soap

Apply sterile dressing

Remove rings and other
  constrictive items

Keep limb at or below level of
  heart

Keep patient quiet, hydrated, and
  comfortable

Suction with Sawyer Extractor

---

and if no other alternative is available.

A healthy adult may become ill from the envenomization but probably will not die. The patient is often at greater danger from the effects of treatment by misinformed rescuers. Pressure bandages, tourniquets, electric shock, ice, and incision of the area can permanently damage tissue that might otherwise remain unaffected. Pressure bandages are appropriate treatment for some exotic snakebites but not for rattlesnake envenomizations, in which local concentration of venom can cause tissue damage.

Studies show that suction devices, such as the Extractor by Sawyer Products, can remove up to 30 percent of venom if applied within 3 minutes. The suction from the Extractor is applied without incision.

Non–North American Snakebite. Snakes outside of North America that are significant sources of envenomization are primarily elapids: cobras, mambas, and kraits; Australian brown snakes, tiger snakes, and taipans; and vipers such as death adders, and rattlesnakes. The potent neurotoxic venoms of some of these snakes can result in altered mental status, unconsciousness, blurred vision, paralysis, seizures, and respiratory and heart failure.

Treatment is the same as for North American rattlesnakes, with the exception of the use of immobilization and a pressure bandage on the bitten extremity. To retard venom absorption, the limb is splinted and wrapped with gauze or an Ace bandage. This wrap is firm, but a pulse should still be present in the foot or wrist.

Bee Stings. The venom apparatus of most species of bees, located on the posterior abdomen, consists of venom glands, a

BEE

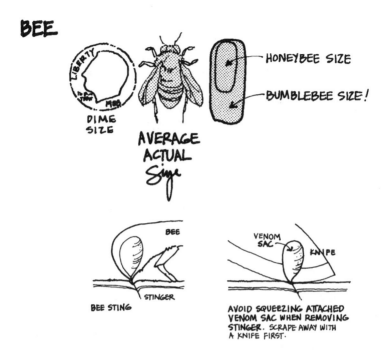

DIME SIZE

HONEYBEE SIZE

BUMBLEBEE SIZE!

AVERAGE ACTUAL Size

BEE

BEE STING

STINGER

VENOM SAC

KNIFE

AVOID SQUEEZING ATTACHED VENOM SAC WHEN REMOVING STINGER. SCRAPE AWAY WITH A KNIFE FIRST.

venom reservoir, and structures for stinging, or injection. The stinger and venom are used in defense and subjugation of prey.

Multiple stings are more dangerous than single stings, and those occurring closely in time are more dangerous than those occurring over a longer duration. Multiple stings, which often result from disturbing a nest, can be life-threatening.

Stings from bees and wasps usually cause instant pain, swelling, and redness. If the stinger remains in the skin, scrape or flick it out. A barb prevents the bee from withdrawing the stinger, so the bee's muscular venom reservoir continues to inject until the stinger is scraped away. Avoid squeezing the attached venom sac.

Treatment of Bee Stings

Scrape or flick off stinger
Clean wound with antiseptic soap
Ice/cool compress may relieve
  pain
If necessary, treat for anaphylaxis

Gently clean the wound with an antiseptic soap. Ice or cool compresses may help relieve pain and swelling. The patient should avoid scratching the stings, as this can cause secondary infection. Applying meat tenderizer to relieve the pain is a folklore remedy not supported by any scientific study.

Bees stings cause more anaphylaxis than do the stings of any other insect. Individuals who are allergic to the sting of one species of bee or wasp may also be allergic to that of different species.

Arachnids. Arachnids are mostly terrestrial and wingless and have four pairs of legs. Spiders, scorpions, tarantulas, and ticks are arachnids. There are over 30,000 spider species worldwide. They live in a variety of habitats, and all are carnivorous.

Poisonous spiders inject venom through hollow fangs. The fangs are primarily for subduing and killing prey and secondarily for defense. The venoms are fast-paralyzing agents that contain enzymes to predigest prey, which is then sucked up.

Black Widow Spiders. The black widow spider has a sinister name yet kills only four to six people a year in the United States. A member of the genus *Lactrodectus,* the venomous adult female is 4 centimeters long and is shiny black with a red "hourglass" marking on the bottom of the abdomen. The adult male is not venomous. There are five species of "widow" spiders, all of which have some type of red marking on the underside of the abdomen, but only three of which are black. Black widows are typically found under stones and logs. They are common in desert overhangs, crawl spaces, outhouses, and barns; they are rare in occupied buildings.

The black widow usually bites only when its web is disturbed. The bite is not initially painful—a pinprick sensation with slight redness and swelling, followed by numbness. Ten to 60 minutes may pass before the onset of toxic symptoms.

Treatment of Spider and Scorpion Bites

Clean wound with antiseptic soap
Ice/cool compress to relieve pain
If systemic symptoms of
  envenomization develop:
  ABCs and supportive care
  Evacuate to antivenin

BROWN SPIDER:

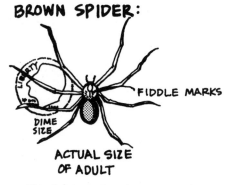

FIDDLE MARKS

DIME
SIZE

ACTUAL SIZE
OF ADULT

- VIOLIN SHAPED MARKS ON TOP OF HEAD
- BOTH MALE and FEMALE ADULTS VENOMOUS

BLACK WIDOW SPIDER:

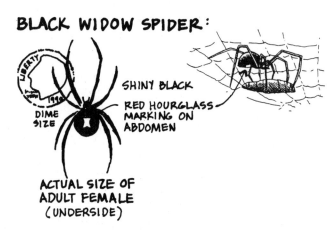

SHINY BLACK

RED HOURGLASS
MARKING ON
ABDOMEN

DIME
SIZE

ACTUAL SIZE OF
ADULT FEMALE
(UNDERSIDE)

- FEMALE ADULTS VENOMOUS;
- LOOK FOR DISTINCTIVE RED HOURGLASS
  MARKING ON THE UNDERSIDE OF
  ABDOMEN !

The venom is primarily a nerve toxin that stimulates muscle contraction, causing large muscle cramps. The abdomen may become boardlike and excruciatingly painful. Weakness, nausea, vomiting, and anxiety are common. Systemic signs include hypertension, breathing difficulty, seizures, and, in the very young or old, cardiac arrest.

The pain generally peaks in 1 to 3 hours and can continue over several days. The natural course of the illness is general recovery after several days. Local cleansing and ice may retard pain and venom absorption. Antivenin is available, as are agents to counteract muscle spasm.

Brown Spiders. The brown spider, genus *Loxosceles,* is rare in the West, especially in Wyoming and Colorado; it is most abundant in the South and Midwest. It has a violin-shaped mark on its head. The spiders average 1.2 centimeters in length with a 5-centimeter leg span. Unlike the black widow, both sexes are dangerous.

Brown spiders live in hot, dry, undisturbed environments, such as vacant buildings and woodpiles. They are nocturnal hunters of beetles, flies, moths, and other spiders, and they are most active from April to October, hibernating in fall and winter. They attack humans only as a defensive gesture.

The venom of the brown spider causes cell and tissue injury. Signs and symptoms vary from a transient irritation to painful and debilitating skin ulcers. Although the bite can be sharply painful, it is often painless. Nausea and vomiting, headache, fever, and chills may be present. In severe envenomizations, redness and blisters form within 6 to 12 hours. Within 1 to 2 weeks, an area of dying skin—a necrotic ulcer—forms and may leave a craterlike scar.

The injury can be difficult to diagnose. The bite often goes unnoticed until a skin ulcer develops. Clean the bite site with an antiseptic soap and evacuate the patient to a physician.

Tarantulas. Except for some species found in the tropics, tarantulas are not dangerous. The tarantula's fangs are too weak to penetrate very deeply, and the effects of the bite are limited to a small local wound. Tarantula bites are rare.

Scorpions. Scorpions first appeared on the earth 300 million years ago. Grasslands and deserts are primary habitat

SCORPIONS

SIZES OF SCORPIONS VARY : CAN BE SMALLER OR LARGER THAN THIS.

DIME SIZE

THE STINGER IS ON THE TAIL !

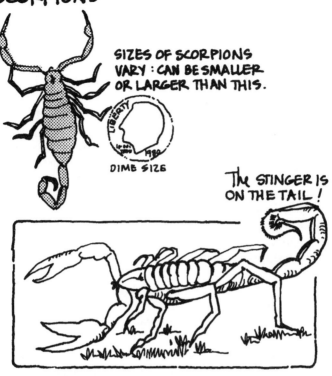

TICKS

DIME SIZE

ACTUAL SIZE OF ADULT

GENUS *DERMACENTOR*
COMMON WYOMING TICK

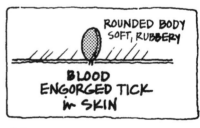

ROUNDED BODY
SOFT, RUBBERY

BLOOD
ENGORGED TICK
in SKIN

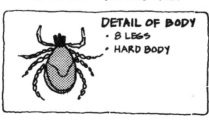

DETAIL OF BODY
• 8 LEGS
• HARD BODY

for more than 600 species of scorpions, some of which carry deadly venoms. In North America, most species are relatively harmless, their stings producing effects similar to those of bee stings.

Only one type of North American scorpion, a small yellowish species of the genus *Centruroides,* is dangerous. It lives in Mexico, Arizona, and New Mexico and has been reported in southern Utah. Fatalities from its venom occur mostly in the young and old.

Scorpions feed at night on insects and spiders, injecting their prey with multiple toxins from a stinger at the tip of the tail. Scorpions like to hide in dark places during the day; beware when reaching into woodpiles or under rocks. Develop a habit of shaking out shoes, clothes, and sleeping bags when in scorpion country.

A scorpion sting produces a pricking sensation. Typical symptoms include burning pain, swelling, redness, numbness, and tingling. The affected extremity may become numb and sensitive to touch.

Treat the sting by applying ice or cool water to relieve the local symptoms. Clean the wound with an antiseptic soap. In the case of severe poisoning, signs and symptoms include impaired speech resulting from a sluggish tongue and tightened jaw, muscle spasms, nausea, vomiting, convulsions, incontinence, and/or respiratory and circulatory distress. Immobilize the extremity and transport the patient to a hospital. An antivenin is available.

Ticks. Ticks are relatives of spiders and scorpions. There are two major families: hard ticks and soft ticks. Most common in the Rockies is the hard tick, genus *Dermacentor.* As with all ticks, it requires blood meals to molt from larva to nymph and from nymph to adult. The various diseases the tick carries are transmitted to the host during the blood meal. These diseases include tick fever, relapsing fever, spotted fever, tularemia, babesiosis, and Lyme disease. Tick season in Wyoming is April through July, although ticks are active throughout the warm months.

Preventing exposure is essential in tick-infested areas. Topical tick repellent is available; look for the chemical ingre-

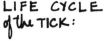

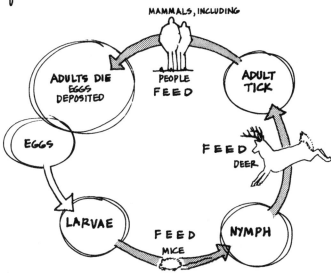

dient premethrin. A visual inspection of all body parts at least twice daily is recommended, as adult ticks generally stay on the body for a few hours before attaching. Even after a tick has attached itself, prompt removal may prevent the transmission of disease.

To remove a tick, grasp it as close to the skin as possible with tweezers or gloved fingers. Pull the tick out with steady pressure, being careful not to squeeze body fluids out of the tick and into the wound. Clean the bite site thoroughly with an antiseptic soap. Traditional tick removal methods (a hot match head, nail polish, or alcohol) may induce the tick to regurgitate into the wound.

Treatment of Tick Bites

Promptly remove the tick with a gentle, steady pull

Clean the bite site with soap and water

In cases of rash, fever, flu, or muscle aches following a tick bite, the patient should be seen by a physician

Diagnosis of tick-caused illness in the field is difficult. If a tick bite is accompanied by a rash, fever, flu symptoms, or muscle aches and pains, the patient should be seen by a physician.

Insects. The bites of mosquitoes, blackflies, midges, horseflies, and deerflies tend to be relatively minor. Usually only localized irritation occurs, although anaphylaxis is a possibility. This group is more significant for its capacity to act as vectors of diseases such as malaria and yellow fever. Worldwide, only the mosquito transmits more disease than the tick.

ALLERGIES AND ANAPHYLAXIS

The immune system is an extensive array of cells, structures, antibodies, and other elements constantly defending us against foreign substances: microorganisms, pollen, dust, food, cat dander—practically all the pieces of the natural world. Normally, the immune system smoothly identifies and neutralizes harmful substances with white blood cells, antibodies, and mild inflammation. It's a wonderful, critical, complex, and efficient system. Among the many things it does is to remember a first encounter with a foreign substance, producing antibodies designed to recognize and neutralize the invader the next time it appears. Normally, this interaction is delicately balanced. An overreaction causes us misery when it triggers an inflammatory response we call an allergy. In an allergic person, reintroduction of the foreign material—an allergen—results in an inappropriately large release of histamine. Histamine causes fluid to leak from blood vessels, resulting in edema and swelling, which can obstruct the airway. It also dilates blood vessels, which can lead to shock.

Allergic reactions range from mild to severe, and they can be immediate or delayed. For most people, the allergic response is mild, though often irritating. Hay fever is one example of a mild allergic response. Hay fever sufferers complain of a runny nose, sneezing, swollen eyes, itching skin, and possibly hives. Antihistamines and decongestants are the usual treatment. An allergic reaction may also be local, the

Mild to Moderate Allergic Reaction

Signs and Symptoms
Local swelling near a sting
Runny nose, sneezing, swollen
    eyes, hay fever
Flushed and itchy skin
Hives or welts on the skin
Mild or no breathing difficulty

**Treatment of a Mild to
Moderate Allergic Reaction**
Remove the allergen from the
    patient, or the patient from
    the offending environment
Oral antihistamines
Hydration
    Monitor for increased breathing
        difficulty

result of insect stings or contact with a plant. The local reaction is red, swollen, and itching, perhaps with hives, but stays near the point of contact.

An anaphylactic response is a massive, generalized reaction of the immune system that is potentially harmful to the body. Common triggers of anaphylaxis are bee stings or other

Anaphylaxis

Signs and Symptoms
Flushed and itchy skin
Hives and welts on the skin
Swollen face, lips, and tongue
Respiratory distress
Shock

Treatment of Anaphylaxis
Remove the allergen or the
    patient from the offending
    environment
Inject epinephrine
When the patient can swallow,
    administer oral
    antihistamines
Watch for a second reaction
Evacuate

insect bites and reactions to drugs and some foods. Instead of the mild symptoms of hay fever, anaphylaxis produces asphyxiating swelling of the larynx, rapid pulse, a rapid fall in blood pressure, rash, itching, hives, flushed skin, swollen and red eyes, tearing of the eyes, swelling of the feet and hands, nausea, vomiting, and abdominal pain. The airway obstruction and shock may be fatal. Onset usually occurs within a few minutes of contact with the triggering substance, although the reaction may be delayed. Any large areas of swelling, typically involving the face, lips, hands, and feet; respiratory compromise; or shock should be treated with epinephrine.

Treatment of anaphylaxis is immediate administration of epinephrine, a prescription medication, to counteract the effects of the histamine. Persons who know that they are vulnerable to anaphylactic shock usually carry injectable epinephrine in an Ana-Kit, Ana-Guard, or EpiPen. Trip leaders should be familiar with their use and seek the advice of a physician adviser when responding to this emergency.

Use of the EpiPen

1. Pull off the safety cap.
2. Place the tip on the outer part of the thigh, preferably on skin, although it will work through thin clothing.
3. Push the unit against the thigh until it clicks. Hold in place for 10 seconds. (On newer models, push the top of the unit.)

Use of Ana-Kit or Ana-Guard

1. Remove the red needle cover.
2. Hold the syringe upright, and push the plunger until it stops. This expels air and excess epinephrine.
3. Rotate the plunger one-quarter turn. This aligns the bar on the plunger with the slot in the syringe.
4. Insert the needle under the skin on the back of the upper arm or thigh.
5. Pull back slightly on the plunger. If a flash of blood appears, you may be in a vein. Pull the needle out and reinsert elsewhere.
6. Push the plunger and inject the epinephrine.
7. Remove the needle and protect it. You may need to inject a second dose.

Hantavirus

Hantavirus is found throughout North America but is most frequently associated with the Southwestern states. It is carried by rodents, primarily deer mice, pinyon mice, brush mice, and chipmunks. The virus produces a serious respiratory disease passed from the rodent reservoir to humans through inhalation of aerosolized microscopic particles of dried rodent saliva, urine, or feces. You can also become infected by touching your mouth or nose after handling contaminated materials. A rodent's bite can also spread the virus.

Symptoms are general and flulike: fever, headache, muscle aches, and sometimes nausea and vomiting. Hantavirus infections progress to breathing difficulty, which is caused by fluid buildup in the lungs.

To minimize the risk of hantavirus infection, follow these precautions:

Check potential campsites for rodent droppings and burrows.

Do not disturb or crawl around in rodent burrows or dens.

Avoid sleeping near woodpiles, burrows, or dens that may be frequented by rodents.

Avoid sleeping on bare ground; use a ground cloth or a tent.

Store foods in rodentproof containers and promptly and appropriately dispose of garbage.

Don't use old cabins until they have been cleaned and disinfected.

FINAL THOUGHTS
Tips for Preventing Poisoning Emergencies
1. Read labels for information on toxic substances.
2. Cook outside or in well-ventilated tents or snow shelters.
3. Identify plants before you eat them.
4. Be aware of foot placement.
5. Look before you reach under logs or overhangs or onto ledges.
6. Shake out clothing, footwear, and sleeping bags.

SUMMARY:
POISONS, STINGS, AND BITES

TREATMENT OF INGESTED POISONS:
PLANTS, DRUGS.
Give 2 tbs syrup of ipecac with ½ liter of water
Repeat dose if no vomiting occurs within 20 minutes
After vomiting ceases, give 5 tbs activated charcoal

If ipecac is unavailable:
2 tbs mild soap or mustard
Tickle back of throat

Do not induce vomiting if:
Corrosive or petroleum products
Altered level of consciousness
Seizures

TREATMENT OF CARBON MONOXIDE POISONING
Move to fresh air
Maintain airway
If possible, administer oxygen

TREATMENT OF ABSORBED POISONS
Dry poisons: brush off, then rinse with water
Wet poisons: rinse thoroughly with water

INJECTED POISONS:
BEES, WASPS, SPIDERS, SNAKES, SCORPIONS
Treatment of Bee and Wasp Stings
Scrape or flick off stinger
Clean wound with antiseptic soap
Ice/cool compress may relieve pain
If necessary, treat for anaphylaxis

• *CONTINUED* •

SUMMARY:
POISONS, STINGS, AND BITES *(continued)*

Treatment of Spider and Scorpion Bites
Clean wound with antiseptic soap
Ice/cool compress to relieve pain

If systemic symptoms of envenomization develop:
ABCs and supportive care
Evacuate to antivenin

Treatment of Rattlesnake Bites
Clean wound with antiseptic soap
Apply sterile dressing
Remove rings and other constrictive items
Keep limb at or below heart level
Keep patient quiet, hydrated, and comfortable
Suction with Sawyer Extractor

Treatment of Tick Bites
Promptly remove the tick with a gentle, steady pull
Clean the bite site with soap and water
In cases of rash, fever, flu, or muscle aches following a tick bite,
    the patient should be seen by a physician

Signs and Symptoms
of Mild to Moderate Allergic Reaction
Local swelling near a sting
Runny nose, sneezing, swollen eyes, hay fever
Flushed and itchy skin
Hives or welts on the skin
Mild or no breathing difficulty

Treatment of Mild to Moderate Allergic Reaction
Remove the allergen from the patient, or the patient from the
    offending environment
Oral antihistamines
Hydration
Monitor for increased breathing difficulty

• *CONTINUED* •

SUMMARY:
POISONS, STINGS, AND BITES *(continued)*

Signs and Symptoms of Anaphylaxis
Flushed and itchy skin
Hives and welts on the skin
Swollen face, lips, and tongue
Respiratory distress
Shock.

Treatment of Anaphylaxis
Remove the allergen or the patient from the offending
    environment
Inject epinephrine
When the patient can swallow, administer oral antihistamines
Watch for a second reaction
Evacuate

CHAPTER 12

MARINE ENVENOMIZATIONS

INJURIES FROM MARINE ANIMALS

Injuries from marine organisms are rarely the result of an aggressive, unprovoked attack. Most injuries occur as a result of accidental contact or when a threatened animal reacts in self-defense. This chapter discusses two broad categories of injuries from aquatic animals: marine spine envenomizations and nematocyst sting envenomizations. Treatment for these two types of injuries is very different: injuries from spines are treated with hot water immersion; stings are rinsed in vinegar.

MARINE SPINE ENVENOMIZATIONS

Marine animals with venom known to be harmful to people include the zebra fish, scorpion fish, stonefish, sea urchin, and stingray, which deliver venom through spines, and the cone shell, which injects venom through a proboscis. Envenomization may cause life-threatening injury or mild irritation, depending on the species, the number of punctures, the amount of venom, the health of the victim, and other factors.

Signs and Symptoms

Signs of marine venom injury include local discoloration, cyanosis, and laceration or puncture wound. Symptoms include numbness, tingling, and intense local pain. In serious envenomizations, nausea, vomiting, paralysis, respiratory distress, heart rhythm irregularities, and shock can occur.

Treatment

Treat marine envenomizations by controlling bleeding, removing imbedded spines, cleaning the wound, and controlling pain with hot water soaks.

Immerse the injury in water as hot as the patient can tol-

Treatment of Marine Spine Envenomizations

Control bleeding
Immerse the injury in water as
  hot as the patient can
  tolerate (usually 115° to
  120°F, 46° to 49°C) for
  30 to 90 minutes or until
  the pain is gone
Remove imbedded spines

Irrigate the wound
Clean the wound
Elevate the extremity to help
  control swelling
Monitor for signs of infection or
  envenomization
Medications for pain

---

erate (usually 115° to 120°F, 46° to 49°C) for 30 to 90 minutes or until the pain is gone. This therapy is thought to inactivate heat-sensitive proteins in the venom. Immersion in a large pot or a plastic bag filled with hot water is best, but hot compresses can also be used.

Clean the wound with irrigation. Remove obvious imbedded spines carefully. Elevate the extremity to help control swelling. Remedies such as meat tenderizer, papain, or mangrove sap are not scientifically confirmed and may irritate the wound.

Removing imbedded spines is against standard treatment for impaled objects, however, the spines are a source of infection and a continued source of venom. Their presence also retards healing and may cause further injury. Removing them is often difficult; the spines are brittle and break easily, leaving a foreign body that may cause infection. Use tweezers or fingers (wear gloves) to remove the spines. If the spine is hard to remove, leave it in place and evacuate the patient to a physician. Medications to control pain are appropriate.

Monitor the patient for signs of generalized envenomization. With severe envenomization, signs and symptoms of shock and respiratory distress will develop. In these cases, our treatment is supportive care and evacuation.

Scorpion Fish
There are three genera in this family—stonefish, zebrafish, and scorpion fish—and several hundred species. The stone-

fish, inconspicuous and possessing a highly toxic venom, is considered to be among the most dangerous of all venomous creatures.

Zebra fish are spectacularly colored; stonefish and scorpion fish less so. All members of the family are found in shallow waters. Zebra fish are free swimmers; stonefish and scorpion fish often hide in cracks, near rocks, or among plants. The stonefish may bury itself under sandy or broken coral bottoms. A dead stonefish is still dangerous! Its venom remains active for 48 hours after death.

The immediate intense pain of stonefish envenomization peaks in 60 to 90 minutes and can persist for days, despite treatment. Stone fish wounds are slow to heal and prone to infection.

Sea Urchins

Sea urchins are nonaggressive, nocturnal, omnivorous feeders that move slowly across the ocean bottom and are often found on rocky bottoms and burrowed in sand and small crevices. The hard spines protecting their vital organs can envenom victims if the urchin is stepped on, handled, or inadvertently bumped. Their grasping organs, called pedicellariae, can also envenom.

Symptoms are usually local and mild; however, infections are possible if pieces of imbedded spines remain in the skin or joint capsules. Spines imbedded in joints or large fragments left in soft tissues should be evaluated by a physician. Severe reactions are rare.

Spines lodged in the skin often turn it a brownish purple color. This reaction is harmless and can be seen regardless of whether a spine has broken off and remains imbedded or not.

Starfish

The venomous crown-of-thorns starfish is found in the Indo-Pacific area, the Red Sea, the eastern Pacific, and the Sea of Cortez. Starfish are scavengers that feed on other echinoderms, mollusks, coral, and worms. The upper surface of the crown-of-thorns starfish is studded with sharp, poisonous spines that can penetrate even the best diving gloves.

CONE SHELL:

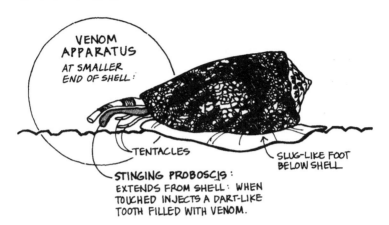

VENOM APPARATUS AT SMALLER END OF SHELL :

TENTACLES

SLUG-LIKE FOOT BELOW SHELL

STINGING PROBOSCIS : EXTENDS FROM SHELL : WHEN TOUCHED INJECTS A DART-LIKE TOOTH FILLED WITH VENOM.

Cone Shells

The shells of these animals, which live in shallow waters, reefs, and tide pools, are beautiful but hide a nasty sting. Cone shells project a long proboscis from the narrow end of the shell and inject venom from its tip. Toxicity to humans varies, but it rarely causes death. Do not handle cone shells. Drop them immediately if the proboscis is observed. Almost all reported envenomizations have come from collectors handling the shells.

The injury resembles a bee sting with pain, burning, and itching. Serious envenomizations produce cyanosis and numbness at the injury site, which progresses to numbness around the mouth, then generalized paralysis.

Treatment of cone shell stings is largely supportive care. Clean and thoroughly irrigate the puncture wound. The benefit of hot water soaks is unproved, but they may provide pain relief. Likewise, the value of circumferential pressure bandages is unconfirmed, but they may slow the spread of the venom.

Stingrays

Stingrays are bottom feeders, often found in shallow waters lying on top of or partially buried under sandy bottoms. Most stingray envenomizations occur when a careless swimmer

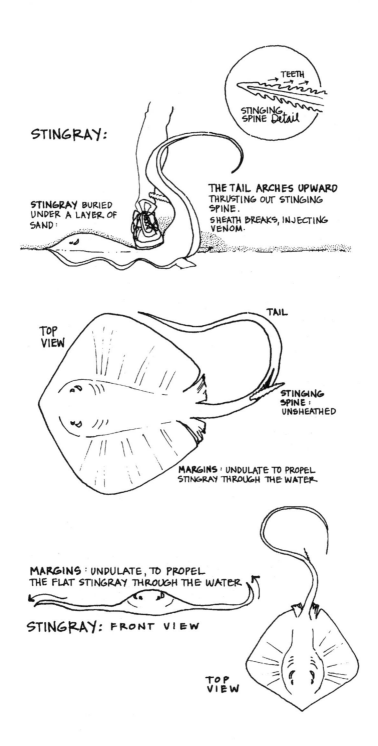

TEETH

STINGING
SPINE *Detail*

STINGRAY:

STINGRAY BURIED
UNDER A LAYER OF
SAND:

THE TAIL ARCHES UPWARD
THRUSTING OUT STINGING
SPINE.
SHEATH BREAKS, INJECTING
VENOM.

TOP
VIEW

TAIL

STINGING
SPINE:
UNSHEATHED

MARGINS: UNDULATE TO PROPEL
STINGRAY THROUGH THE WATER

MARGINS: UNDULATE, TO PROPEL
THE FLAT STINGRAY THROUGH THE WATER

STINGRAY: FRONT VIEW

TOP
VIEW

or wader steps on a buried ray. The stingray's tail whips up, and its serrated barbs inflict a nasty wound. Such defensive attacks usually cause wounds to the leg or ankle, and pieces of barbs may remain imbedded in the wound. Wounds often take the form of bleeding soft tissue lacerations or punctures. Intense local pain may last up to 48 hours.

NEMATOCYST STING ENVENOMIZATIONS

Nematocysts are specialized stinging capsules found in members of the phylum Coelenterata, which includes the sea anemones, jellyfish, Portuguese man-of-wars, and some corals. The nematocyst discharges an incapacitating venom, allowing the animal to kill and digest its prey. Some nematocysts produce a sticky venomous substance; others deliver a barbed, venomous stinger.

Nematocyst discharge is triggered by contact with the skin or by changes in osmotic pressure, as can occur when the nematocyst is rinsed with fresh water. Nematocysts are generally found around the animal's mouth or on the tentacles, and nematocysts from dead jellyfish can still envenom.

Signs and Symptoms

Signs and symptoms range from mild skin irritations to rapid death and vary considerably with the venomous species. In general, contact with a nematocyst produces painful local swelling, redness, and a stinging, prickling sensation that progresses to numbness, burning, and throbbing pain. Pain may radiate from the extremities to the groin, abdomen, or armpit. The contact site may turn a reddish brown-purple color, marked by swelling. In more serious cases, blisters may occur.

Severe envenomization may produce headache, abdominal cramps, nausea, vomiting, muscle paralysis, and respiratory or cardiac distress.

Treatment

Treat nematocyst injury first by protecting yourself and second by inactivating and removing nematocysts from the skin. Rinse the injury with sea water to begin removing remaining nematocysts. Do not scrape, rub, or rinse with fresh water, as this will cause any nematocysts on the skin to release more venom. Soak the injury in vinegar for at least 30 minutes. Alcohol, meat tenderizer, and baking soda are less effective, although a baking soda slurry is effective in treating the sting of the Chesapeake sea nettle.

> **Treatment of Nematocyst Sting Envenomizations**
>
> Rinse with sea water to remove remaining nematocysts
>
> Soak in vinegar for at least 30 minutes
>
> After soaking, remove all visible tentacles

After soaking, remove all visible tentacles with tweezers. Sticky tentacles may be easier to remove if you first apply a drying agent such as baking soda, talc, or sand. Nematocysts can also be removed with adhesive tape or by shaving gently with a razor and shaving cream. Remember: Be careful. Rescuer injury is common both in the water and when removing nematocysts on shore.

Anemones
Stinging cells surround the mouths of these sessile organisms. Contact often occurs from accidentally brushing into the anemone. Anemone nematocysts usually produce only very mild local symptoms.

Jellyfish
These animals vary in size from tiny (2 millimeters) to big (2 meters with 40-meter tentacles). Most produce mild local signs and symptoms; however, some produce very potent venom. The box jellyfish *(Chironex fleckeri),* found in the Pacific Ocean off Australia, can cause death within 1 minute.

Portuguese Man-of-War
This large colony of animals usually lives on the surface of the open ocean, its long, transparent tentacles dangling for prey. It is transported by winds and currents, and the animal or

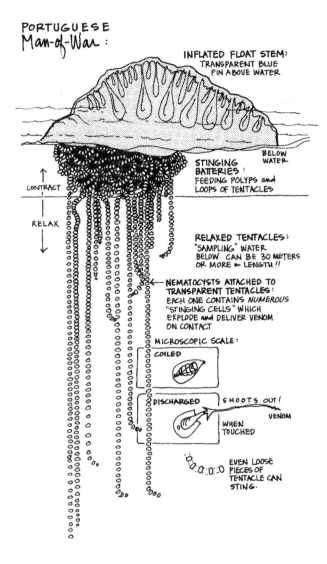

PORTUGUESE
Man-of-War :

INFLATED FLOAT STEM:
TRANSPARENT BLUE
FIN ABOVE WATER

BELOW WATER

STINGING BATTERIES:
FEEDING POLYPS and LOOPS OF TENTACLES

CONTRACT
RELAX

RELAXED TENTACLES:
"SAMPLING" WATER BELOW. CAN BE 30 METERS OR MORE in LENGTH !!

NEMATOCYSTS ATTACHED TO TRANSPARENT TENTACLES:
EACH ONE CONTAINS NUMEROUS "STINGING CELLS" WHICH EXPLODE and DELIVER VENOM ON CONTACT

MICROSCOPIC SCALE:

COILED

DISCHARGED SHOOTS OUT!
VENOM
WHEN TOUCHED

EVEN LOOSE PIECES OF TENTACLE CAN STING.

pieces of its tentacles can sometimes be pushed into coastal waters. Contact with pieces of tentacle usually causes only mild, superficial reactions. However, contact with a large number of tentacles from an intact animal can provoke massive envenomization and cause serious reactions.

Fire Coral

Fire corals are so named because they make you feel as if you've touched hot coals. They are found in coral reefs in tropical waters. Their nematocyst sting causes immediate pain, often described as burning, and small raised red areas on the skin. The localized pain usually lasts 1 to 4 days.

Hard Coral

Hard corals are not highly venomous but often have very sharp edges that can cause abrasions or even lacerations. The wounds heal slowly, especially if pieces of coral are imbedded in the skin. Some species can cause rashes. Vigorous irrigation of the wound is helpful to remove coral pieces. Imbedded pieces of coral often cause slow-healing wound infections known at NOLS as "coast disease."

Traumatic Wounds

Wounds in a marine environment are treated like any other soft tissue wound, with an emphasis on cleansing and prevention of infection. See chapter 3 ("Soft Tissue Injuries"). Research shows that seawater contains many potentially dangerous contaminants. Soft tissue wounds in fresh or seawater should be vigorously cleaned to reduce the chance of infection.

Sea Cucumbers

These creatures are bottom scavengers found in both shallow and deep water. Sea cucumbers often feed on nematocysts, so they may secrete coelenterate venom as well. They also produce a liquid toxin that causes skin irritations and often severe inflammatory reactions (swelling, raised patches, itching, oozing). To treat, rinse the skin thoroughly with water, and soak the injured area in vinegar.

FINAL THOUGHTS

Learn to identify marine animals and to understand their habits. When wading, shuffle your feet to alert stingrays to your presence. Touching marine animals or coral formations is not necessary to enjoy them. When swimming and diving, avoid standing or walking on coral reefs or banging against them. A minimum-impact approach protects not only you but also the fragile underwater environment.

SUMMARY:
MARINE ENVENOMIZATIONS

Treatment of Marine Spine Envenomization
Immerse the affected area in hot water (usually 115° to 120°F,
46° to 49°C) for 30 to 90 minutes or until pain is relieved

Treatment of Nematocyst Sting Envenomization
Soak the affected area in vinegar for 30 minutes
Remove all visible tentacles with tweezers
Remove obvious imbedded spines
Rinse and irrigate the wound thoroughly
Monitor closely for signs and symptoms of systemic involve-
ment; if these are present, consider evacuation

CHAPTER 13

COLD WATER IMMERSION AND DROWNING

INTRODUCTION

NOLS students participating in river crossings, sea kayaking, sailing, white-water rafting and kayaking, sailboarding, snorkeling, and canoeing are exposed to the hazards associated with being on or near water. These hazards include cold water immersion, immersion hypothermia, and drowning.

COLD WATER IMMERSION

The body's responses to cold water immersion are many. Sudden immersion in cold water causes a gasp for air, constriction of blood vessels in the extremities, and an increase in breathing and heart rate. The initial gasp may result in water inhalation, and the rapid breathing rate makes it more difficult to hold the breath underwater.

Death caused by heart rhythm abnormalities is possible, and as strength and coordination diminish, the chance of drowning increases. What's more, as the brain cools, we think less clearly and may do foolish things, such as removing a personal flotation device (PFD) or swimming aimlessly.

The danger of cold water immersion is widely present in the wilderness environment. Water conducts heat 25 times faster than air. In North America, most water remains below 77°F (25°C) year-round. Lakes in the Rocky Mountains warm only to the mid-50s (13°C) in summer. In Mexico, the Sea of Cortez averages 58°F (14.5°C) in winter. We are unable to remain warm at any of these temperatures unless we wear protective clothing.

IMMERSION HYPOTHERMIA

The common image of immersion hypothermia is that of a victim floating for hours in a cold ocean or lake. The body can also cool quickly in the cold moving water of a mountain stream.

Although there may be subtle differences between hypothermia on land and in the water, these differences are not relevant to field treatment. Treat immersion hypothermia by removing the victim from the water. Handle the patient gently, as rough handling may trigger lethal heart rhythm abnormalities. Treat the patient for hypothermia as discussed in chapter 9 ("Cold Injuries"). Dry and insulate the patient; prevent further heat loss; ensure adequate airway, breathing, and circulation; and place the patient in a sleeping bag, possibly with another person or with hot water bottles as heat sources.

DROWNING

Drowning is the second most common cause of accidental death in children and the third leading cause of death in young adults. A majority of drowning victims are young males. Alcohol is involved in over half of drowning accidents. Freshwater drowning, especially in pools, is more common than saltwater drowning.

Aspects of a Typical Drowning

Panic and Struggle. The victim frantically tries to keep his or her head above water, often using a vertical breast-

---

Risk Factors Related to Drowning

Age—toddlers and teenage males are at highest risk
Location—private swimming pools, small streams, ponds, and irrigation ditches are common drowning sites
Gender—males dominate all age groups

Alcohol—a factor in one-third to two-thirds of drownings
Injury—cervical spine injury, as from diving or surfing
Seizure disorder—risk is greatest if poorly controlled; hyperventilation may cause predisposition to seizures
PFD—failure to wear one

stroke, with the head held back and the mouth open. The victim attempts to hold his or her breath when submerged but eventually gasps for air.

Aspiration. Inhalation of water causes intense vomiting and further inhalation of water and vomit. Approximately 85 to 90 percent of victims experience a "wet" drowning in which they inhale water into their lungs. The other 10 to 15 percent experience a "dry" drowning: spasm of the larynx that obstructs the airway.

Unconsciousness. The victim becomes unconscious and stops breathing. Cardiac arrest and death may follow.

Treatment

For first aid purposes, the type of water (salt, fresh, clean, dirty) or type of drowning (wet or dry) does not matter. Airway maintenance and, if necessary, rescue breathing and chest compressions are essential to the treatment of unconscious drowning victims. If you have any doubts about how long the victim was submerged, attempt resuscitation. There are rare case reports of people surviving submersion in ice water for more than 15 minutes, with 66 minutes being the longest documented survival.

The goals of treatment are to remove the victim from the water, protect the cervical spine, prevent cardiac arrest, and stabilize the patient's temperature.

Treatment of Drowning

Remove the victim from the water	Monitor vital signs
Handle gently	Evacuate any person who required resuscitation, was unconscious in the water, exhibits shortness of breath, or has a history of lung illness
Check the ABCs	
Protect the cervical spine	
Perform a focused exam and history	
Treat for hypothermia	

Remove the Victim from the Water. Remove the victim from the water as quickly as possible. Rescuer safety is a priority. Remember the lifesaving adage "reach, throw, row, tow, and go." First try reaching for the victim, remaining in contact with the shore or boat. Second, throw a lifeline. Third, row or paddle to the victim. Attempt a swimming rescue only as a last resort.

Handle the Patient Gently. A patient who was submerged in cold water may be hypothermic.

Check the ABCs. Assess and check the ABCs. Aggressive initiation of airway, breathing, and circulation is the standard in drowning rescue. If available, administer oxygen.

Protect the Cervical Spine. Unless injury can be ruled out, assume that the victim has a neck injury and use the jaw thrust technique to open the airway. Neck injuries can be caused from surfing, diving in shallow water, or flipping a kayak or decked canoe in rapids.

Perform a Focused Exam and History. A complete patient exam is warranted to assess for injury.

Treat for Hypothermia. Remove wet clothing and dry and insulate the patient to prevent further heat loss.

Evacuate the Patient. Outside the wilderness, any victim of involuntary submersion should be evaluated by a physician, as lung injury from inhaled water may not be immediately evident. In the wilderness, we don't evacuate every asymptomatic person who swims through a rapid or takes a dunking during a river crossing and comes up coughing. Evacuate the victim of a submersion incident if that person required resuscitation, was unconscious in the water, exhibits shortness of breath or other symptoms of respiratory difficulty, or has a history of lung disease.

The mode of transport and speed of the evacuation should be based on the seriousness of the patient's condition. For example, a patient who is unconscious following submersion should be quickly evacuated.

FINAL THOUGHTS

Safety around lakes, rivers, and the ocean begins with respect for the power of moving water and the debilitating effects of cold water. Cold water, failure to wear a PFD, and the inability to swim are, according to the Coast Guard, the most common factors in white-water deaths.

In two out of three drownings, the victims could not swim, had no intention of entering deep water (and thus were ill prepared), and were affected by alcohol or drugs. Most drownings occur 10 to 30 feet from safety; only 10 percent of drownings occur in a guarded pool.

While awaiting rescue, assume the HELP (heat escape lessening posture) position by bringing your knees to your chest and crossing your arms over them. If you're with a group of people awaiting rescue, everyone in the group should face inward and huddle with arms interlocked. You must be wearing a PFD to assume either of these positions. If possible, get out of the water onto an overturned or partially submerged boat. It is always better to keep as much of yourself or the victim out of the water as possible, even when the wind is blowing.

Clothing selection for paddling or other activities around water requires finding a balance between overdressing—and overheating—and protecting the body against sudden immersion in cold water. Extra clothing should be easily accessible in the cockpit of your boat or in your pack and should be donned if developing conditions increase the likelihood of a cold dunking.

Well-developed safety and rescue programs exist for swimming, sea kayaking, white-water boating, and sailing. If you're involved in any of these activities, seek out these programs for further training.

SUMMARY:
TREATMENT OF DROWNING

Remove the victim from the water
Handle gently
Check the ABCs
Protect the cervical spine
Perform a secondary survey
Treat for hypothermia
Monitor vitals
Evacuate any person who required resuscitation, was uncon-
  scious in the water, exhibits shortness of breath, or has a
  history of lung illness.

CHAPTER 14

ALTITUDE ILLNESS

INTRODUCTION

Each year thousands of people trek in Nepal, South America, and Africa at altitudes over 13,000 feet. In the United States, thousands of people climb Mount Ranier (14,408 feet) and Denali (18,000 feet) each year. Skiers in the Rocky Mountains often ski within 24 hours of leaving low elevations. All these people are at risk for altitude sickness.

NOLS expeditions have managed life-threatening cerebral edema at 21,000 feet on Cerro Aconcagua in Argentina and pulmonary edema at 9,000 feet in Wyoming's Wind River Range. Prevention through acclimatization provides some protection from altitude illness, but there is no immunity. If you travel in mountains, you need to know how to prevent, recognize, and treat altitude illness.

Lack of oxygen is the number-one cause of health problems at altitude. Normally, oxygen diffuses from the alveoli into the blood because the gas pressure is greater in the alveoli than in blood. At altitude, diminished air pressure (barometric pressure) reduces the pressure in the alveoli and decreases the amount of oxygen diffusing into the blood. For example, in a healthy person at sea level, blood is 95 percent saturated with oxygen. At 18,000 feet, it is only 71 percent saturated; that is, it is carrying 29 percent less oxygen.

As altitude increases, barometric pressure falls logarith-

> **Altitudes are defined as:**
>
> High altitude
>   8,000–14,000 feet
> Very high altitude
>   14,000–18,000 feet
> Extreme altitude
>   Above 18,000 feet

mically. Distance from the equator, seasons, and weather also affect barometric pressure.

The greater the distance from the equator, the lower the barometric pressure, given the same elevation. For example, if Mount Everest were located at the same latitude as Denali, the corresponding drop in barometric pressure would make an ascent without oxygen impossible.

As for seasons and weather, air pressure is lower in winter than in summer, and a low pressure trough reduces pressure. Although temperature does not directly affect barometric pressure, the combination of cold stress and lack of oxygen increases the risk of cold injuries and altitude problems.

ADAPTATION TO ALTITUDE

The body undergoes numerous changes at higher elevation in order to increase oxygen delivery to cells and improve the efficiency of oxygen use. These adaptations usually begin almost immediately and continue to occur for several weeks. People vary in their ability to acclimatize. Some adjust quickly; others fail to acclimatize, even with gradual exposure over a period of weeks.

In general, the body becomes approximately 80 percent acclimatized after 10 days at altitude and approximately 95 percent acclimatized by 6 weeks. The respiratory rate peaks in about 1 week and then slowly decreases over the next few months, although it tends to remain higher than its normal rate at sea level. After 10 days, the heart rate starts to decrease.

When we descend, we begin losing our hard-won adaptations at approximately the same rate at which we gained them; 10 days after returning to sea level, we have lost 80 percent of our adaptations.

Increased Respiratory Rate. During the first week of adaptation, a variety of changes takes place. Respiratory rate and depth increase in response to lower concentrations of oxygen in the blood, causing more carbon dioxide to be lost and more oxygen to be delivered to the alveoli. The increased respiratory rate begins within the first few hours of arriving at

---

Adaptation to Altitude

Early changes	*Later changes*
Increased respiratory rate	Increased red blood cell
Increased heart rate	production
Fluid shifts	Increased 2, 3-DPG production
	Increased number of capillaries

---

altitudes as low as 5,000 feet. The lost carbon dioxide causes the body to become more alkaline.

To compensate for the body's increasing alkalinity, the kidneys excrete bicarbonate—an alkaline substance—in the urine. This adaptation occurs within 24 to 48 hours after hyperventilation starts.

Increased Heart Rate. Cells require a constant supply of oxygen, so the heart beats more quickly to meet the demand. Except at extreme altitudes, heart rate returns to near normal after acclimatization.

Fluid Shifts. Blood flow to the brain increases to provide the brain with its required volume of oxygen (equivalent to that available at sea level).

In the lungs, the pulmonary capillaries constrict, increasing resistance to flow through the lungs and raising pulmonary blood pressure. Dangerously high blood pressure in the pulmonary artery may cause fluid to escape from the capillaries and leak into the lungs (pulmonary edema).

Increased Red Blood Cell Production. As acclimatization continues, the bone marrow contributes by increasing red blood cell production. New red blood cells become available in the blood within 4 to 5 days, increasing the blood's oxygen-carrying capacity. An acclimatized person may have 30 to 50 percent more red blood cells than a person at sea level.

Increased 2, 3-DPG Production. Within the blood cells 2, 3-diphosphoglycerate (DPG) increases. This is an organic phosphate that helps oxygen combine with red blood cells.

Production of myoglobin, the intramuscular oxygen-carrying protein in red blood cells, also increases.

Increased Number of Capillaries. The body develops more capillaries in response to altitude. This improves the diffusion of oxygen by shortening the distance between the cell and the capillary.

ALTITUDE ILLNESS

Altitude illness results from a lack of oxygen in the body. Anyone who ascends to high altitude will become hypoxic (the condition of having insufficient oxygen in the blood). Why some people become ill and others don't is not known. It is known, however, that most people who become ill do so within the first few days of ascending to altitude.

Treatment of altitude illness is based on four principles: (1) stop ascent when symptoms develop; (2) descend if there is no improvement or condition worsens; (3) descend immediately if shortness of breath, loss of coordination, or changes in consciousness are present; and (4) don't leave alone people with altitude sickness. The definitive treatment of all forms of altitude illness is descent.

Six Factors That Affect the Incidence and Severity of Altitude Illness

1. Rate of ascent—the faster you climb, the greater the risk
2. Altitude attained (especially sleeping altitude)—the higher you sleep, the greater the risk
3. Length of exposure—the longer you stay high, the greater the risk
4. Level of exertion—hard exertion, without rest or hydration, increases the risk
5. Hydration and diet—high-fat and high-protein diets and dehydration increase the risk
6. Inherent physiological susceptibility—some people are more likely to become ill, and we don't know why

---

Management requires early diagnosis and prompt intervention. There are several medications used for the prevention and treatment of altitude illness: acetazolamide (Diamox), dexamethasone (Decadron), and nifedipine (Procardia). Check with your physician adviser for recommendations on the use of these drugs. NOLS brings these medications on high-altitude expeditions for the treatment of altitude illness during descent. We do not use medications to prevent altitude illness. We focus on slow ascent and acclimatization as the cornerstones of prevention.

The three common types of altitude illness are acute mountain sickness (AMS), high-altitude pulmonary edema (HAPE), and high-altitude cerebral edema (HACE). AMS is the most common. It is not life-threatening, but if not treated, it can progress to HAPE or HACE. HAPE is less common but more serious. HACE is rare but can be sudden and severe.

Acute Mountain Sickness (AMS)

Acute mountain sickness is a term applied to a group of symptoms. It is more apt to occur in people not acclimatized who make rapid ascents to above 8,000 feet. It also occurs in people who partially acclimatize then make an abrupt ascent to a higher altitude.

Signs and Symptoms. Signs and symptoms tend to start 6 to 72 hours after arrival at high altitude. They usually disappear in 2 to 6 days. Symptoms are worse in the morning, probably due to the normal decrease in the rate and depth of breathing during sleep, which lowers blood oxygen saturation. Symptoms include the following:

Headache. Increased cerebral blood flow helps the brain

Signs and Symptoms of AMS
Headache
Malaise
Loss of appetite
Nausea, vomiting
Peripheral edema
Disturbed sleep
Cyanosis
Ataxia

maintain its oxygen supply, but the expanded volume causes pain as the system adapts.

Malaise. This uneasy feeling, drowsiness, and lassitude occur because of decreased oxygen in the blood.

Loss of Appetite, Nausea, and Vomiting. Loss of appetite and nausea commonly accompany AMS and contribute to the overall sensation of feeling lousy.

Peripheral Edema. Persons with AMS tend to retain fluid, resulting in edema, especially of the face and hands.

Disturbed Sleep. During sleep, a person's rate and depth of respiration may gradually increase until it reaches a climax. Breathing then ceases entirely for 5 to 50 seconds. This phenomenon is called Cheyne-Stokes respiration. Cheyne-Stokes breathing further decreases the level of oxygen in the blood.

Cyanosis. This bluish appearance in the fingernail beds, in the mucous membranes, and around the mouth occurs as a result of decreased oxygen saturation of the blood.

Ataxia. Ataxia, or difficulty maintaining balance, is a good sign—some experts say the most useful sign—of significant AMS. The test is simple. Have the patient stand straight with boots together and eyes closed. If the patient wobbles, falls, or has to open the eyes to maintain balance, he or she has ataxia.

Treatment. Limit your activity during the first 3 days at altitudes greater than 8,000 feet; it may take 3 to 4 days to acclimatize. Stay well hydrated to help the kidneys excrete bicarbonate. Aspirin, acetaminophen, or ibuprofen may ease the headache. If symptoms worsen, signs of ataxia or pulmonary edema become apparent, or there is a change in the level of consciousness, descend to the altitude where symptoms began.

Treatment of AMS

Hydrate
Rest (light exercise okay)
Use pain medication for
    headache
Avoid sedatives

Descend if:
Symptoms worsen
Signs of HAPE or HACE develop

High-Altitude Pulmonary Edema (HAPE)

HAPE is abnormal fluid accumulation in the lungs resulting from maladaptation to altitude. The cause is not clearly understood. HAPE rarely occurs below 8,000 feet and is more common in young males.

Signs and Symptoms. The symptoms of HAPE result from the decreasing ability of the lungs to exchange oxygen and carbon dioxide. The symptoms usually begin 24 to 96 hours after ascent.

HAPE may initially appear with mild symptoms similar to AMS. The patient complains of a dry cough and shortness of breath and fatigue while climbing uphill. The heart and respiratory rates increase. Cyanosis of the fingernail beds may occur.

As HAPE worsens, the shortness of breath, weakness, and fatigue occur while walking on level ground. The patient complains of a harsh cough, headache, and loss of appetite. The heart and respiratory rates remain elevated. The nail beds become cyanotic. Rales (rattles) can be heard with a stethoscope. The patient may be ataxic. Signs and symptoms may be mistaken for the flu, bronchitis, or pneumonia.

As HAPE becomes severe, the patient complains of a productive cough, extreme weakness, and shortness of breath while at rest. The heart rate is greater than 110 beats per minute, and the respiratory rate is greater than 30 breaths per minute. Facial and nail bed cyanosis may be apparent. Rales can be heard without a stethoscope. The patient coughs up frothy, blood-tinged sputum. The patient becomes ataxic, lethargic, or unconscious.

Signs and Symptoms of HAPE

Signs of acute mountain sickness

Shortness of breath on exertion, progressing to shortness of breath at rest

Fatigue

Dry cough, progressing to wet, productive cough

Increased heart rate and respiratory rate

Rales, sounds of fluid in the lungs

Ataxia

HAPE, like AMS, becomes worse at night due to Cheyne-Stokes respirations. HAPE is a life-threatening illness.

Treatment. Descend to a lower altitude as quickly as possible. Immediate descent is essential. Give oxygen, if available, during the descent. If the symptoms do not improve, descend until they do. Keep the patient warm, as cold stress can worsen the condition. The patient should avoid exercise for 2 to 3 days so the fluid in the lungs can be reabsorbed. People with mild HAPE may attempt to ascend again when the condition disappears. Watch for a relapse. A patient with moderate to severe HAPE must be evacuated from the mountain to a hospital.

Treatment of HAPE

Descend at least 2,000–3,000 feet
until symptoms abate

If you are unable to descend and have oxygen available, give the patient 100 percent oxygen at a flow rate of 4 to 6 liters per minute. If the condition does not improve, increase the flow of oxygen. Descend as soon as possible.

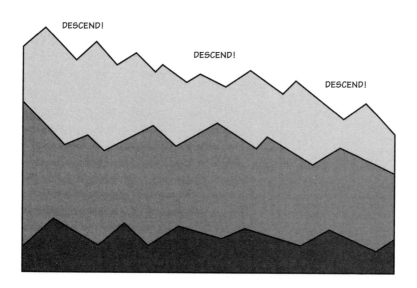

High-Altitude Cerebral Edema (HACE)

HACE is swelling of the brain thought to be caused by hypoxia damage to brain tissue. HACE generally occurs above 12,000 feet but has been recorded at 10,000 feet in the Wyoming's Wind River mountains.

Signs and Symptoms. The classic signs of HACE are change in the level of consciousness, ataxia, and severe lassitude. The patient may become confused, lose his or her memory, or slip into unconsciousness. Ataxia is evident in the lower extremities first, then in the upper extremities. In severe cases, the patient may be unable to hold a cup.

Signs and Symptoms of HACE

Signs of acute mountain sickness
Changes in level of consciousness
Ataxia
Severe lassitude
Headache
Nausea and vomiting
Vision disturbances
Paralysis
Seizures
Hallucinations
Cyanosis

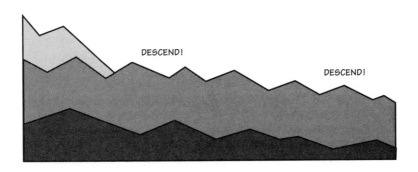

Treatment of HACE
DESCEND, DESCEND, DESCEND!

Other signs and symptoms may include headache, nausea, vomiting, cyanosis, seizures, hallucinations, transient blindness, partial paralysis, and loss of sensation on one side of the body.

Treatment. Descend. Do not hope the condition will get better if you wait. Waiting and hoping may be fatal. Descend to a lower elevation as soon as you notice any ataxia or change in the level of consciousness. Give oxygen if available.

Hyperbaric Bags. Portable hyperbaric (greater atmospheric pressure than normal) chambers are used in the treatment of altitude illness. These bags, the best known of which is the Gamow Bag, are made of nonpermeable nylon. Inflated with a foot pump to greater than atmospheric pressure, these bags are believed to increase oxygen diffusion into the blood. They simulate a descent of several thousand feet.

Hyperbaric bags are temporary treatment for emergencies—intended for use during evacuation to lower altitudes or if you are unable to descend immediately.

Thrombophlebitis

Studies have shown that there is an increased tendency for blood to thrombose (clot) in arteries and veins at high altitudes. Dehydration, increased red blood cells, cold, constrictive clothing, and immobility during bad weather have been cited as possible causes.

Signs and Symptoms. Clots most commonly occur in the deep veins of the calf. The calf is swollen and painful. The

DESCEND!

lower leg may be pale or cyanotic with decreased pulses in the foot. Flexing the foot upward or walking increases calf pain. If the clot breaks lose, it can travel to the lungs and cause a pulmonary embolism.

Treatment. Loosen constrictive clothing. Give aspirin (1 or 2) every 4 hours for pain and to decrease the blood's ability to clot. The patient should be carried down from altitude.

Prevention. Dehydration can predispose one to blood clots. Hydration is important for prevention. Exercise feet and legs a few minutes every hour if bad weather confines the group to tents. Be careful of constrictive clothing, such as tight gaiters.

FINAL THOUGHTS

Acclimatization is key. Start out sleeping at altitudes below 10,000 feet and spend 2 to 3 nights there before going higher. For every 2,000 to 3,000 feet gained, plan to spend an extra night acclimatizing to the new altitude.

Climb high and sleep low. It is best not to increase the sleeping altitude by more then 2,000 feet at a time. Set up camp at lower elevations and take day trips to high points.

Acclimatization
Ascend slowly
Climb high, sleep low
High-carbohydrate diet
Hydrate

Ferry loads up to a high camp and then return to the low camp to sleep as you acclimatize.

Eat a high-carbohydrate diet. Carbohydrates require less oxygen for metabolism than do fats and proteins. However, a diet exclusively of carbohydrates does not meet the body's overall nutritional needs. Eat protein and fat on rest days. Avoid eating fats and protein at night. The combination of decreased respiratory rate during sleep and increased requirement for oxygen to metabolize fats and proteins increases the risk of altitude illness.

Drink copious amounts of fluid. Urine should be clear, not yellow. Avoid sleeping pills, which decrease the respiratory rate, aggravating the lack of oxygen.

SUMMARY: ALTITUDE ILLNESSES

The risks of altitude illness can be reduced by acclimatizing to altitude. Ascend slowly, climb high, sleep low, eat a high-carbohydrate diet, and stay hydrated.

The only definitive treatment of altitude illness is to

DESCEND

DESCEND

DESCEND!

CHAPTER 15

ATHLETIC INJURIES

INTRODUCTION

Living and traveling in the wilderness, carrying a pack, hiking long distances, climbing, and paddling can be the sources of sprains, strains, and tendinitis. Athletic injuries account for 50 percent of injuries on NOLS courses and are a frequent cause of evacuations.

When faced with an athletic injury, the first-aider in the wilderness has to choose between treating the injury in the field—possibly altering the expedition route and timetable to accommodate the patient's loss of mobility—or evacuation. If evacuation is indicated, the first-aider must decide between walking the patient out or carrying the patient out on a litter.

Athletic injuries can be difficult to diagnose if initial pain and swelling confuse the extent of the injury. The most common athletic injuries on NOLS courses are ankle and knee sprains, Achilles tendinitis, and forearm tendinitis. Most of the athletic injuries we experience are minor, but even a moderate ankle sprain can take a week to heal. It is difficult for

Common Causes of Athletic Injury on NOLS Courses	
Playing games such as hug tag and hacky sack	Lifting a kayak or raft
Tripping while walking in camp	Falling or misstepping while hiking with a pack (on any terrain)
Stepping over logs	
Crossing streams, including shallow rock hops	Falling while skiing with a pack
	Shoveling snow
Putting on a backpack	Bending over to pick up firewood

General Treatment of Athletic Injuries (RICE)

Rest: allows time for healing

Ice: 20 to 40 minutes every 2 to 4 hours for 24 to 48 hours

Compression: elastic bandage to reduce swelling

Elevation: reduces swelling

Take acetaminophen or ibuprofen for pain and inflammation

---

a NOLS student to rest for 7 days without affecting a course traveling through the wilderness.

GENERAL TREATMENT (RICE)

Athletic injuries are generally treated with RICE: rest, ice, compression, and elevation. Allowing these injuries to heal until they are free of pain, tenderness, and swelling prevents aggravation of the condition. Gently rub the injured area with ice, wrapped in fabric to prevent frostbite, for 20 to 40 minutes every 2 to 4 hours for the first 24 to 48 hours. Cooling decreases nerve conduction and pain, constricts blood vessels, limits the inflammatory process, and reduces cellular demand for oxygen.

Compression with an Ace bandage helps reduce swelling. Care must be taken when applying the wrap not to exert pressure on an injury that swells dramatically or to cut off blood flow to the fingers or toes.

Elevating the injury above the level of the heart reduces swelling. Nonprescription pain medications such as acetaminophen and ibuprofen may help as well.

SPRAINS

Sprains are categorized as grades one, two, or three. With a grade one injury, ligament fibers are stretched but not torn. A partly torn or badly stretched ligament is a grade two injury. Completely torn ligaments are grade three injuries. Grade one and two sprains can be treated in the field. Grade three injuries require surgery to repair the severed ligament.

Assessment

A thorough assessment includes an evaluation of the mechanism of injury, as well as the signs and symptoms. Knowing the mechanism helps you determine whether the occurrence was sudden and traumatic, indicating a sprain, or whether it was progressive, suggesting an overuse injury.

Signs and Symptoms of Sprains
Swelling and discoloration
Pain
Instability at joint
Loss of range of motion
Inability to bear weight

Signs and symptoms of a sprain include swelling, pain, and discoloration. Point tenderness and obvious deformity suggest a fracture. Ask the patient to try to move the joint through its full range of motion. Painless movement is a good sign. If the patient is able to use or bear weight on the affected limb and pain and swelling are not severe, he or she can be treated in the field.

Severe pain, the sound of a pop at the time of injury, immediate swelling, and inability to use the joint are signs of a serious sprain, possibly a fracture. This injury should be immobilized and the patient evacuated from the field.

Ankle Sprains

Uneven ground, whether boulder fields in the backcountry or broken pavement in the city, contributes to the likelihood of ankle sprains. Of all ankle sprains, 85 percent are inversion injuries—those in which the foot turns in to the midline of the body and the ankle turns outward. Inversion injuries usually sprain one or more of the ligaments on the outside of the ankle.

Ankle Anatomy. The bones, ligaments, and tendons of the ankle and foot absorb stress and pressure generated by both body weight and activity. They also allow for flexibility and accommodate surface irregularities so that we don't lose our balance.

Bones. The lower leg bones are the tibia and the fibula. The large bumps on either side of the ankle are the lower ends of these bones—the fibula on the outside, and the tibia on the inside. Immediately under the tibia and fibula lies the talus bone, which sits atop the calcaneus (heel bone). The talus and calcaneus act as a rocker for front-to-back flexibility of the ankle. Without them, we would walk stiff-legged.

In front of the calcaneus lie two smaller bones, the navicular (inside) and the cuboid (outside). They attach to three small bones called the cuneiforms. Anterior to the cuneiforms are five metatarsals, which in turn articulate with the phalanges (toe bones).

Ligaments. Due to the number of bones in the foot, ligaments are many and complex. For simplicity, think of there being a ligament on every exterior surface of every bone, attaching to the adjacent articulating bone.

There are four ligaments commonly associated with ankle sprains. On the inside of the ankle is the large, fan-shaped deltoid ligament joining the talus, calcaneus, and several of the smaller foot bones to the tibia. Rolling the ankle inward, an eversion sprain, stresses the deltoid ligament. Spraining the deltoid requires considerable force, and due to its size and strength, it is seldom injured. In fact, this ligament is so strong that if a bad twist occurs, it frequently pulls fragments of bone off at its attachment points, causing an avulsion fracture.

On the outside, usually the weaker aspect, three ligaments attach from the fibula to the talus and the calcaneus.

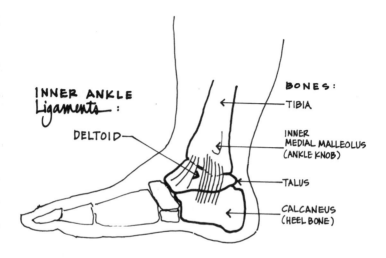

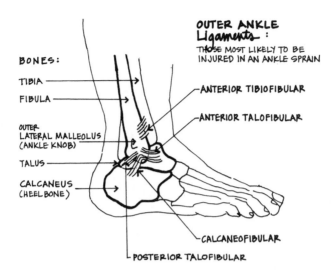

OUTER ANKLE Ligaments :
THOSE MOST LIKELY TO BE INJURED IN AN ANKLE SPRAIN

BONES:

TIBIA

FIBULA

OUTER LATERAL MALLEOLUS (ANKLE KNOB)

TALUS

CALCANEUS (HEEL BONE)

ANTERIOR TIBIOFIBULAR

ANTERIOR TALOFIBULAR

CALCANEOFIBULAR

POSTERIOR TALOFIBULAR

Together these three ligaments protect the ankle from turning to the outside.

Muscles and Tendons. Muscles in the lower leg use long tendons to act on the ankle and foot. The calf muscles—the gastrocnemius and soleus—shorten to point the toes. These muscles taper into the largest tendon, the Achilles, which attaches to the back of the calcaneus. The peroneal muscles in the lower leg contract and pull the foot laterally and roll the ankle outward. Muscles in the front of the lower leg turn the foot inward and extend the toes.

Treatment of Ankle Sprains. Sprains should have the standard treatment of rest, ice, compression, and elevation to limit swelling and allow healing. If a severe sprain or a fracture is suspected, immobilize the ankle. Aggressively treating a mild sprain with RICE for the first 24 to 48 hours and letting it rest for a few days may allow a patient to stay in the mountains rather than cut the trip short. A simple method

Treatment of Ankle Sprains
RICE
Taping for support

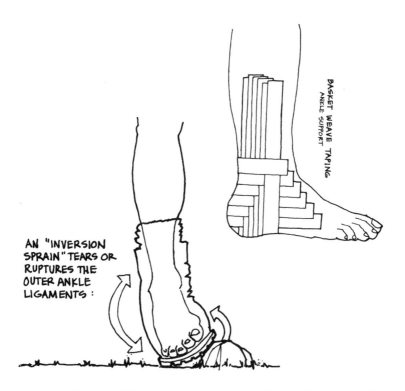

AN "INVERSION SPRAIN" TEARS OR RUPTURES THE OUTER ANKLE LIGAMENTS :

BASKET WEAVE TAPING
ANKLE SUPPORT

for providing ankle support is to tape the ankle using the basket weave.

Knee Pain

Pain in the knee from overuse can be treated by ceasing the activity causing the discomfort and controlling pain and inflammation with RICE. In the event of a traumatic injury resulting in an unstable, swollen, and painful knee, splint and evacuate. If the injury is stable and the patient can bear weight, use RICE to control pain and inflammation. If the patient can walk without undue pain, wrap the knee with foamlite for support.

TENDINITIS

A tendon is the fibrous cord by which a muscle is attached to a bone. Its construction is similar to that of kernmantle rope, with an outer sheath of tissue enclosing a core of fibers. Some tendons, such as those to the finger, are long. The activating muscles are in the forearm, but the tendons stretch from the forearm across the wrist to each finger. These tendons are surrounded by a lubricating sheath to assist their movement.

Tendinitis is inflammation of a tendon. When the sheath and the tendon become inflamed, the sheath becomes rough, movement is restricted and painful, and the patient feels a grating of the tendon inside the sheath. Fibers can be torn or, more commonly, irritation from overuse or infection can inflame the sheath, causing pain when the tendon moves. There may be little pain when the tendon is at rest.

Tendons are poorly supplied with blood, so they heal slowly. Tendons are well supplied with nerves, however, which means that an injury will be painful. Tendons can be injured by sudden overloading but are more frequently injured through overuse. Factors contributing to tendinitis include poor technique, poor equipment, unhealed prior injury, and cool and unstretched muscles.

Assessment

Tendinitis, in contrast to ankle sprains, is a progressive overuse injury, not a traumatic injury. Common sites for tendinitis are the Achilles tendon and the tendons of the forearm. The Achilles, the largest tendon in the body, may fatigue and become inflamed during or following lengthy hikes, especially with significant elevation gain. Boots that break down and place pressure on the tendon can provide enough irritation in one day to initiate inflammation.

Forearm tendinitis is common among canoeists and kayakers. Poor technique and inadequate strength and flexibility contribute to the injury. Similar tendinitis comes with repetitive use of ski poles, ice axes, and ice climbing tools.

Signs and Symptoms of Tendinitis
Redness
Warmth
Crepitus
Localized pain

Tendinitis may also occur on the front of the foot, usually caused by tightly laced boots or stiff mountaineering boots. The tendons extending the toes become irritated and inflamed. Tendinitis causes swelling, redness, warmth, pain to the touch (or pinch), painful movement, and sounds of friction or grinding (crepitus).

Treatment
Treat tendinitis with RICE: rest, ice, compression, and elevation. It may be necessary to cease the aggravating activity until the inflammation subsides. Prevent or ease tendinitis of anterior muscles by varying boot lacing. Lace boots more loosely when hiking and more tightly when climbing.

Achilles Tendinitis. To relieve stretch on the Achilles tendon, provide a heel lift. To relieve direct pressure from the boot, place a 6-inch by 1-inch strip of foamlite padding on either side of the Achilles tendon. The placement should take the pressure off without touching the Achilles.

Treatment of Achilles Tendinitis
RICE
Heel lifts
Pads on ankle to protect the tendon

Forearm Tendinitis. Forearm tendinitis is primarily associated with the repetitive motion of paddling. Pay close attention to proper paddling technique. Keep a relaxed, open grip on the paddle. On the forward stroke, keep the wrist in line with the forearm during the pull and push, and avoid crossing the upper arm over the midline of the body.

Other paddling techniques that may help prevent forearm tendinitis include keeping the thumb on the same side of the paddle as the fingers and switching a feathered paddle for an unfeathered paddle. The

Treatment of Forearm Tendinitis
RICE
Taping wrist to limit range of motion

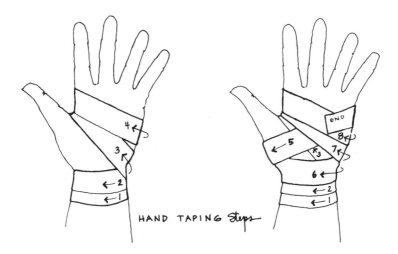

HAND TAPING Steps

feathered paddle requires a wrist movement that can sometimes aggravate tendinitis.

Tendinitis of the forearm is treated with RICE. Also, the wrist can be taped to limit movement that aggravates the condition.

MUSCLE STRAINS
Muscles can be stretched and torn from overuse or overexertion. Initial treatment is RICE, followed by heat, massage, and gentle stretching. Radiating muscle pain, strong pain at rest, pain secondary to an illness, or pain from a severe trauma mechanism is a reason to evacuate the patient for evaluation by a physician.

FINAL THOUGHTS
Errors in technique and inadequate muscular conditioning or warm-up produce injury. Overuse of muscles and joints (when there is no single traumatic event as the cause of injury) generates many of the sprains and strains on NOLS courses.

Jerky movements, excessive force, or an unnecessarily tight grip on the paddle while kayaking contribute to forearm tendinitis. Performing the athletic movements required for difficult rock climbs without warming up or paying attention to balance and form can cause injury. Even the seemingly simple actions of lifting a backpack or boat, stepping over logs, and wading in cold mountain streams can be dangerous.

Steep terrain and wet conditions contribute to injuries. Slippery conditions make it harder to balance and can cause falls. Falls that occur in camp and while hiking are the cause of many athletic injuries. Surprisingly, injuries are just as likely to occur when backcountry travelers are wearing packs as when they are not. Possibly this is because people are more attentive to technique when hiking or skiing with a pack.

You are more likely to be injured when you are tired, cold, dehydrated, rushed, or ill. You're not thinking as clearly, and your muscles are less flexible and responsive. Injuries happen more frequently in late morning and late afternoon, when dehydration and fatigue reduce awareness and increase clumsiness. Shifting from a three-meal-a-day schedule to breakfast and dinner plus three or four light snacks during the day helps keep food supply constant.

Haste, often the result of unrealistic timetables, is frequently implicated in accidents. Try to negotiate the more difficult terrain in the morning, when you are fresh. Take rest breaks before difficult sections of a hike or paddle. Stop at the base of the pass, the near side of the river, or the beginning of the boulder field. Drink, eat, and stretch tight muscles. Check equipment: for loose gaiters that may trip you, and for poorly balanced backpacks.

The sustained activity of life in the wilderness and the need for sudden bursts of power when paddling, skiing, or climbing necessitate physical conditioning prior to a wilderness expedition. A regimen of endurance, flexibility, and muscle strength training will help prevent injuries and promote safety and enjoyment of the wilderness activity.

SUMMARY:
ATHLETIC INJURIES

Signs and Symptoms of Sprains
Swelling and discoloration
Pain
Instability at joint
Loss of range of motion
Inability to bear weight

General Treatment of Athletic Injuries (RICE)
Rest: allows time for healing
Ice: 20 to 40 minutes, every 2 to 4 hours for 24 to 48 hours
Compression: Ace bandage to reduce swelling
Elevation: reduces swelling
Acetaminophen or ibuprofen for pain and inflammation

Treatment of Ankle Sprains
RICE
Taping for support

Signs and Symptoms of Tendinitis
Redness
Warmth
Crepitus
Localized pain

Treatment of Achilles Tendinitis
RICE
Heel lifts
Pads on ankle to protect the tendon

Treatment of Forearm Tendinitis
RICE
Taping wrist to limit range of motion

CHAPTER 16

GENDER-SPECIFIC MEDICAL CONCERNS

INTRODUCTION

Women have participated in NOLS expeditions since the beginning of the school and take their place among the school's most senior field instructors. Both women and men have enjoyed the challenges and rewards of climbing the highest peaks, paddling the wildest rivers and coastlines, and exploring the world's most remote wilderness.

During these trips, both genders have experienced injury and illness to reproductive and urinary systems. Men can experience epididymitis and testicular torsion. Women, with their more complex reproductive anatomy and physiology, may experience a variety of medical conditions ranging from changes in their menstrual cycles to vaginal infections, pelvic inflammatory disease, and ectopic pregnancy. The wilderness leader should be knowledgeable about the prevention, assessment, and field treatment of these conditions, and know when to evacuate.

MALE-SPECIFIC MEDICAL CONCERNS

Male Anatomy

The male external genitalia consist of the penis and scrotum. The penis provides a route for urine to be expelled from the bladder and sperm expelled from the testes. The scrotum is a pouchlike structure located to the side of and beneath the penis. The testes lie within the scrotum and are the site of sperm and testosterone production.

Sperm travels out of the testes via the epididymis, a comma-shaped organ that lies behind the testes. The epididymis is composed of approximately 20 feet of ducts. From

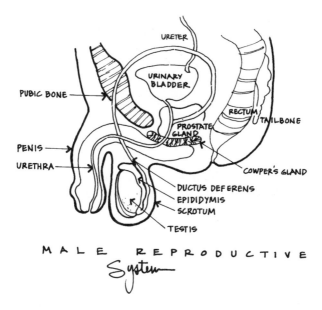

MALE   REPRODUCTIVE System

the epididymis, sperm travel through the ductus deferens, a tube approximately 18 inches long that loops into the pelvic cavity. Sperm can be stored there for many months.

Epididymitis
Epididymitis is an inflammation of the epididymis and can be caused by gonorrhea, syphilis, tuberculosis, mumps, prostatitis (inflammation of the prostate), or urethritis (inflammation of the urethra).

Signs and Symptoms. The patient suffers from pain in the scrotum, possibly accompanied by fever. The scrotum may be red and swollen. Epididymitis tends to come on slowly, unlike torsion of the testis, which comes on rapidly.

Treatment. The treatment is bed rest, support or elevation of the testes, and antibiotics. Diagnosis can be tricky. The pain and swelling often prevent any activity; thus, evacuation is recommended. Acetaminophen, aspirin, or ibuprofen may decrease the fever and pain.

Torsion of the Testis

Torsion of the testis is a twisting of the testis within the scrotum. The ductus deferens and its accompanying blood vessels become twisted, decreasing the blood supply to the testis. If the blood supply is totally cut off, the testis dies. After 24 hours without blood supply, the prognosis for saving the testis is poor.

Signs and Symptoms. The scrotum is red, swollen, and painful, and the testis may appear slightly elevated on the affected side.

Treatment. Cool compresses and pain medication provide some relief. The patient must be evacuated for treatment. A jockstrap made from a triangular bandage will elevate the scrotum and may increase blood flow to the testis.

FEMALE-SPECIFIC MEDICAL CONCERNS
Female Anatomy

The female reproductive organs lie within the pelvic cavity. The vagina, or birth canal, is approximately 3 to 4 inches long. The vagina is continuously moistened by secretions that keep it clean and slightly acidic.

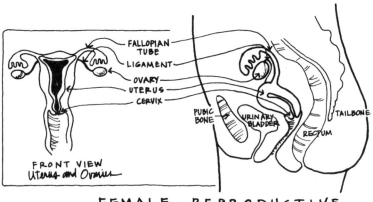

FEMALE REPRODUCTIVE System

At the top of the vagina is the cervix, a circle of tissue pierced by a small hole that opens into the uterus. The cervix thins and opens during labor to allow the baby to be expelled.

The uterus is about the size of a fist and is located between the bladder and rectum. Pregnancy begins when a fertilized egg implants in the tissue of the uterus. The uterus is an elastic organ that expands with the growing fetus.

On either side of the uterus are the ovaries, which lie approximately 4 or 5 inches below the waist. The ovaries produce eggs and the female sex hormones estrogen and progesterone. Each month an egg (ovum) is released from one of the ovaries and travels down the fallopian tube to the uterus. The fallopian tubes are approximately 4 inches long and wrap around the ovaries but are not directly connected to them. When the egg is released from the ovary, the fimbriae (finger-like structures at the end of the fallopian tube) make sweeping motions across the ovary, sucking the egg into the fallopian tube.

The Menstrual Cycle
As early as 12 years of age, a woman starts her menstrual cycle, the monthly release of ova. Hormones regulate the cycle, which continues until menopause, or cessation of the menstrual cycle, at approximately 52 years of age.

The endometrial tissue that lines the uterus undergoes hormone-regulated changes each month during menstruation. The average menstrual cycle is 28 days long, with day 1 being the first day of the menstrual period. From days 1 through 5, the endometrial tissue sloughs off from the uterus and is expelled through the vagina. The usual discharge is 4 to 6 tablespoons of blood, tissue, and mucus. During days 6 through 16, the endometrial tissue grows in preparation for implantation of an ovum, becoming thick and full of small blood vessels.

Ovulation usually occurs around day 14; the egg takes approximately 6½ days to reach the uterus. On days 16 through 26, the endometrium secretes substances to nourish the embryo. If conception has not occurred, the hormones progesterone and estrogen decrease, causing the uterine blood supply to decrease and the lining of the uterus to be shed.

Mittelschmerz. Some women experience cramping in the lower abdomen on the right or left side or in the back when the ovary releases an egg. The pain is sometimes accompanied by bloody vaginal discharge. This is called mittelschmerz (*mittel* = middle; *schmerz* = pain).

Signs and Symptoms. The pain may be severe enough to be confused with appendicitis or ectopic pregnancy, but a careful assessment should allow the first-aider to distinguish between the two. Ask the patient where she is in her menstrual cycle. Has she ever had this pain before? Typically, a woman will have had similar cramping in the past. Any light bleeding or pain should cease within 36 hours. The abdomen is soft. Women taking birth control pills do not ovulate, so they cannot have mittelschmerz.

Dysmenorrhea. Dysmenorrhea is painful menstruation (cramps). Possible causes include prostaglandins, which cause the uterus to cramp, endometriosis (inflammation of the endometrium), pelvic inflammatory disease, or anatomic anomalies such as a displaced uterus.

Treatment. Antiprostaglandins such as ibuprofen reduce the pain as well as the volume of flow and the length of the period. Relaxation exercises such as yoga and massaging the lower back or abdomen help reduce pain. Applying heat to the abdomen or lower back may also help reduce pain.

A change in diet may help. Decreasing the amount of salt, caffeine, and alcohol in the diet while increasing the B vitamins—especially B_6 (found in brewer's yeast, peanuts, rice, sunflower seeds, and whole grains)—or drinking raspberry leaf tea (1 tablespoon for each cup) can offer some relief during the acute phase of the cramps. Because exercise causes endorphins (natural opiates) to be released by the brain, many women find that cramps diminish when they participate in strenuous exercise.

Secondary Amenorrhea. Secondary amenorrhea is the absence of menstrual periods after a woman has had at least one period. Causes of secondary amenorrhea include pregnancy, ovarian tumors, intense athletic training, excessive weight loss or gain, altitude, and stress (physical and emotional). Changes in the menstrual cycle are common in the backcountry and may be normal adjustments to unfamiliar stresses.

Signs and Symptoms of a Vaginal Infection

Curdy white discharge or grayish milky discharge
Malodorous discharge
Redness, soreness, itching of vaginal area
Burning sensation upon urination

Vaginal Infection

The normal vagina contains a plethora of microorganisms. Most of the time these organisms are in balance. The normal pH of the vagina is slightly acidic. Vaginal infections can occur when the normal balance of bacteria and the pH are upset. Antibiotics, birth control pills, diabetes, and physical or emotional stress may cause an infection to develop. Cuts and abrasions from intercourse or tampons, not cleaning the perineal area, or not changing underwear can also lead to an infection.

The two most common causes of vaginal infections are candidiasis (yeast) and bacterial vaginitis.

Symptoms. Symptoms of a yeast infection generally include curdy white discharge and itching. The vulva may be swollen and excoriated from scratching. The patient may complain of a burning sensation upon urination. Symptoms of bacterial vaginitis include a grayish, milky, thin discharge. The discharge may be malodorous, and the patient may complain of vaginal pain but not itching. For the purposes of field diagnosis, the symptoms are similar, and initial treatment is the same.

Treatment. Vaginal infections can be treated with over-the-counter medications such as Gyne-Lotrimin and Monistat 1 (vaginal suppository), or with prescription Diflucan (oral pill). If these treatments don't provide relief within 48 hours, the patient should be

Treatment of Vaginal Infection

Gyne-Lotrimin, Monistat 1, or Diflucan
Evacuate if symptoms persist for 48 hours

**Prevention
of Vaginal Infection**

Stay hydrated

Decrease sugar, caffeine, and
alcohol intake

Wear loose-fitting underwear or
running shorts for ventilation

Wash perineal area daily

Change tampons regularly

Decrease stress

---

evacuated. An untreated infection can develop into pelvic inflammatory disease.

Prevention. The best prevention for vaginal infections is education. To help prevent vaginal infections, wipe front to back, clean the perineal area (between the vagina and anus) daily with plain water or a mild soap, and promote ventilation by wearing loose-fitting nylon or cotton underwear or running shorts. Women with a history of vaginal infection should decrease their caffeine, alcohol, and sugar intake.

Urinary Tract Infection

Urinary tract infections are common in women due to the closer proximity of the urethra to the vagina and rectum and the shorter length of the urethra. The infection can affect the urethra, ureters, or bladder.

Signs and Symptoms. Urinary tract infections cause increased frequency or urgency of urination and/or a burning sensation during urination. The patient complains of pain above the pubic bone and a heavy urine odor with the morning urination. Blood and/or pus may be present in the urine. Urinary tract infections can progress to kidney infections. If the kidneys are infected, the patient complains of rebound tenderness in the small of the back and may have a fever.

**Signs and Symptoms
of Urinary tract Infection**

Increase in frequency of urination

Urgency and a burning sensation
during urination

Treatment. The best treatment (also good for prevention) is to drink lots of water every day and empty the bladder often. A good way to tell if you are drinking enough is by the color of your urine.

Unless you are taking vitamins, the urine should be clear, not yellow colored. Persons taking vitamins tend to have yellow-colored urine.

The perineal area should be cleaned with water or mild soap daily. Taking 500 milligrams of vitamin C daily and/or eating whole grains, nuts, and fruits may make the urine more acidic, which prevents bacteria from growing. Curry, cayenne pepper, chili powder, black pepper, caffeine, and alcohol should be avoided because these irritate the bladder. Vitamin B_6 and magnesium or calcium supplements help relieve spasms of the urethra.

> **Treatment of Urinary Tract Infection**
>
> Increase fluid intake
> Give vitamin B_6, calcium, and magnesium supplements to relieve bladder spasms
> Change diet
> Avoid sugar and foods that irritate the bladder
> Antibiotics

On extended expeditions, consider carrying antibiotics such as Bactrim or Macrobid to treat urinary tract infections. If an infection persists for more than 48 hours despite the use of antibiotics, the patient should be evacuated. Evacuate patients with symptoms of a kidney infection for further evaluation.

Pelvic Inflammatory Disease (PID)

PID is an inflammation of the fallopian tubes, ovaries, and/or uterus. It is caused primarily by gonorrhea, chlamydia, and *E-coli* or streptococcal infection. PID is more commonly seen in young, sexually active women. IUDs may increase the risk of PID. Birth control pills and barrier methods of contraception decrease the risk of PID.

Signs and Symptoms. Because PID affects the reproductive organs bilaterally, the patient complains of diffuse pain in the middle of the lower abdomen. The pain begins gradually and develops into a constant ache. She may also complain of pain in the right upper quadrant due to a bacterial irritation of the tissues surrounding the liver. Lower back or leg pain may also occur.

> ### Signs and Symptoms of PID
>
> Diffuse pain in the middle of the lower abdomen; possibly in the upper right quadrant, lower back, or leg
>
> Swollen abdomen and lymph nodes
>
> Watery, malodorous discharge
>
> Acnelike rash on back, chest, neck, face
>
> Fever, nausea, vomiting
>
> Vaginal bleeding
>
> Signs and symptoms of shock

The patient may have a fever, nausea, vomiting, anorexia, and swollen abdomen and lymph nodes. There may be a watery, foul-smelling discharge from the vagina. She may complain of irregular bleeding, an increase in menstrual cramps, and pain or bleeding during or after intercourse. Some women develop acnelike rashes on the back, chest, neck, or face. Usually these signs and symptoms start within a week following the menstrual period.

Treatment. The treatment for PID is evacuation. Untreated PID can lead to peritonitis (inflammation of the lining of the abdomen), scarring of the fallopian tubes, and sterility. PID is treated with antibiotics.

Ectopic Pregnancy

Ectopic pregnancies occur outside the uterus, most commonly in the fallopian tubes. Sperm usually fertilizes the egg in the upper two-thirds of the tube. Due to congenital anomalies or scarring caused by infection, the egg starts growing in the tube.

> ### Signs and Symptoms of Ectopic Pregnancy
>
> Rapid onset of unilateral lower abdominal pain
>
> Vaginal bleeding
>
> Signs and symptoms of peritonitis and shock

Signs and Symptoms. The patient experiences abdominal pain and bleeding. The onset of pain is rapid and on one side of the abdomen. The fallopian tube ruptures in 4 to 6 weeks when the embryo becomes too large for the tube. The pain then becomes agonizing, and signs and symptoms of peritonitis develop. The patient may hemorrhage and die from shock, although slow bleeding is more common.

   Treatment. Treat for shock and evacuate immediately.

Toxic Shock Syndrome (TSS)

TSS is an infection caused by the bacterium *Staphylococcus aureus.* Tampons have been suggested as one of the possible causes of TSS.

   Superabsorbent tampons that dry the vagina or cause backflow of blood into the peritoneal cavity may predispose a woman to TSS. Since 1980, TSS in menstruating women has declined, but the number of cases in men and nonmenstruating women has increased. This may be due to better reporting. The highest incidence is still in 10- to 30-year-old menstruating white females.

   Signs and Symptoms. The onset of TSS is abrupt. The patient has a high fever, chills, muscle aches, sunburnlike rash, abdominal pain, sore throat, vomiting, diarrhea, fatigue, dizziness, and/or fainting. In some people, the onset may be gradual and the characteristic rash does not appear for 1 or 2 days. Mucous membranes are beet red. The rash appears on the palms or all over the body. It typically peels, just like a sunburn, 1 to 2 weeks later.

   Treatment. Remove any tampon in use, treat for shock, and evacuate.

   Prevention. To decrease the risk of TSS, women should change their tampons frequently and use pads at night and on light flow days. Pads and tampons should be carried out of the mountains or burned in a very hot fire. The staphylococcus organism is frequently found on the hands; good handwashing prior to inserting a tampon is a must. If the patient has had TSS previously, there is a 30 percent chance of recurrence.

ASSESSMENT TIPS

If you're leading or participating in wilderness trips, you will encounter people with gender-related medical concerns. A young male experiencing scrotal pain for the first time may be embarrassed and hesitant to inform the leader, especially if the leader is of the opposite gender. Likewise, a woman with a urinary tract infection may not know the signs and symptoms or that you have the means to treat it in the field, and she may be reluctant to inform a male trip leader.

If a gender-specific medical problem arises, provide a private place to talk. Maintain eye contact; be straightforward, respectful, and nonjudgmental. Use proper medical terminology or terms that you both understand—no jokes or slang. A member of the patient's sex should be present before and during any physical exam.

For female patients, gather information about the patient's menstrual and reproductive history. When was her last menstrual period? How long is her cycle? What is normal for her? Does she use contraception? Has she had sexual intercourse in the past? Has she experienced this problem in the past, and if so, how was it treated?

TIPS FOR WOMEN'S HYGIENE IN THE WILDERNESS

Wear-loose fitting shorts that allow for adequate ventilation. Cotton underwear breathes better than nylon and may reduce the risk of infection. With washings, two or three pairs of underwear will be sufficient for a 30-day expedition.

During menstruation, change tampons and pads frequently, and remember to wash your hands prior to inserting a tampon.

If you are prone to vaginal infections, consider decreasing the amount of sugar in your diet. Drink tea instead of cocoa, water instead of fruit drinks, and eat nuts instead of candy bars.

Wipe from the front to the back to limit introduction of bacteria into the vaginal area. Wash the vaginal area with water or mild soap daily.

A "pee rag" has become popular among women backpackers to conserve toilet paper. Usually a bandanna, it's tied onto the outside of the pack while hiking. If it gets rained on, fine.

If not, women rinse them out every few days. It makes a big difference in staying clean.

Used tampons and pads are bagged and carried out of the backcountry. Having a designated system makes proper disposal of tampons, pads, and toilet paper easier. A small stuff sack with a couple of extra plastic bags allows personal organization and privacy. Some women prefer widemouthed water bottles or plastic containers for this. Include a small wad of toilet paper in this kit. An aspirin or two placed in the bag or container will help dissipate odor.

How many extra tampons or pads to bring? Bring a little extra for heavier flow, in case your cycle changes and you experience your period twice in a monthlong trip, or if pads or tampons get wet. If each woman in a group brings a bit extra, almost any emergency can be covered by the group without adding a lot of bulk.

An added note: There is no evidence that bears are attracted to women during their period.

SUMMARY:
GENDER-SPECIFIC MEDICAL CONCERNS

TESTICULAR TORSION AND EPIDIDYMITIS
Signs and Symptoms
Pain in the scrotum
Red, swollen scrotum

Treatment
Give pain medication
Provide supportive care during evacuation

VAGINAL INFECTION
Signs and Symptoms
Excessive, malodorous discharge
Redness, soreness, itching of vaginal area
Burning sensation upon urination

Treatment
Douche with vinegar or povidone-iodine
Evacuate if symptoms persist for 48 hours

Prevention
Stay hydrated
Decrease sugar intake
Wear loose-fitting underwear or running shorts for ventilation
Wash perineal area daily
Change tampons regularly
Decrease stress

URINARY TRACT INFECTION
Signs and Symptoms
Increase in frequency of urination
Urgency and a burning sensation during urination

Treatment
Increase fluid intake
Change diet; avoid sugar and bladder-irritating foods
Give vitamin B_6, calcium, and magnesium supplements to
    relieve bladder spasms

• *CONTINUED* •

SUMMARY:
GENDER-SPECIFIC MEDICAL CONCERNS
(continued)

SIGNS AND SYMPTOMS OF PID
Diffuse pain in the middle of lower abdomen; possibly in the
    upper right quadrant, lower back, or leg
Swollen abdomen and lymph nodes
Watery, malodorous discharge
Acnelike rash on back, chest, neck, face
Fever, nausea, vomiting
Vaginal bleeding
Signs and symptoms of shock

SIGNS AND SYMPTOMS OF ECTOPIC PREGNANCY
Rapid onset of unilateral pain
Vaginal bleeding
Signs and symptoms of shock

Treatment of Ectopic Pregnancy and PID
Provide supportive care during evacuation

TOXIC SHOCK SYNDROME (TSS)
Signs and Symptoms
Abdominal pain
High fever, chills, muscle aches
Sunburnlike rash
Vomiting, diarrhea
Fatigue, dizziness, fainting
Beet-red mucous membranes
Signs and symptoms of shock

Treatment
Remove tampon
Treat for shock and evacuate

CHAPTER 17

HYGIENE AND WATER DISINFECTION

INTRODUCTION

Twenty-five years ago, we assumed that clear, flowing mountain streams were pristine and clean. We now know that this is not necessarily true. In fact, we should assume that all natural water sources are populated with disease-causing bacteria, viruses, and protozoa.

People from developed countries live with the luxury of clean tap water and effective sanitation systems. In other parts of the world, water contamination continues to be a major health problem, and diarrheal illness is a leading cause of death. Wilderness expeditions leave behind modern sanitation and reliably disinfected tap water. Healthy people raised with Western medical standards may not understand the debilitating power of diarrheal illness. For them, maintaining strict hygiene practices in what appears to be pristine wilderness can be difficult. On NOLS courses, diarrhea and closely related flu symptoms are the most common illnesses. Contaminated water and poor personal hygiene are the two main causes of these preventable illnesses.

WATERBORNE ILLNESS

Worldwide, waterborne microorganisms account for many cases of infectious diarrhea. The microorganisms causing diarrhea include bacteria, protozoa, viruses, and parasitic worms. Diseases that are spread through contaminated water include typhoid, cholera, campylobacteriosis, giardiasis, and hepatitis A.

Although a frequently diagnosed diarrhea-causing microorganism in the United States is the protozoan *Giardia,* other bacteria and viruses are being identified with increasing frequency. In Wyoming's Teton Range, the bacterium *Campylobacter* causes more diarrhea than *Giardia*. Recently the protozoan *Cryptosporidium* has received attention as a cause of municipal waterborne outbreaks, but it is unclear how much risk it poses in wilderness water sources.

Giardia

Giardia is a microscopic protozoan. It has a two-stage life as cyst and trophozoite. The cyst, excreted in mammalian feces, is hardy and can survive 2 to 3 months in near-freezing water. If swallowed, the warmer internal environment causes the cyst to change into its active stage, the trophozoite. The trophozoite attaches itself to the wall of the small intestine and is the cause of the diarrhea associated with *Giardia* infections.

Humans are a major carrier of *Giardia*. It has also been identified in both domestic and wild animals, specifically in beavers, cats, dogs, sheep, cattle, deer, and elk, and in reptiles, amphibians, and fish. It is not clear whether contamination from *Giardia* is increasing or whether it is being diagnosed more frequently as a cause of diarrhea.

Giardia is difficult to diagnose due to the wide variation in symptoms. For a reliable diagnosis, three stool samples should be examined. Most infections are without symptoms,

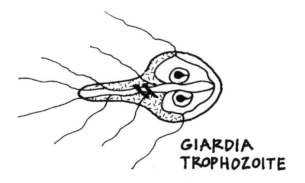

GIARDIA
TROPHOZOITE

and the unwitting patient becomes a carrier of *Giardia,* inadvertently spreading the illness.

The incubation period—from ingestion to the onset of infection—is 1 to 3 weeks. Symptoms include recurrent and persistent malodorous stools and flatus, abdominal cramping, bloating, "sulfur burps," and indigestion. Serious infections produce explosive watery diarrhea with cramps, foul flatus, fever, and malaise.

Although drug therapy is available, prevention through hygienic habits and water disinfection makes much more sense. *Giardia* is sensitive to heat, is easily filtered, and can be killed with chemical disinfection.

Cryptosporidium

Also a microscopic protozoan, *Cryptosporidium* is spread by drinking contaminated water, by eating contaminated raw or undercooked food, or by hand-to-mouth transfer of cysts picked up from fecal matter.

Some people may not have symptoms. Most have an illness lasting 1 to 2 weeks that starts 2 to 10 days after infection and includes watery diarrhea, headache, abdominal cramps, nausea, vomiting, and low-grade fever. In persons with suppressed immune systems, such as AIDS or cancer chemotherapy patients, the infection may continue and become life-threatening.

Cryptosporidium cysts are sensitive to heat and can be filtered but are not reliably killed by iodine or chlorine. People with suppressed immune systems should consider boiling water or using a filtration system to protect them from infection.

WATER DISINFECTION

Purifying water eliminates offensive odors, tastes, and colors but does not kill microorganisms. Sterilization kills all life-forms. Disinfection removes or destroys disease-causing microorganisms. What we commonly refer to as water purification is really disinfection. There are three main methods of water disinfection: heat, chemical treatment, and filtration.

Methods OF WATER DISINFECTION:

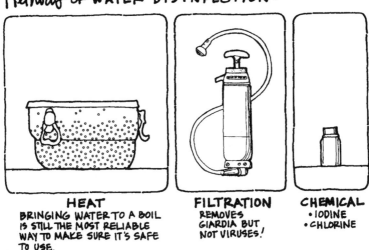

HEAT
BRINGING WATER TO A BOIL
IS STILL THE MOST RELIABLE
WAY TO MAKE SURE IT'S SAFE
TO USE.

FILTRATION
REMOVES
GIARDIA BUT
NOT VIRUSES!

CHEMICAL
• IODINE
• CHLORINE

Heat

Incorrect information persists on how long to boil water before it is disinfected. The common diarrhea-causing microorganisms are sensitive to heat and are killed immediately by boiling water. The protozoa *Giardia* and *Amoeba,* (which causes amebiasis) die after 2 to 3 minutes at 140°F (60°C). Viruses, diarrhea-producing bacteria, and *Cryptosporidium* cysts die within minutes at 150°F (65°C). By the time water boils, it is safe to drink.

Boiling point decreases with increasing elevation, but this does not affect disinfection. The boiling point at 19,000 feet is 178°F (81°C), sufficient for disinfecting water.

The advantage of boiling is its effectiveness. However, it is inconvenient on the trail, takes time, and consumes fuel.

Chemical Treatment

Chemical treatment is the addition of halogens—either iodine or chlorine—to water. Halogens kill viruses, diarrhea-causing bacteria, and most protozoa cysts, with the exception of

Cryptosporidium. Bacteria are highly sensitive to halogens. Viruses and *Giardia* require greater doses or longer contact time. The concentration of halogen and its contact time in water determine the degree of disinfection. In general, a halogen dose can be halved if the contact time for the recommended dosage is doubled.

Factors that can affect halogen treatment include pH, chemical binding with material in the water, and water temperature. Halogens are affected by pH, but the pH levels of most natural water sources don't significantly influence the activity of iodine or chlorine.

When iodine or chlorine binds with organic and inorganic particles in water, less halogen is available to destroy the diarrhea-causing microorganisms. Reduce debris before adding halogen; filter murky water with a manufactured filter or use an improvised strainer such as a coffee filter or a clean bandanna. You can also let water sit until the floating particles settle to the bottom or use alum to clear the water. To compensate for halogen bonding with organic matter in cloudy water, increase the amount of halogen (see the recommendations in the table at the end of this section).

Halogens are also affected by temperature. Cold water slows the chemical reaction. Compensate for a slower reaction in cold water by increasing contact time. On the safe side, wait 30 minutes in warm water (86°F [30°C]), 60 minutes in cold water (59°F [15°C]).

Iodine. Iodine, the most commonly used halogen, is available as a tablet—tetraglycine hydroperiodide—sold commercially as Globuline or Potable Aqua. Iodine crystals, 2 percent iodine (tincture), and 10 percent povidone-iodine solutions are also effective.

Iodine is affected less by pH than is chlorine and has less effect on the taste of the water. Wilderness medicine experts believe that at the levels used to disinfect water, iodine is safe for most people on prolonged wilderness trips. Iodine is not recommended for persons with thyroid disease, a known iodine allergy, or during pregnancy.

HALOGEN DOSES PER LITER OF WATER

	Clear Water	Cloudy Water
Iodine		
Tetraglycine hydroperiodide		
(Potable Aqua)	1 tablet	2 tablets
2% iodine solution (tincture)	0.2 ml (5 drops)	0.5 ml (10 drops)
10% povidone-iodine	0.4 ml (8 drops)	0.8 ml (16 drops)
Iodine crystals, aqueous		
(Polar Pure)	15 ml	30 ml
Chlorine		
4% to 6% chlorine bleach	0.1 ml (2 drops)	0.2 ml (4 drops)
Aquaclear		1 tablet
AquaCure		1 tablet

1 drop = 0.05 ml
Source: Backer, H. "Field Water Disinfection." Syllabus, World Congress on Wilderness Medicine/Wilderness Medical Society Meeting, Whistler, British Columbia, August 1999.

The aftertaste of iodine and chlorine in water can be improved by adding flavoring. However, the sugar in drink mixes also binds the halogen. Add flavoring after disinfection. An ascorbic acid (vitamin C) tablet, added after disinfection, improves flavor by chemically reducing the iodine and chlorine to iodide and chloride, which have no taste.

Chlorine. Chlorine has been used as a disinfectant for over 200 years. Chlorine bleach (4 to 6 percent) is commonly used to disinfect water. Halazone, AquaCure, and Aquaclear are all chlorine tablets that can disinfect water.

Filtration
Filters remove particulate matter and large organisms. Several types of filters are available with pore sizes small enough

to filter *Giardia* and *Cryptosporidium* cysts. Viruses are too small to be reliably eliminated by field water filtration. Some filters kill viruses by passing water through an iodine-impregnated resin.

Filters are more convenient on the trail than boiling water, and filtration may reduce the amount of iodine or chlorine necessary to chemically purify water. Filters can be expensive, costing from $40 to $250. Also, they may clog or develop undetectable leaking cracks. Because of their inability to remove viruses, some experts do not recommend filters as the sole water disinfection system for foreign travel, where additional treatment with halogens or boiling may be necessary.

FOODBORNE ILLNESS

Microbes such as bacteria, viruses, and fungi live everywhere. They're in the soil, in water, on our hands, in our noses and mouths. Many are harmless to us. Some cause illness either through the toxins they produce or as a side effect of colonizing the digestive tract. We can expose ourselves to these organisms by drinking contaminated water or through poor hygiene practices in the kitchen. Bacteria such as *Staphylococcus, Shigella,* and *Salmonella* are common sources of foodborne illness. If we give these creatures a place to live, such as a dirty cookpot, they can quickly multiply or produce enough toxin to make us sick.

With the luxury of modern sanitation, we don't give much thought to hygiene. We're protected by flush toilets, effective waste disposal and sewer systems, reliably disinfected tap water, readily available hot water, and proximity to advanced medical care. Proper human waste disposal, hand and utensil washing, food preparation, and water disinfection need to become habits in the wilderness. A river guide with poor kitchen hygiene was the source of food poisoning for many of the people on his trip. We suspect that most episodes of flulike and diarrheal illness on NOLS courses are caused by poor kitchen and personal sanitation.

Hygiene in the Wilderness Kitchen

These are practices NOLS has found helpful in reducing the incidence of foodborne illness on our expeditions.

Cook Food Thoroughly. Food that is dry or has a high salt or sugar content inhibits bacterial growth. Moist food that is low in salt and sugar is a good medium for growth, especially if it is warm. Protect yourself by cooking food completely; boil your pasta, beans, and rice; cook your meat until it is no longer red (ideally 170°F or 77°C).

Eat Cooked Food Promptly. Heat destroys most bacteria. Cold keeps bacteria from multiplying. Keep cooked food hot or cold, but don't keep it long. The optimal temperature zone for bacterial growth is between 45° and 140°F (7° and 60°C). In only a short period—within an hour in ideal warm and moist conditions—bacteria can multiply to become the source of diarrhea.

Avoid Leftovers. Storing cooked food without refrigeration invites disaster. Plan meals so that all food is consumed when served. Besides promoting bacterial growth, keeping leftovers creates a waste disposal problem and attracts animals such as bears.

Cold weather trips have an advantage of natural refrigeration. If leftovers are quickly cooled in air temperatures that stay below 38°F (3.5°C) and the meal is reheated completely, your risk of foodborne illness is less, but not zero. It's always safer to avoid leftovers. Heat-resistant toxins and microbes may colonize stored cooked food. If you do eat leftover food, make sure that the food is hot throughout the dish, not just on the surface. A crispy exterior does not mean that the interior has been well heated.

Clean Pots, Pans, and Utensils. Dirty pots, pans, and utensils are ideal surfaces for microbial life. Cleaning grease and food in the wilderness can be a challenge, especially if water is scarce. Plan ahead to minimize leftovers. Use sand or snow to scour pots, then rinse with hot water. Hard work to remove food residue can minimize the water needed for a final rinse.

Dish soap helps clean, but it must be rinsed well to avoid diarrhea and must be disposed of properly to leave no trace. Use a strainer to filter out large food particles, which are packed out. Scatter the remaining waste water widely away from camp and water sources.

Boil cooking utensils daily. Immersing clean utensils in your water pot as you boil the morning hot drink water will help continue the sanitizing process. Bacteria, viruses, and protozoa will be killed as the water is disinfected by the heat.

Large groups frequently use group cooking setups with chlorine rinses as an important step in keeping utensils clean. The three-bucket method begins with a hot soapy water scrub, then a warm water rinse, and finally a 1-minute immersion in a chlorine rinse bucket. Prepare this 100 to 150 ppm solution by adding 1 tablespoon of 4 to 6 percent chlorine bleach per gallon of water or one-quarter tablet of Effersan, a commercially available chlorine tablet. Air dry the cooking gear.

Keep Kitchen Surfaces and Utensils Clean. Keep the food preparation surface and your utensils clean. In between the grocery store and dinner, your food can be contaminated many different ways. Dirty hands can reach inside, touch, and contaminate the food. Avoid this by pouring food from a bag or box. The spoon used to taste the soup may also be the spoon used to stir or serve. The cook may sneeze or cough and spread germs over dinner. The spatula may be placed on the ground or in a grubby food sack, then used to stir your pasta. An organized and clean kitchen reduces the chance of this cross-contamination.

Rinse Fresh Fruit and Vegetables. The surfaces of fruit and vegetables can be contaminated. A rule of thumb is peel it, boil it, cook it, or avoid it.

Protect Food from Insects and Animals. Insects and animals are vectors of disease. Keeping flies and rodents from your food both protects you from disease and keeps the animal from becoming habituated to humans as a source of food.

Don't Share. Sharing your resources, energy, wisdom, and companionship is good expedition behavior. Sharing your microbes with your tent mate is not. Keep your handkerchief, water bottle, cup, bowl, spoon, and lip balm to yourself. Instead of reaching into a plastic bag for a handful of raisins and contaminating the entire bag, pour the raisins into your hand. Serve food with the serving utensil, not your personal spoon. An ill person or one with open cuts on his or her hands should not prepare food. It takes only one person to be the source of a groupwide illness.

Wash Your Hands. Lastly, but most importantly, wash your hands! Keep nails trimmed and clean. Microbes live on the skin. Hands are an excellent and common tool for transporting these creatures from person to person. Regular handwashing does not sterilize your hands, but it does reduce the chance of infection. Ideally, you should use hot water, lots of soap, and a thorough rinse after using the latrine. Practically speaking, in the wilderness, you'll wash with cold water. At a minimum, you should do this before preparing, serving, or eating food. Large expeditions or base camps often set up a handwashing station near a latrine or outhouse or in a central camp location. Waterless soaps are an option when water is not available or as an extra precaution after hands have been rinsed of grease and dirt.

Using natural toilet paper—leaves, sticks, rocks, or snow—reduces the paper you use and when done properly, this method is as sanitary as regular toilet paper. But you need to be proficient to avoid contaminating your hands with fecal material. And of course, always wash your hands afterward.

FINAL THOUGHTS

Medical authorities think that contaminated water accounts for most infectious diarrhea in the U.S. wilderness. At NOLS, we think that person-to-person exchange from poor kitchen and personal hygiene practices is also a leading cause. Outside the wilderness, the most common route for infection is believed to be from person to person via hand-to-mouth contact or from contaminated utensils. Infection rates increase with close contact and poor hygiene. Habits of cleanliness and hygiene are essential to health and safety in the wilderness.

Your choice among boiling, filtering, or chemically disinfecting your water will depend on how contaminated the water might be, personal preference, fuel availability, group size, cost, and reliability. None of the water disinfection methods is foolproof. Each has its limitations, and each must be done correctly. They reduce but do not eliminate the risk of getting sick from drinking water. Their benefit is a reduced chance of becoming ill from bad water.

CHAPTER 18

RESPIRATORY AND CARDIAC EMERGENCIES, SEIZURES, DIABETES, AND UNCONSCIOUS STATES

INTRODUCTION

The topics typically discussed in first aid texts as medical emergencies include heart disease, heart attacks, and congestive heart failure; respiratory illnesses such as asthma, emphysema, and pneumonia; as well as diabetes, epilepsy, and drug and alcohol abuse. These are common emergency runs for ambulance crews but less common on wilderness expeditions, although they do occur. Supported by modern medicine, people with heart and lung disease, seizures, and diabetes are able to enjoy the wilderness.

RESPIRATORY AND CARDIAC EMERGENCIES

A history of asthma, heart disease, or even a heart attack does not, by itself, prevent someone from paddling a river, climbing a peak, or hiking the Wind River Range. The wilderness first-aider will see these medical conditions and should be knowledgeable in their assessment and treatment.

Hyperventilation Syndrome

Hyperventilation syndrome is an increased respiratory rate caused by an overwhelming emotional stimulus. The patient becomes apprehensive, nervous, or tense. For example, a person may normally have a fear of heights, and the thought of rock climbing triggers a hyperventilation episode, or a climber may fall and suffer a minor injury but begin to hyperventi-

CARPOPEDAL SPASMS
HYPERVENTILATION SYNDROME :

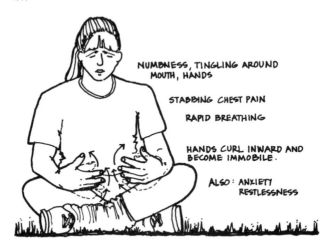

NUMBNESS, TINGLING AROUND
MOUTH, HANDS

STABBING CHEST PAIN

RAPID BREATHING

HANDS CURL INWARD AND
BECOME IMMOBILE.

ALSO: ANXIETY
RESTLESSNESS

late out of fear and anxiety. The hyperventilation can quickly become the major condition affecting the patient.

Signs and Symptoms. Signs and symptoms of hyperventilation include a high level of anxiety, a sense of suffocation without apparent physiological basis, rapid and deep respiration, rapid pulse, dizziness and/or faintness, sweating, and dry mouth.

As the syndrome progresses, the patient may complain of numbness or tingling of the hands or around the mouth. Thereafter, painful spasms of the hands and forearms—carpopedal spasms—may occur. The hands curl inward and become immobile. The patient may complain of stabbing chest pain. Rapid respiration increases the loss of carbon dioxide, which causes the blood to become alkaline. The alkaline blood causes the carpopedal spasms.

Treatment. To treat hyperventilation syndrome, attempt to resolve the emotional concern, and treat the respiratory problem. Your objectives are to increase the carbon dioxide level in the blood and slow the patient's respiratory rate. Breathing into a stuff sack, or any bag, will make the patient reinhale exhaled carbon dioxide. Reassure the patient by explaining what you are doing and why.

Pulmonary Embolism

A pulmonary embolism occurs when a clot (usually from a leg vein) breaks loose and lodges in the blood vessels of the lung. Decreased mobility—lying in a tent waiting out a storm, for example—may predispose a person to a blood clot. Fat embolism occurs when fat globules are released from broken bones (usually the femur), enter the circulatory system via a lacerated vessel, and lodge in the vessels of the lung. The clot or globules impair normal blood flow, resulting in tissue damage and shock.

Signs and Symptoms. The patient complains of a sudden onset of shortness of breath and pain with inspiration. Respiratory distress may develop, including anxiety and restlessness; shortness of breath; rapid breathing and pulse; signs of shock, including pale, cool, and clammy skin and cyanosis of the skin, lips, and fingernail beds; and labored breathing using accessory muscles of the neck, shoulder, and abdomen to achieve maximum effort.

Treatment. First-aiders can't dissolve the embolism in the field. You can identify the respiratory distress, administer oxygen if it is available, and evacuate the patient promptly.

Pneumonia

Pneumonia is a lung infection that can be caused by bacteria, viruses, fungi, and protozoa. The inflammation of the alveolar spaces causes swelling and fluid accumulation. Difficulty breathing can result. People weakened by an illness, chronic disease, fatigue, or exposure are especially at risk. Pneumonia can be a serious infection and is a leading cause of death.

Signs and Symptoms. Signs and symptoms of pneumonia are shortness of breath, fever and chills, a productive cough with green-yellow or brown sputum, and pain on inspiration or coughing. The patient may have a recent history of upper respiratory infection and the lung sounds, if you can listen with a stethoscope, may be noisy.

Pneumonia	
Signs and Symptoms	**Treatment of Pneumonia**
History of upper respiratory infection	Encourage patients to cough
Sweating, fever, chills	Hydrate
Productive cough	Administer oxygen
Pain on inspiration or coughing	Evacuate
Shortness of breath	
Wet lung sounds	
General illness	

Treatment. Patients with pneumonia should be evacuated. Encourage the patient to cough and breathe deeply to keep the lungs clear. Hydration is important, and oxygen, if available, will be helpful. The patient may be more comfortable sitting up.

Asthma

Asthma is an allergic response characterized by narrowing of the airways, increase in mucus production, and bronchial edema. Asthma's exact cause is unknown. We do know that allergy and environmental factors such as molds, cold air, chemical fumes, cigarette smoke, exercise, and infections play a role.

Asthma is usually a reversible condition. The airway narrowing can improve spontaneously or in response to medication. A prolonged, severe asthma attack that is not relieved by treatment is an emergency requiring rapid transport. There are other chronic lung diseases, such as emphysema and bronchitis, in which the breathing impairment is persistent because of destruction of lung tissue and chronic inflammation.

Signs and Symptoms. Signs and symptoms of mild to moderate asthma are wheezing, chest tightness, and shortness of breath. The heart and breathing rates are increased. When

---

Asthma

**Signs and Symptoms
of Mild to Moderate Asthma**
Chest tightness
Wheezing and coughing
Shortness of breath
Increased heart and breathing
rates
Increased mucous production
Fatigue

**Signs and Symptoms
of Severe Asthma**
Use of accessory muscles to
breathe
Decreasing breath sounds
progressing to absence of
sounds

Speaking in one- to two-word
clusters
Sleepiness
Cyanosis

Treatment of Asthma
Bronchodilators
Warm, humidified oxygen
Hydration and rest
Avoidance of antihistamines

---

asthma becomes severe, the patient may be hunched over, bracing the upper body and working to breathe. The patient may be able to speak only in one- or two-word clusters. Lung sounds may be diminished or absent. If the patient becomes sleepy or too fatigued to breathe, the situation is dire.

Treatment. Usually the patient treats the asthma by self-administering medication, commonly a bronchodilator, with an inhaler. You may need to help the patient relax and use the inhaler properly; shake it first, hold it in the mouth, exhale, and then depress the device and inhale the mist deeply, holding the breath for 5 to 10 seconds before exhaling. Warm, humidified air can help relax airways and clear mucus. Avoid antihistamines, which can dry the airways. Severe asthma episodes require medications usually not available in the wilderness, and such patients should be evacuated promptly.

Chest Pain and Heart Disease

Heart disease is a leading cause of death in the United States. Atherosclerosis, a common form of heart disease, slowly builds deposits on arterial walls that narrow the artery and impede blood flow. The narrowed artery can spasm, constrict, or lodge a clot, depriving tissue of blood. If this happens in the brain, the result may be a stroke. If it happens in the heart, it causes chest pain, also known as angina pectoris, or a myocardial infarction, a heart attack. Angina is pain from diminished blood flow. A myocardial infarction is heart muscle damage from blocked blood flow. Sudden death from a heart that beats erratically, or not at all, can be a result of this disease.

Signs and Symptoms. Cardiac chest pain is often described as crushing, tight, pressing, viselike, and constricting. It is below the breastbone and can radiate into the left arm and jaw. Shortness of breath, anxiety, pale sweaty skin, nausea, and dizziness are also common complaints. The pulse rhythm may be irregular. If the pain is brought on by physi-

---

Cardiac Chest Pain

Signs and Symptoms	Treatment of Suspected Cardiac Chest Pain
Persistent chest pain: crushing, tight, pressing, viselike, constricting	Reduce anxiety and activity
Shortness of breath	Oxygen
Anxiety and denial	Aspirin
Pain radiating to arm or jaw	Evacuation
Nausea and vomiting	
Lightheadedness	
Pale, cool, sweaty skin	
Rapid, slow, weak, or irregular heartbeat	
History of angina, heart attack, or risk factors	

cal or emotional stress and is relieved by rest, it may be angina. If it is unprovoked and persists, it may be a myocardial infarction.

Treatment. Figuring out whether nontraumatic chest pain is a heart condition can be difficult under the best of circumstances. Inflammation of the stomach or esophagus, chest muscle strains, rib injury, lung problems, bronchitis, and coughing can all cause chest pain. To complicate the situation, cardiac pain does not always fit the classic pattern and description. A patient with chest pain symptoms that cannot be attributed to a chest injury, lung problem, stomach upset, or muscle strain should be given one 325-milligram aspirin every 12 hours and evacuated. Reduce the demands on the heart by calming the patient and making him or her rest. If available, administer oxygen.

SEIZURES
A seizure is a disruption of the brain's normal activity by a massive paroxysmal electrical discharge from brain cells. The seizure begins at a focus of brain cells, then spreads through the brain and to the rest of the body through peripheral nerves. This electrical disturbance may cause violent muscle contractions throughout the body or result in localized motor movement and possible loss of consciousness.

The causes of seizures include high fever, head injury, low blood sugar, stroke, poisoning, and epilepsy. Low blood sugar is a cause of seizures in diabetics. Brain cells are sensitive to low oxygen and sugar levels, and if these fall below acceptable levels, a seizure may be triggered. The most common cause of seizures is epilepsy, a disease that manifests as recurring seizures.

The onset of epilepsy is not well understood. Often it begins in childhood or adolescence, but it can also be a consequence of a brain injury. Most persons with epilepsy control their seizures with medication. Interruption of the medication or inadequate dosage is frequently the cause of seizures.

At one time, seizures were attributed to mental illness. The source of these misperceptions may have been the dramatic visual impact of a writhing, moaning person having a seizure. Educating bystanders and group members about epilepsy and seizures can help alleviate such misunderstandings.

Assessment. The typical generalized seizure begins with a short period, usually less than a minute, of muscle rigidity, followed by several minutes of muscle contractions. The patient may feel the seizure approaching and warn bystanders or cry out at the onset of the episode. The patient suddenly falls to the floor, twitching and jerking.

As muscular activity subsides, the patient remains unconscious but relaxed. He or she may drool, appear cyanotic, and become incontinent. Pulse and respiratory rate may be rapid. The patient may initially be unconscious or difficult to arouse, but in time—usually within 10 to 15 minutes—the patient becomes awake and oriented.

When the seizure has subsided, open the airway, assess for injuries, and take vital signs. Place the patient on his or her side during the recovery phase to help maintain an open airway.

Treatment. Treatment for a seizure is supportive and protective care. You cannot stop the seizure, but you can protect the patient from injury. The violent muscle contractions of a seizure may cause injury to the patient and to well-meaning bystanders who attempt to restrain the patient. Move objects that the patient may hit. Pad or cradle the head if it is bouncing on the ground.

A patient in seizure will not swallow the tongue; however; the airway may become obstructed by saliva or secretions, and the patient may bite his or her tongue. Most seizures happen without warning, with no opportunity to protect the airway. If you can, insert a padded object between the teeth to protect the tongue. This may be difficult because of the tightness of the jaw. Once the seizure starts, do not force the mouth open.

An accurate description of the seizure tells the physician much about the onset and extent of the problem. In most cases, a seizure runs its course in a few minutes. Repeated seizures, especially repeated seizures in which the patient does not regain consciousness in between, and seizures associated with another medical problem such as diabetes or head injury are serious medical conditions.

An epileptic patient with an isolated seizure requires evaluation by a physician but does not require a rapid evacuation. These occasional seizures are often due to changes in the patient's need for medication or failure to take the medication as prescribed. After recovering from the seizure, the patient should be well fed and hydrated and assessed for any injury that may have occurred during the seizure.

DIABETES

Diabetes is a disease of sugar metabolism, affecting, by conservative estimates, 10 million Americans. It is a complex disease characterized by a broad array of physiological disturbances. In the long term, diabetic complications include high blood pressure and heart and blood vessel disease; it can also affect vision, kidneys, and healing of wounds. In the short term, the disturbance in sugar metabolism can manifest itself as too much or too little sugar in the blood.

Diabetes is thought to be caused by genetic defects, infection, autoimmune processes, or direct injury to the pancreas. The pancreas produces the hormones, most notably insulin, that help regulate sugar balance. Insulin facilitates the movement of sugar from the blood into the cells. An excess of insulin promotes the movement of sugar into the cells, lowers the blood sugar level, and deprives the brain cells of a crucial nutrient. This disorder is known as hypoglycemia (low blood sugar) or insulin shock.

In contrast, a deficit of insulin results in cells that are starved for sugar and an excess of sugar in the blood, disturbing fluid and electrolyte balance. This disorder is known as hyperglycemia (high blood sugar) or diabetic coma.

A healthy pancreas constantly adjusts the insulin level to the blood sugar level. The pancreas of a person with diabetes produces defective insulin or no insulin. To compensate for this, a diabetic takes medication to stimulate endogenous insulin or takes artificial insulin.

Hypoglycemia (Insulin Shock)

Hypoglycemia results from the treatment of diabetes, not the diabetes itself. If a diabetic takes too much insulin or fails to eat sufficient sugar to match the insulin level, the blood sugar level will be insufficient to maintain normal brain function.

Hypoglycemia can occur if the diabetic skips a meal but takes the usual insulin dose, takes more than the normal insulin dose, exercises strenuously and fails to eat, or vomits a meal after taking insulin.

Assessment. Hypoglycemia has a rapid onset. The most prominent symptoms are alterations in level of consciousness due to a lack of sugar to the brain. The patient may be irritable, nervous, weak, and uncoordinated; may appear intoxicated; or, in more serious cases, may become unconscious or have seizures. The pulse is rapid; the skin pale, cool, and clammy.

Treatment. Brain cells need sugar and can suffer permanent damage from low blood sugar levels. The treatment of hypoglycemia is to administer sugar. If the patient is conscious, a sugar drink or candy bar can help increase the blood sugar level. If the patient is unconscious, establish an airway, then place a small paste of sugar underneath the patient's tongue. Sugar is absorbed through the oral mucosa. Improvement is usually quick after the administration of sugar.

Hyperglycemia (Diabetic Coma)

Diabetics who are untreated, who have defective or insufficient insulin, or who become ill may develop a high level of sugar in the blood. Consequences of this may be dehydration and electrolyte disturbances as the kidneys try to eliminate the excess sugar, and acid-base disturbances as cells starved for sugar turn to alternative energy sources.

Assessment. In contrast to the rapid onset of hypoglycemia, hyperglycemia develops slowly. The first symptoms are loss of appetite, nausea, vomiting, thirst, and increased volume of urine output. The patient's breath may have a fruity odor from the metabolism of fats as an energy source. The patient may also have abdominal cramps or pain and signs of dehydration, including flushed, dry skin and intense thirst. Loss of consciousness is a late and very serious symptom.

Treatment. This patient has a complex physical disturbance and needs the care of a physician. Treatment is supportive: airway maintenance, vital signs, and treatment for
shock. Dehydration is a serious complication of hyperglycemia.
If the patient is alert, give oral fluids.

Hypoglycemia or Hyperglycemia?
Hypoglycemia usually has a rapid onset; the patient is pale,
cool, and clammy and has obvious disturbances in behavior
or level of consciousness. Hyperglycemia has a gradual onset.
Often, the patient is in an unexplained coma, with flushed,
dry skin. A fruity breath odor may be present. A patient with
hypoglycemia will respond to sugar; a hyperglycemic patient
will not, but the extra sugar will cause no harm.

Two questions to ask any diabetic patient are: Have you
eaten today? and Have you taken your insulin today? If the
patient has taken insulin but has not eaten, you should suspect hypoglycemia. The patient will have too much insulin, not
enough sugar, and a blood sugar level that is too low to sustain
normal brain function. If the patient has eaten but has not
taken insulin, hyperglycemia should be suspected. This person
has more sugar in the blood than can be transported to the
cells.

Most persons with diabetes are very knowledgeable about
their reactions and intuitively know if they are getting into
trouble. Many diabetics measure their blood sugar levels daily;
almost all diabetics test their urine for sugar daily.

It is important for persons with diabetes to eat at regular
intervals. If there is a possibility that a diabetic's insulin
could be lost or destroyed—for example, by a boat flipping on
the river—make sure that someone else in the group is carrying an extra supply. With control and care, diabetics can participate without problems in any activity.

UNCONSCIOUS STATES
A conscious patient can react to the environment and protect
himself or herself from sources of pain and injury. An unconscious patient is in danger. He or she is mute and defenseless,
unable to rely on even the gag reflex to protect the airway.

Many conditions cause unconsciousness: head injury, stroke, epilepsy, diabetes, alcohol intoxication, drug overdose, and fever.

A patient who is unconscious for unexplained reasons poses a difficult diagnostic problem. The medical history may provide clues; use AEIOUTIPS as a guideline for a complete assessment of common conditions that may cause unconsciousness.

Often, all you can do is support the patient and transport him or her to a physician for further evaluation. Care for an unconscious patient includes airway maintenance and cervical spine precautions unless trauma can be ruled out entirely. If you are unsure as to why a patient is unconscious, place some sugar under the tongue. This will help a hypoglycemic patient and won't hurt a patient who is unconscious for any other reason.

FINAL THOUGHTS

Persons with diabetes and epilepsy routinely participate in wilderness expeditions. The adverse consequences of these diseases—seizures and sugar imbalances—can be prevented through care and education. Paul Petzoldt, NOLS founder, worked with physicians in the early 1970s to support diabetic students attending our remote monthlong wilderness expeditions. At that time, this was a bold initiative.

The physical and emotional stress, new physical and social environment, heavy packs, altitude, sun, and battle against dehydration in the wilderness may be new challenges, but they are ones that can be managed.

Discuss the illness beforehand with the diabetic or epileptic person undertaking the expedition. Make sure that you both understand the disease, the timing and side effects of medications, the appropriate emergency treatment, and any other health needs. It is important to inform the rest of the group—especially the person's tent mates—about the condition and how to deal with it in an emergency.

SUMMARY:
RESPIRATORY AND CARDIAC EMERGENCIES, SEIZURES, DIABETES, AND UNCONSCIOUS STATES

SIGNS AND SYMPTOMS OF PNEUMONIA
History of upper respiratory infection
Sweating, fever, chills
Productive cough
Pain on inspiration or coughing
Shortness of breath
Wet lung sounds
General illness

Treatment of Pneumonia
Encourage patient to cough
Hydrate
Administer oxygen
Evacuate

ASTHMA
Signs and Symptoms of Mild to Moderate Asthma
Chest tightness
Wheezing and coughing
Shortness of breath
Increased heart and breathing rates
Increased mucous production
Fatigue

Signs and Symptoms of Severe Asthma
Use of accessory muscles to breathe
Decreasing breath sounds progressing to absence of sounds
Speaking in one- to two-word clusters
Sleepiness
Cyanosis

• *CONTINUED* •

SUMMARY:
RESPIRATORY AND CARDIAC EMERGENCIES, SEIZURES, DIABETES, AND UNCONSCIOUS STATES *(continued)*

Treatment of Asthma
Bronchodilators
Warm, humidified oxygen
Hydration and rest
Avoidance of antihistamines

SIGNS AND SYMPTOMS OF CARDIAC CHEST PAIN
Persistent chest pain: crushing, tight, pressing, viselike,
    constricting
Shortness of breath
Anxiety and denial
Pain radiating to arm or jaw
Nausea and vomiting
Lightheadedness
Pale, cool, sweaty skin
Rapid, slow, weak, or irregular heartbeat
History of angina, heart attack, or risk factors

Treatment of Suspected Cardiac Chest Pain
Reduction of anxiety and activity
Oxygen
Aspirin
Evacuation

SEIZURES are caused by epilepsy, high fever, head injury, low blood sugar, stroke, and poisoning.

Treatment
Supportive and protective
Move objects the patient may hit; protect the head
When the seizure subsides:
    Open the airway
    Assess for injuries

• *CONTINUED* •

SUMMARY:
RESPIRATORY AND CARDIAC EMERGENCIES, SEIZURES, DIABETES, AND UNCONSCIOUS STATES *(continued)*

HYPOGLYCEMIA (low blood sugar) associated with diabetes is caused by missing a meal but taking insulin, taking an insulin overdose, exercising strenuously without eating, or eating and then vomiting a meal. The low blood sugar affects the brain.

HYPERGLYCEMIA (high blood sugar) associated with diabetes is caused by lack of treatment, insufficient or ineffective insulin, or the onset of illness. The high blood sugar causes dehydration and electrolyte disturbances.

Signs and Symptoms

Hypoglycemia	*Hyperglycemia*
Rapid onset	Gradual onset
Pale, cool, clammy skin	Flushed, dry skin
Disturbances in LOC	Unconscious or coma
Possible seizures	Fruity breath odor
Irritability, nervousness	Abdominal cramps, nausea
Weakness	
Lack of coordination	

Treament

Hypoglycemia	*Hyperglycemia*
ABCs	ABCs
Sugar under tongue	Fluids if conscious
	Treat for shock
	If unsure, give sugar

CHAPTER 19

HYDRATION

INTRODUCTION

NOLS instructors constantly harp on hydration, urging their students to drink, drink, drink. They issue liter water bottles and large insulated mugs. They carry water in the desert and melt snow with a passion in winter environments. To the inexperienced outdoorsperson, this appears to be an unnecessarily exaggerated process when in fact it is based on need and experience. More than one NOLS student has been evacuated from the mountains with dehydration as the primary diagnosis. Most of our evacuations for illness are in part complicated by underlying dehydration. Addressing daily episodes of dehydration on the trail is a fact of life for wilderness travelers.

Dehydration is a contributing factor to hypothermia, heat exhaustion, heatstroke, altitude illness, and frostbite. Dehydration worsens fatigue, decreases the ability to exercise efficiently, and reduces mental alertness. Often the fatigue, irritability, poor thinking, body aches, and headache at the end of a day are the first signs of dehydration. Even by itself, dehydration can be a life-threatening medical problem.

PHYSIOLOGY OF WATER BALANCE

Humans are bags of water. We hear through a medium of water, the brain is cushioned by fluid, and the joints are lubricated by fluid. Blood is 90 percent water, and every biochemical reaction takes place in a medium of water.

Outside the wilderness, we give little thought to hydration. Air conditioning, heating, and lack of exercise enable us to avoid fluid stress most of the time. In the outdoors, we exercise daily at high levels. Exercise causes water loss through sweating, breathing, and metabolism. In the outdoors, we adjust directly to the environment, whether hot or cold. In the desert, we sweat to lose heat. In the cold, we lose water to moisten the cold air we breathe.

In the outdoors, hydration is not as simple as turning on the tap. In the desert, we carry water, ration water, and spend a lot of time searching for water. Our activity patterns may be altered to reduce heat loss. We rest during the hours of the hot, midday sun; we work in the cool dawn and evening. In the winter, we must melt the water we drink—a time-consuming process. There is always the difficulty of disinfecting potentially contaminated water sources.

It's harder to get water in the outdoors, we lose more of it responding to the environment, and we need more of it to maintain health. Many people in the outdoors are dehydrated—more so at high altitudes and in winter.

Assessment

Dehydration is often overlooked as a cause of illness or injury in the outdoors. The signs and symptoms mimic altitude illness, hypothermia, fatigue, heat exhaustion, and shock. Severe dehydration can cause significant mental deterioration, causing us to think that the patient might have a serious brain problem. The key to assessment is suspicion. Dehydration is so common that it must be considered in every patient treated in the outdoors.

General symptoms of a negative water balance are fatigue, heat oppression, thirst, irritability, dizziness, dark concentrated urine, and headache. A seriously dehydrated patient appears to have signs of shock: rapid pulse; pale, sweaty skin; weakness and nausea. Mental deterioration presents itself as loss of balance and changes in mental awareness. Tenting—in which the skin forms a tent shape when pinched—is a sign of serious dehydration. Normal skin is sufficiently hydrated to collapse; the tent stays in place in severe dehydration.

With a 2 percent fluid deficit, we experience mental deterioration, decreased group cooperation, vague discomfort, lack of energy and appetite, flushed skin, impatience, sleepiness, nausea, an increased pulse rate, and a 25 percent loss in efficiency.

A 12 percent fluid deficit results in an inability to swallow, a swollen tongue, sunken eyes, and decreased neurological function. Dizziness, tingling in the limbs, absence of salivation, and slurred speech may also be present. A fluid deficit greater than 15 percent is potentially lethal. Signs include delirium, vision disturbances, and shriveled skin.

Treatment

A mildly dehydrated patient—and all wilderness travelers—should drink clear water to replace fluids. It is the best fluid for hydration. Cold water is absorbed faster than warm water.

Electrolyte replacement drinks are acceptable but should be diluted to reduce their sugar content. Sugar increases the time it takes for fluid to be absorbed from the stomach. Coffee, tea, and alcohol should be avoided. Coffee and tea contain caffeine, a diuretic that stimulates the kidneys to excrete fluid. Alcohol also increases urine production and fluid loss.

A severely dehydrated patient may have electrolyte imbalances as well as a fluid deficit. Such a patient cannot be rehydrated in the field and must be evacuated to a hospital for intravenous fluid therapy.

Hyponatremia
It is possible to drink too much, or, more accurately, to drink enough water to replace water loss but at the same time lose salt in sweat without replacing it. The scenario is a hot weather hiker drinking lots of water but not consuming enough electrolytes, such as sodium. Your hydration status is good, yet your blood sodium is low and you have a case of hyponatremia, also known as water intoxication.

Signs and symptoms vary among individuals and depend on the patient's hydration and sodium levels. The patient seems to have heat exhaustion: headache, weakness, fatigue, lightheadedness, muscle cramps, nausea with or without vomiting, sweaty skin, normal core temperature, and normal or slightly elevated pulse and breathing rates.

The assessment of hyponatremia versus heat exhaustion or dehydration depends on an accurate history. Be suspicious if the patient has eaten relatively little salty food recently, combined with a high fluid intake—several liters in the last few hours.

Patients with an altered mental status should be evacuated. Patients with mild to moderate symptoms and a normal mental status can be treated in the field. Have the patient rest in the shade with moderate fluid intake and a gradual intake of salty foods while the kidneys reestablish a sodium balance. Oral electrolyte replacement drinks are low in sodium and high in water and may not help as much as you anticipate. If you're not sure whether it's heat exhaustion or hyponatremia, give the patient electrolyte replacement drinks and salty food and monitor closely for improvement.

FINAL THOUGHTS

There are several cornerstones to good health in the outdoors: staying warm and dry, eating well, resting, camping comfortably, washing hands, climbing slowly at altitude, and, most important, staying hydrated.

How much water should you drink to stay healthy? Probably more than you usually drink. Three to 4 liters a day is the minimum, with another liter added for cold or high-altitude conditions. Thirst is a poor indicator, alerting you to a fluid deficit after you are already dehydrated and indicating that you are satiated before you are fully rehydrated. Urine color and volume are helpful indicators; darker, more concentrated urine is an indicator of dehydration. Again, this is a later sign, appearing after the body has decided to conserve fluid.

Fluids must be forced to maintain hydration in the wilderness. Measure your daily fluid intake. Tank up to buffer your hydration margin. Drink early, anticipating fluid loss during the day. Drink often, preventing the subtle mental and physical deterioration of dehydration. Drink more than you think you need. Oral electrolyte replacement drinks help but may not add sufficient salt to your diet. Eat salty foods while exercising, especially in the heat. Drink before you become dehydrated. DRINK, DRINK, DRINK (and drink some more)!

SUMMARY: HYDRATION

SIGNS AND SYMPTOMS OF DEHYDRATION
Early Signs
Fatigue
Heat oppression
Thirst
Irritability
Dizziness
Dark, concentrated urine
Headache
Loss of group cooperation

Later Signs
Rapid pulse
Pale, sweaty skin
Weakness and nausea
Loss of balance
Changes in mental awareness
Tenting

Serious Signs
Inability to swallow, swollen tongue
Sunken eyes
Loss of consciousness
Delirium

TREATMENT FOR DEHYDRATION
DRINK, DRINK, DRINK
In severe cases, evacuation may be necessary

CHAPTER 20

DENTAL EMERGENCIES

INTRODUCTION

Enduring a dental problem in the wilderness, several days from a dentist, can be an uncomfortable experience. There are simple field treatments for broken teeth or fillings, toothaches, and gum irritations that can make life more comfortable during the evacuation. Although we do not experience many dental problems on NOLS courses, they account for 10 percent of problems seen among trekkers visiting the Himalayan Rescue Association clinics.

BROKEN TEETH OR FILLINGS

Lost fillings cause discomfort if hot or cold liquids or spicy foods touch the exposed tooth tissue. Exposure of the nerve, pulp, artery, or vein by a lost filling or a broken tooth causes pain. Various temporary filling materials are available for stopgap treatment of broken teeth or fillings. Cavit is a premixed compound available from your dentist. A nonprescription temporary filling available in many dental emergency kits is a combination of zinc oxide powder (not the ointment) and oil of cloves. The oil of cloves is a topical anesthetic. NOLS staff have even had success using sugarless gum and ski wax to cover loose fillings and broken teeth.

Rinse the broken tooth or filling thoroughly before covering with a temporary filling. Roll the temporary material into a small ball and gently press it into the hole in the tooth, sealing the exposed tissue.

A broken or avulsed tooth should be gently rinsed off and slowly and gently placed back in the hole. Irrigate the tooth, but don't scrub it—you may remove tissue that can help the tooth survive. If you can't replace it, save the tooth for replacement. Wrap the tooth in gauze and have the patient carry it between the cheek and gum or in a cool place. For a good prognosis, a tooth must be replaced within 30 minutes and receive the care of a dentist within a week.

If the socket is bleeding, it can be packed to place pressure on the tissue. A slightly moist tea bag makes an acceptable packing material. In fact, the tannic acid in nonherbal tea promotes clotting.

TOOTHACHES

Exposure of the pulp from a dental cavity can cause pain. In the backcountry, treatment is limited to pain medications, antibiotics, and avoiding excessively hot, cold, or spicy foods. A temporary filling material may protect the pulp and any exposed nerve. Oil of cloves may be helpful for pain relief.

ORAL IRRITATIONS AND INFECTIONS

General mouth irritation is usually due to poor hygiene and can be treated with vigorous brushing and rinses with salt water (a teaspoon of salt per glass of water) three to four times a day.

Swelling around teeth or gums is an indicator of an infection. On remote expeditions, treatment with antibiotics and drainage of the infection may be considered. Evacuation to a dentist is the best treatment and the only choice on less remote trips in which there is no access to a physician or antibiotics.

FINAL THOUGHTS

Preparation for a wilderness expedition includes a visit to your dentist to identify and treat any potential problems. In the field, brush and floss regularly. Anyone who has experienced the woes of a toothache, loose filling, or dental infection in the wilderness knows that the need for dental hygiene does not cease when we venture into the woods.

CHAPTER 21

STRESS
AND THE RESCUER

INTRODUCTION

First aid training has traditionally concentrated on treatment and transport: the nuts and bolts of assessment, splinting, and airway maintenance. The human elements of emergency medical care are equally important. We are beginning to recognize the impact of emergency stress on the rescuer as well as the victim.

Although there is limited data on wilderness rescuers, there is a growing body of literature on the effects of stress on emergency workers. Caring for the ill or injured, having responsibility for the lives and safety of others, is considered a significant stressor. Research is showing that high attrition rates, burnout, and stress-related illness are common in emergency personnel.

EFFECTS OF STRESS

A perceived threat or challenge or a change in the environment can cause stress—a state of physical or psychological arousal. Beneficial stress affects all living creatures and can be a positive factor in change, creativity, growth, and productivity. Healthy exercise that increases your physical capability is a good stress. Continuous hard exercise without rest or adequate nutrition can become a destructive force with negative effects on your health, your family, and your life.

You may be stressed by noises, confined spaces, extremes in weather, and other aspects of the environment. In the social environment, conflicts within a group, and conflicts with the boss or family members are all stressors. You're also stressed by inactivity and boredom.

Stress produces intricate biochemical changes in the body. The brain becomes more active; chemicals secreted by the endocrine system cause muscles to tighten, pupils to dilate, and heart rate, breathing rate, and blood pressure to increase. Protein, glucose, and antibody levels in the blood rise.

These physiological changes prepare you to meet a challenge by making you more alert and ready for physical activity. In the short term, they can be helpful. In the long term, or if the short-term stress is significant, the effects of stress can adversely affect your physical and psychological health by wearing you down and making you susceptible to a variety of physical and psychological problems. The surgeon general estimates that 80 percent of nontraumatic causes of death are actually stress-related disease such as coronary artery disease, high blood pressure, ulcers, and cancer.

STRESS ON THE JOB

Research on stress suggests that dedicated people who work hard and have high standards and deep personal interest in their work are vulnerable to stress.

The job demands of emergency personnel create an environment in which turnover and stress-related illness are common. Emergency situations may subject them to noise such as wind, rushing water, screams, and sirens; to the confusion of the emergency scene; to having responsibility for the health and safety of patients and fellow rescuers in prolonged weather extremes; to difficult bystanders who may never be satisfied with the rescuer's performance; to equipment failures and inadequate equipment, which add to the difficulty of the situation; and to long hours of hard physical work. Lengthy rescues, rescues in which the patient dies, multiple-casualty incidents, and incidents in which emergency workers or friends are injured are particularly stressful.

Personality profiles of emergency personnel developed by Jeffrey Mitchell, Ph.D., show a tendency toward personality traits that make these individuals susceptible to stress. Emergency personnel are often perfectionists and risk-takers who are highly motivated and goal- and action-oriented; they feel the need to be in control. They are dedicated, take great personal satisfaction and interest in their work, and feel a great need to be needed. These are traits that also apply to many outdoor leaders and educators.

Certainly, emergency stress affects an outdoor leader or anyone thrown into the role of rescuer. Experience may help a person cope with these stresses, but it does not make him or her immune.

The leader of a notably difficult expedition experiences significant extra stress when weather, group dynamics, faulty equipment, or complex logistics combine to create a high-pressure situation. In addition to caring for the ill or injured under these difficult conditions, the leader continues to be responsible for the safety and welfare of the group.

ASSESSMENT: RECOGNIZING STRESS REACTIONS
Stress in the short term may produce fatigue, nausea, anxiety, fear, irritability, lightheadedness, headache, memory lapses, sleep disturbances, changes in appetite, loss of attention span, and indecision. These are normal reactions by normal people to abnormal events. A person experiencing an acute stress reaction may wander aimlessly on the scene, sit or stare blankly, or engage in erratic or irrational behavior.

Long-term effects of stress include difficulty concentrating, intrusive images (recurring dreams or sensations of the traumatic event), sleep disturbance, fatigue, and diseases such as ulcers, diabetes, and coronary artery disease. Emotional signs include depression, feelings of grief and anger, and a sense of isolation. Emergency workers suffering from cumulative stress may respond by avoiding emergency situations, taking excessive sick leave, or being easily aroused or startled. It is beyond the scope of this book to discuss intervention for cumulative stress reactions.

TREATMENT: MANAGING STRESS IN THE FIELD
Preparation for stress management includes anticipation of the difficulties of rescue and a realistic appraisal of your

ability to cope. Among emergency personnel on the scene of a serious rescue, 97 percent will experience at least some symptoms of stress. Rescuers need to remember that a successful outcome is not guaranteed, particularly if the patient is far from modern medical care. Rescue work, especially wilderness rescue, can be long and tedious. Recognition and thanks for the efforts of the rescuer are often sparse, whereas criticism from bystanders is common.

Short-term stress symptoms can be managed by attending to the physical needs for rest, food, and hydration; by briefing the group on the sights, sounds, and emotions they may experience during a long evacuation; and by debriefing the group after the incident.

Acute stress reactions on the scene can be managed by removing an overstressed person from the site. Give simple, clear directions to the stressed person, and assign productive tasks that can help shift his or her focus away from the immediate incident. Such tasks might include providing food and drink, building a litter, and setting up tents.

If an emergency care giver is overly distressed, detached from reality, or disruptive, someone may need to stay with him or her to lend a sympathetic ear. You can help such persons cope by talking with them and offering assurances that their feelings are valid, real, and perfectly appropriate. Provide emotional support with honesty and direct, factual answers to their questions.

The Field Debriefing

In a critical stress incident—one involving the death of the patient, a coworker, or a fellow expedition member; a particularly long, frustrating, or arduous rescue; or an incident involving children, multiple casualties, or gruesome injuries— consider involving people trained as stress debriefers. Teams of critical incident stress debriefers (CISD) are set up throughout North America to help rescuers who have experienced critical stress incidents. They can usually be contacted through your local hospital or emergency services.

If the debriefing team is not available or the incident,

though stressful, does not reach the critical threshold, you can still assist stress management by conducting a less formal but valuable debriefing.

Following a rescue, first attend to the physical needs of the rescuers by providing food, water, clean clothing, and shelter. Light aerobic exercise, such as a hike or a game of hacky sack, may help relieve tension built up over the course of the rescue.

Debriefings are designed to provide a forum in which rescuers and/or group members can share their experiences, emotions, and thoughts following a stressful situation. A debriefing seems to provide best results if it is conducted within 24 hours of the close of the rescue. The debriefing allows for ventilation and validation of feelings, encourages discussion, and helps the facilitator gauge the well-being of the participants. It can be helpful in identifying who needs further support to manage the emotional impact of the experience.

Debriefing should never include a critique of performance. A critique has a separate role in evaluating a emergency response. It should be conducted at a separate time and place.

To debrief, gather the group in a quiet place. Set a tone of support and openness. You want to discuss the impact of the incident, not critique performance. Your communication and group facilitation skills will be helpful during the debriefing. If an individual does not want to talk, that's acceptable as long as he or she has been given the opportunity. Begin by having each group member discuss his or her role in the incident. This provides a starting point for a debriefing and common ground for people who may have had different roles. This stage often fills in gaps in the story and serves to bring a sense of closure to the incident. Then, ask for each person's first thoughts after he or she had finished with the rescue and the excitement had abated. This is often a clue as to what affected the person the most and opens a discussion of the emotional and physical impact of the event. The facilitator and the peers who shared this experience can offer their insights and personal experience as support. A debriefing should last long enough to give everyone a chance to talk. End with a talk about stress and the physical and emotional reactions the group may experience. Share some of the information in this chapter on stress reactions, and give the participants information on other support services they can contact if needed, such as local mental health professionals, counselors, or pastoral support.

FINAL THOUGHTS
Emotional reactions to accidents are perfectly normal and should be expected. People who don't know this may compound their own anxieties, making the stress even worse for themselves. The majority of reactions are short term, with no lasting consequences. For both patients and rescuers, the emotional first aid we provide is as important to their ultimate recovery as the physical care.

SUMMARY: ACUTE STRESS REACTIONS

Physical	*Emotional*	*Cognitive*
Fatigue	Anxiety	Memory loss
Muscle tremors	Fear	Indecision
Nausea	Grief	Difficulty problem
Profuse sweating	Depression	solving
Glassy eyes	Hopelessness	Confusion between
Chills	Irritability	trivial and major
Difficulty	Feeling over-	issues
breathing	whelmed	Loss of attention
Dizziness	Anger	span

Delayed Stress Reactions
Macabre humor
Excessive use of sick leave
Reluctance to enter stressful situations
Intrusive images
Obsession with the stressful incident
Withdrawal from others
Suicidal thoughts
Feelings of inadequacy

CHAPTER 22

LEADERSHIP, TEAMWORK, AND COMMUNICATION

INTRODUCTION

In 1989, the center engine on a DC-10 passenger aircraft with 296 people on board malfunctioned over the Great Plains. Severed hydraulic lines crippled the pilot's ability to control the plane. The three-person crew's response to this crisis was a model of effective communication and teamwork. Working together, and using input from a pilot traveling as a passenger, they improvised a means of controlling the aircraft with the throttles.

Skilled aircrews, rescue teams, and wilderness leaders have found themselves in challenging situations in which communication, teamwork, and leadership are not optimum and things don't work out well. Aircraft have crashed because flight crews failed to perform a routine task or a team member didn't speak up to report a problem. Ineffective communication of snowpack and terrain observation has contributed to avalanche incidents. Maps and headlamps left behind have embarrassed wilderness travelers caught in approaching darkness. Experts have unclipped from their climbing anchors, avoiding a dangerous situation only when their observant partners noticed the error.

Human error is a prominent cause of many accidents and critical incidents in team activities. NASA estimates that 70 percent of airline accidents involve some degree of human error. The Teton Park rescue rangers estimate that human error contributes significantly to most backcountry and mountain incidents. When the airline industry realized that well-trained and technically proficient crews could crash airworthy aircraft because of inadequate crew communication or inteaction, it developed a series of programs—known as crew resource management or human factors in aviation—to focus on teamwork, communication, and leadership. The DC-10 crew had this training, and they credit it with helping them manage their emergency. Law enforcement, the nuclear power industry, surgical teams, and wilderness rescue groups are beginning to recognize the impact of human factors in risk management.

If you're involved in a medical situation in the wilderness, you will work with the members of your expedition or with outside rescue groups. You may find yourself needing to work fast in an emergency, or work slowly to plan a wilderness evacuation. You can use the concepts from crew resource management to enhance how you serve patients in the wilderness by combining medical and wilderness skills with effective leadership and teamwork.

NOLS LEADERSHIP SKILLS
Leadership at NOLS means timely, appropriate actions that guide and support your group to set and achieve realistic goals. Leadership is a complex blend of skills. For teaching purposes, we organize our leadership skills into seven groups.
1. Competence
2. Self-awareness
3. Judgment and decision making
4. Tolerance for adversity and uncertainty
5. Expedition behavior
6. Communication
7. Vision and action

Crew resource management has identified a number of behaviors demonstrated by well-functioning teams, including:
1. Sharing knowledge and experience
2. Avoiding self-imposed workloads
3. Recognizing and resolving fatigue and work overloads
4. Using advocacy, feedback, and questioning
5. Preparing for contingencies
6. Building teamwork
7. Setting appropriate tone

8. Addressing conflict
9. Stating decisions clearly
10. Briefing effectively
11. Prioritizing and staying vigilant

In a wilderness medical scenario, leadership may involve assessing and treating a patient; protecting him or her from the cold and rain or heat and dust; and calling for help. Or it may involve leading a litter carry or technical rescue in remote terrain. We can take each NOLS leadership skill area, weave in lessons from crew resource management, and discuss how they apply to leadership, teamwork, and communication in a wilderness medical situation.

Competence

Competence refers to proficiency in technical (outdoor and first aid) and group management skills. Ideally, your outdoor, first aid, and group management skills are sharp, and you train to keep them fresh. The level of technical skill needed is situationally dependent.

The leader must manage the group to capitalize on the abilities of the team. You do not need to be a master of group management or technical skills; however, you must have sufficient skill in both areas to fill the leadership role. For example, in a large rescue operation, a leader may not be the most experienced medical person. He or she can delegate this task. However, the leader needs information from the medical people to make decisions about the organization of the evacuation. The leader needs group management skills to ensure that communication, decision making, and leadership are effective.

Share Knowledge and Experience. In a crisis, it is common to utilize a leadership style with one person overtly leading the group. A directive leader, however, does not have to act in isolation. Ideally, the leader utilizes the team's skill and experience to make the best decisions. The leader both leads and teaches. He or she takes the initiative and time to make sure that pertinent details on the medical or evacuation plan are shared with team members. Techniques can be explained and practiced before use on the patient. This knowledge and communication strengthen the team. Everyone feels respected and engaged. Higher-quality decisions are more likely to be made.

Self-Awareness

Self-aware leaders learn from their experiences by acknowledging their abilities and successes, facing their limitations, admitting their mistakes, seeking feedback from others, and working to understand themselves. They know themselves well enough to know their bad habits and their tendencies to slip into the procrastination syndrome, the hurry-up syndrome, the do-it-all syndrome, or the perfectionist syndrome. The following are some behaviors that help avert these patterns.

Avoid Self-Imposed Workloads. Avoid self-imposed workloads and stress. A lack of situational awareness when mountaineering (e.g., ignoring building afternoon thunderheads) may self-impose a hasty descent in rain, wind, and lightning. Conversely, watch for a self-imposed hurry-up syndrome—working fast when you don't need to, and missing details or failing to complete procedures. Plan ahead, and prepare for the night shift. Will you need to rest, feed people, or find fresh folks to help carry the litter?

Recognize and Resolve Fatigue. Actively plan and schedule for transition and rest periods. In the excitement of an emergency, you tend to ignore the effect of fatigue on your performance. Pilots and rescue personnel have unrealistic attitudes about their invulnerability to stress and fatigue. Coauthor Tod Schimelpfenig learned a valuable lesson when he was assigned to the night shift on a multiday search. Not wanting to rest when others were working hard, he found something to do. The incident commander noticed this, confirmed that he was on his night shift, and told him in no uncertain terms, "It's your job to sleep. I need you at 100 percent tonight."

Recognize and Report Work Overloads. Avoid trying to fix everything yourself and taking on too many tasks. Leaders need to be able to step back and keep their eyes on the big picture. The culture of emergency services and outdoor leadership can drive a strong work ethic and a sense that it is inappropriate for the helper to ask for help. It's a measure of wisdom and maturity to be able to say, "I'm getting loaded up here. Can you take over?"

Judgment and Decision Making

The best medical protocols and practices cannot anticipate every situation, especially in wilderness. Leaders have to use their judgment by blending their knowledge, experience, character, situational awareness, and the knowledge of other resources into a decision. Wilderness medical teams need leaders who make wise decisions, and who can choose from a variety of decision-making styles. Leaders help a group put vague or complex information into a framework that makes sense. Leaders, regardless of their role as the designated person-in-charge or a team member, seek clarity, question assumptions, solicit input, listen, and thoughtfully share their observations and impressions.

Use Situationally Appropriate Decision-Making Styles. Effective leaders balance authority and teamwork. They choose from a range of decision-making styles, knowing when each is situationally appropriate. They tell others what style they and/or the group will use to make a decision: directive, consultative, a group decision, or a decision delegated to another. As a general principle, they take stands and are directive as needed while working toward maximum team participation.

Use Appropriate Advocacy and Assertion. Foster an environment in which your team can speak up and state their information, until there is resolution and decision. There are sad tales of a team member or leader making a mistake and another team member having the correct information but not speaking up or asserting his or her perspective. For example: "I'm uncomfortable with your delay in starting an evacuation. John has a persistent high fever. I think we should take him to a doctor."

You may need to provide a forum for communicating views. As a leader, model advocacy by checking in with your team and listening to their responses. "Are you getting enough direction from me about what you need to be doing? If anyone disagrees, please speak up."

Tolerance for Adversity and Uncertainty

The common definition of wilderness medicine includes lengthy transport times, arduous conditions, inclement weather, and lack of resources—a test of any leader's tolerance for adversity and uncertainty. Wilderness medical leaders must be able to live with uncertainty, endure hard work and challenge, and make do or improvise what they lack.

Prepare for Contingencies. Weather will turn bad. Helicopters will be delayed. Radios will break. Stable patients will take turns for the worse. Spring snow that's firm and supports weight in the morning can become soggy pudding in the afternoon. Stay ahead of the curve by analyzing your plan over and over and asking, what if? What if one of us sprains an ankle? It's sunny and warm now, but can I keep the patient dry if it rains?

Get Ready for the Long Haul. It's easy to be focused during the initial stages of a crisis. However, in wilderness medicine, the rubber often meets the road when you move into the long hours of work in difficult conditions as you carry a litter or wait through a storm for the helicopter. Leaders understand this change. They stay connected to the group, keeping everyone informed and focused on the task. They make sure that team members are eating, drinking, and staying warm and dry. They keep the process moving and energy and enthusiasm high.

Expedition Behavior

You may be on a wilderness expedition when you have to practice your wilderness medicine. You may be part of a rescue group sent into the wilderness. In both cases, the style of the expedition—the respect the team members show for one another and their work and the effectiveness of the communication within the group—is a critical component of the quality of the leadership. NOLS values good expedition behavior—a balance among teamwork, personal initiative, and responsibility. Team members take care of one another. They watch for fatigue and hazards, lend a helping hand without being asked, yet ask for help when they need it. They treat everyone with dignity and respect and support leadership while they work toward accomplishing the mission. Each person does his or her share, and more. They're honest and polite; they listen, yet they speak up and share their thoughts with the group. They're flexible, take responsibility, and work hard.

Build a Team Environment. Build an environment that acknowledges and respects the skills, experiences, and contributions of team members. Your team members should clearly understand their roles and tasks: "Sandy, thanks for staying alert for hazards. I'll stay at the head of the patient and monitor the airway and c-spine. Jack, finish the head-to-toe assessment and measure the vital signs. Jill, find a foam pad and sleeping bag for the patient."

Establish a team concept and environment for open communication. If there is an urgent need for action, you may need to focus someone who is rambling or talking about a nonpertinent issue. In general, listen with patience, do not interrupt or "talk over," and do not rush through a discussion. Include as many team members as possible in the communication flow: brief and update them as needed on weather, delays, plans, and schedules. Students in outdoor education groups, clients in guided trips, helpful bystanders, and local rescue personnel may all be part of your team.

Set an Appropriate Tone to the Situation. Set an appropriate tone of urgency. If the situation isn't dire, you may need to slow down your team. "Folks, let's take it easy. We've finished the assessment, and the scene is safe. Next we have to splint Bill's fractured leg, then log-roll him onto a sleeping bag and treat for shock. Let's take it one step at a time." Conversely, you may have to remind them to keep conversation and attention on the situation at hand. "Let's worry about dinner later. Right now, let's RICE and evaluate this ankle sprain." Leaders ensure that nonoperational factors such as social interaction or conversation do not interfere with necessary tasks (e.g., small talk does not interfere with climbing signals).

Address Conflict. Disagreements may occur. Personalities may clash. Unresolved conflicts can impede communication and cooperation and contribute to accidents. The leader may need to step in, identify the issue, and ask the team to put aside interpersonal differences until the emergency is over, addressing only immediate issues that are impeding progress. Later, when the crisis has passed, it's important to debrief these issues and emotions, work to resolve the conflict, and increase the team's ability to deal with its differences. A conflict during a crisis often means that expectations, roles, and responsibilities are unclear. People don't know what is expected of them or others, are missing information, or don't have a sense of the big picture. It's the leader's job to clarify structure and expectations.

Communication

Effective leaders master communication skills. They have the courage to state what they think, feel, and want and to listen with openness to different viewpoints. Leaders keep their groups informed and give clear, usable, and timely feedback. They provide a safe forum where each group member can discuss ideas and contribute to the decision-making process.

Clearly State and Acknowledge Decisions. Clearly state and acknowledge operational decisions to team members. Restate communications, clarify, and question to see if everyone understands: "We're going to rig an anchor here and use it to belay the patient to the ground. Let's go around the group and have everyone say what they will do."

Effective Inquiry: Ask and Listen. Foster an environment where questions are asked regarding actions and decisions. If people do not understand, they should be encouraged to speak up, to ask for clarification of unclear instructions or confusing or uncertain situations. For example:

I don't understand this technique. . . . I'm not sure what you want me to do. . . . Why are we putting a tourniquet on this snakebite wound? I thought tourniquets weren't indicated for snakebite. . . . You said you can't hear breath sounds. Do you mean it's too noisy to listen or the patient is not breathing?

Give and Accept Appropriate Feedback. Give positive and negative performance feedback at appropriate times. Make it a positive learning experience for the whole crew—feedback must be specific to the issue at hand, objective, based on observable behavior, and given with respect and politeness. Likewise, accept feedback objectively and nondefensively. Inhibiting communication by having an unreceptive response to feedback has played a role in accidents.

Vision and Action

Leaders assure that the group knows the mission. They keep team members informed about the plan and each person's task. They are decisive when the situation requires decisiveness and patient when it is appropriate to wait or gather more information. They are forward looking and flexible, revising the plan as necessary.

Workload Management: State Clear Expectations of Roles and Responsibilities. Make clear roles, responsibilities, and the big picture: "I'll keep myself visible and in the open in case the rest of the group comes by. John, you're in charge of Fred and Sally. Scout for the best trail through these boulders back to camp. Check back with me before a half hour is up. Allison, you're in charge of patient care. Stay with the patient and monitor vitals. Blow your whistle three times if you need me." A team works well when people know what they have to do and have a sense of where this fits into the big picture. As well, this prevents people from doing unnecessary tasks or getting in one another's way. Let others know what you expect of them, and what they can expect from you. "Folks, let's splint this arm first, then move the patient to the litter."

Provide adequate time for completion of tasks. Half-

completed tasks—for example, flaps not adjusted on takeoff—
have caused aircraft accidents. Backboard straps left loose
when a team stops one task to start another are a real possibility on an emergency scene. Identify your key tasks, tell
people what needs to be done, allow enough time, and complete
each task—one by one.

Brief Effectively. Briefings are clear, complete, and
interesting and address team coordination and planning for
potential problems. The team puts aside social conversation
or low-priority tasks, pays attention, and asks clarifying
questions. If it's an urgent situation, you may need to be concise. Expectations are set for handling possible deviations
from normal operations or unusual conditions. For example:
"We sent four people walking to the roadhead to ask for help
carrying Pete. They should arrive tonight. If we don't hear
from them by tomorrow noon, we'll send a second team."

*Stay Vigilant during Both High and Low Work-
loads.* Look around, check details, and check in with people
when you're busy and when workload is low. It's easy to focus
your attention when you're on duty and in the middle of the
event. It's harder in the routine situation or when the initial
excitement ebbs and the work of a long but apparently routine situation sets in. Accidents can happen when you overlook
the obvious, missing the moment when you could have inter-
vened or prevented a problem. How many of us have walked
away from a rest break without looking around and noticing
the water bottle and map left on the rock?

Prioritize Secondary Tasks. Prioritize secondary tasks
to allow sufficient resources for dealing effectively with the
important tasks. Talking about whether you will be able to
continue your trip in the face of this illness may be the secondary task, the distraction. Feeding your team, having them
gather personal gear, and preparing camp may be the primary
tasks. Effective leaders keep their teams' eyes on the ball.

A WILDERNESS SCENARIO

Cindy, the designated leader, and her coleaders Pete, Sandy,
and Juan were leading ten teenagers on a ski trip. They

planned to ski across the pass from Arapaho Basin to Dodge Creek. The weather was warm and blustery, with alternating periods of sun and clouds. They moved as one big group.

Shortly after noon, as the group approached the top of the pass, the weather deteriorated into whiteout conditions. The leaders, concerned about a possible cliff band on the descent route, searched for almost an hour for a route off the pass. The students, in what to them was an exposed, cold, confusing, and new situation, were left alone. Standing around, the students became frightened, wet, and cold.

Cindy told Pete and Sandy to continue to try to find a route off the saddle, but to return in 20 minutes, regardless of their success. Cindy and Juan returned to the group to find several students excitedly pointing out two hypothermic students sitting hunched over on their packs. "They're really cold. We need to get out of here!" Juan began to pull out sleeping bags and tarps to treat the hypothermia. Cindy said, "Juan, first check everyone out. Let's be sure they're hypothermic."

A few minutes later, Juan reported that although cold and scared, everyone could walk and was still alert and oriented. Their hands and feet were still warm. "OK," said Cindy, "let's get everyone together and get extra layers on people. Have them eat some trail food. Have the cold people jog in place. We need to wait for Pete and Sandy before we descend the slope."

Pete returned shortly and said that he had found a good route to the saddle and a decent campsite in the trees. Sandy wanted to dig in on the pass, arguing that people were tired and the descent would take too long. Cindy listened and also asked Pete what he thought. Pete said, "People still have energy. Let's descend to better shelter before it's too late."

Cindy said, "I agree, that's what we'll do—descend to the trees in the saddle."

Cindy clarified details on the route and the campsite, checking the map and Pete's compass bearing. They pulled Juan aside for a moment and told him this information and the plan—emphasizing the need to stay together and planning what to do if someone was really slow on the descent. Cindy then briefed the entire group. "Let's move. Pete will lead. Juan will be tail person. We will stay close together and not lose sight of each other. The weather is nasty, but we can deal with it. We're doing fine, and we will be in camp shortly."

The group descended to the saddle slowly but without incident and quickly rigged tarps. Within the hour the teenagers were enjoying hot drinks and stories of their adventure.

This incident has several examples of effective leadership and crew management:

1. Appropriate decision-making style. Cindy was directive when needed, and consulted with Pete, Sandy, and Juan before making the plan to descend the slope.
2. Effective inquiry. Cindy and Juan checked the report of hypothermia and thus avoided acting on misinformation. Cindy confirmed the route, compass bearing, and map with Pete.
3. Effective briefing. Everyone was told the plan before the descent. Roles and expectations were clear: Pete in front, Juan in back, everyone staying together.
4. Good situational awareness and an appropriate tone. The leaders knew that they had a challenge but not an emergency.
5. Appropriate advocacy. Sandy spoke up with her plan to stay on the pass, then deferred to the leader when her idea had been discussed.
6. Good preparation for contingencies. Layers and food were accessible, and the group was kept together. The leaders talked through possible problems on the descent.
7. Workloads were managed and tasks prioritized. Everyone stayed together. No one else became lost or cold during the descent to camp.

FINAL THOUGHTS

You may find yourself alone with a patient or in a small team performing wilderness first aid within a larger team of local rescue resources. The quality of your leadership, teamwork, and communication will determine how well you work within your team and with others. People working together add redundancy and synergism; one person may notice something that escapes the attention of others, and everyone can contribute knowledge and experience to the decision-making process. The team members must be effective advocates, and the leader must be an effective listener; multiple perspectives on an event are useless unless the information is shared. As well, we need to understand the impact of fatigue, the distraction of multiple tasks, and the value of effective briefing. Teamwork is enhanced, and many problems averted, when people are clear on their roles, responsibilities, and expectations. Effective leadership, teamwork, and communication are characteristics that lead to excellence.

FIRST AID KIT

These are the contents of a standard first aid kit designed for a group of twelve on a monthlong trip. Obviously, requirements will vary with group size, medical qualifications, trip length, location, and remoteness.

Bandaging Material

2" × 2" sterile gauze pad	12 ea
4" × 4" sterile gauze pad	6 ea
3" gauze roller bandage	2 ea
Cravats	2 ea
Adhesive bandages (various sizes)	12 ea
Butterfly or Steri-strip	12 ea
35cc syringe	1 ea

Blisters and Athletic Injuries

1½" athletic tape	4 rolls
3" elastic bandage	1 ea
Moleskin	1 ea 6" × 12" sheet
Molefoam	1 ea 6" × 12" sheet
Second Skin	1 package

Miscellaneous

Bandage scissors	1 ea
Zephiran/povidone-iodine	4 oz
Topical antibiotic cream	4 oz
Subnormal thermometer	1 ea
Tweezers	1 pr
Cortizone cream	4 oz
Latex gloves	4 pr

Signal mirror	1 ea
Sawyer Extractor	1 ea
Nonprescription pain medications	
Aspirin, ibuprofen, or	
acetaminophen	50 tablets

SUGGESTIONS

Protect the sterile dressings from moisture by sealing them in groups of three or four in clear plastic.

If you have a planned resupply of food and fuel, consider including extra tape and blister material.

The kit should be accessible. Everyone should know its location.

Label all containers. Include instructions for all medications.

Thermometers break easily. A strong package is imperative; a spare thermometer a good idea.

The kit should be packaged in a distinctly colored and labeled bag that is durable, waterproof, and not heavy or bulky.

If your first aid kit is too big, you will have a tendency to leave it behind. Many NOLS instructors carry in their summit packs a small package of the most frequently needed items, including tape, moleskin, Second Skin, and povidone-iodine. Others slide a small roll of tape, cravat, and 4 × 4 into their helmet lining.

NOLS first aid kits do not include premade splints, such as airsplints or SAM splints. Premade splints may be carried in the first aid kit or suitable splints can be improvised from foamlite pads.

Keep a note pad, pencil, change for phone calls, evacuation report forms, and emergency instructions with the first aid kit.

EMERGENCY PROCEDURES FOR OUTDOOR GROUPS

INTRODUCTION

This is an outline for organizing an emergency scene and a wilderness evacuation. It is not a checklist; it is a list of considerations we have found helpful in leading evacuations.

Think

1. A wilderness evacuation is a mental as well as physical challenge. Paul Petzoldt's wise advice to step aside and carefully review the situation is always pertinent.
2. Details are important; small omissions in planning can have great consequences. The evacuation team spending the night out because maps were forgotten is a liability, not an asset.
3. Errors in organization and technique have a tendency to multiply over time.
4. Time is an asset and a liability in the outdoors. Rapid transport is not possible. Use the time to think and plan.

Preplan

1. Research possible resources and evacuation options before the trip begins. Under what circumstances is self-rescue an option, and when must outside help be called upon. Know who is responsible for rescue in your wilderness area.
2. Be knowledgeable and proficient in first aid.
3. Prepare for the emergency by carrying water, shelter, matches, and a first aid kit.

Emergency Medical Care
Address the physical and psychological needs of the patient. A thorough patient assessment is essential to making a wise decision regarding method and urgency of evacuation.

LEADERSHIP
In any evacuation, many things begin happening simultaneously. The following topics—organization, decision making, communication, and reports—are presented as related elements rather than as a sequence of events.

Organization
As leader, you must assume the leadership role, delegate responsibilities, consider the circumstances, determine the type of evacuation, and prepare for and execute the evacuation.

Assume Leadership.
1. Review scene safety. Prevent situations that might create additional victims.
2. If the injury or illness is not serious, consider making an educational exercise of the rescue.
3. Organize the members of the group.

Delegate Responsibilities. Keeping everyone purposefully occupied reduces stress. In a complex evacuation there are always more tasks than people. Every task is important. Possible tasks include:
1. Feed the group. Cook food. Prepare hot drinks.
2. Prepare the evacuee's pack.
3. Build a litter.
4. Scout trail; break trail.
5. Find and mark landing site for helicopter evacuation; clear or pack soft ground if necessary.
6. Prepare evacuation and medical reports.
7. Gather and inventory all available gear: maps, first aid kits, food, water, stoves, shelters, technical climbing or boating gear.
8. Feed, shelter, hydrate the rescuers.

The PACKFRAME LITTER:

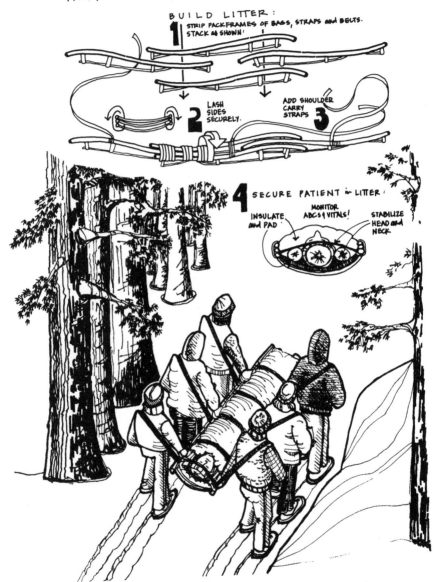

BUILD LITTER:

1 STRIP PACKFRAMES OF BAGS, STRAPS and BELTS. STACK as SHOWN.

2 LASH SIDES SECURELY.

3 ADD SHOULDER CARRY STRAPS

4 SECURE PATIENT in LITTER:

INSULATE and PAD

MONITOR ABCS & VITALS!

STABILIZE HEAD and NECK

Decision Making

Consider the following when determining the type of evacuation:

Severity of Injury. How soon does this patient need to be in the hospital? Does the injury threaten life (ABC systems) or limb?

Distance to Roadhead. What is the distance to the phone or additional help? What are the distance and time of the evacuation considering a 1- to 2-miles-per-hour rate of travel?

Difficulty of Terrain. When will you reach the rough country? In the beginning when you are fresh or later when you're exhausted?

Group's Physical Strength and Stamina.

Group's Technical Abilities and Experience, the Weather. Will you be able to deal with deteriorating weather or technical terrain?

Communication Possibilities. Can you communicate quickly with outside resources by telephone or radio, or must your message be carried by foot?

Outside Assistance. What are available rescue services—horsepackers, snowmobilers, etc.?

Transportation Schedule. Who will meet you at the roadhead?

Plan for Mechanical Failures.

Suitability of Landing or Loading Site.

Determine the Type of Evacuation. The following are common modes of evacuation:

Walking or Skiing. For the patient who is able, this is easiest and least complex.

Simple Carries. Whether or not you can carry the patient on your back depends on your strength and the nature of the patient's injuries. Such carries can be faster and easier than litter carries.

Litter. Requires a larger group—at least ten people—and is slow but safe and effective.

Request More Manpower. Consider starting for the roadhead and meeting support en route.

Horsepacking. Injury-dependent but fast; commonly used in Western states.

Helicopter. Fast but expensive; risky in poor weather and mountains; requires special permission in wilderness areas.

Ski Sled Litter. Improvised sled litters can be fast and effective.

Snowmobile. Limited by snow conditions.

Boat / Vehicle (4WD).

Execute the Evacuation.

1. Arrange for the evacuation party:
   Make sure you have enough people to carry out a safe and effective evacuation.
2. Be prepared with food, extra clothing, sleeping bags and marked maps.

Communication

Assuming that no radio or telephone communication is available, messages must be delivered on foot. They are generally one-way and must be accurate, concise, and complete.

1. Determine whether messengers should be sent.
2. Designate messengers and leader.
3. Send sufficient number of messengers to ensure safety and effectiveness.
4. Consider: physical stamina, night travel, map, navigation and first aid skills, foul weather experience.
5. Send written instructions including medical and evacuation report form with a time control plan.

Reports

The full evacuation report should include both a medical report and the field evacuation report.

Medical Report. The medical report should include the following:

Age and gender
Chief complaint
Physical exam/vital signs
Present illness/injury

Past history
Treatment
Medications administered
Changes in patient's condition
    Evacuation Report. The evacuation report should include:
Type of evacuation (walk, helicopter, litter)
Marked maps showing:
    1. Location of accident
    2. Present location of group and victim
    3. Anticipated route out of mountains
    4. Roadhead destination
Estimated date and time of arrival and return
Any special requests (doctor, litter, etc.)
Plans for messengers returning to expedition and plans
    for the group remaining in the field
    Important! Always include an alternate plan in your report!

GLOSSARY OF FIRST AID TERMS

Anaphylaxis. A hypersensitive reaction of the body to a foreign protein or drug.

Anorexia. A lack of appetite.

Appendicular. Refers to the limbs, the legs and arms.

Avulsion. A forcible tearing away of a body part. It can be a piece of skin, a finger, toe, or entire limb.

Ataxia. Incoordination of muscles. Usually seen when voluntary movement is attempted; e.g., walking.

Axial. Referring to the midline through the skeleton, the skull, vertebrae, and pelvis.

Axillary. Referring to the armpit.

Bacteria. Unicellular organisms lacking chlorophyll.

Basal metabolic rate. The metabolic rate of a person at rest. Usually expressed in kilocalories per square meter of body surface per hour.

Basal metabolism. The amount of energy needed to maintain life when the body is at rest.

Brachial. Refers to the arm, usually the brachial artery or nerve.

Brain stem. The portion of the brain located below the cerebrum, which controls automatic functions such as breathing and body temperature.

Campylobacter. A genus of bacteria implicated in diarrheal illness.

Capillary. The smallest of the blood vessels, the site of oxygen, nutrient, and waste product exchange between the blood and the cells.

Cerebellum. The portion of brain behind and below the cerebrum, which controls balance, muscle tone, and coordination of skilled movements.

Cerebrum. The largest and upper region of the brain. Responsible for higher mental functions such as reasoning, memory, and cognition.

Comminuted. A fracture in which several small cracks radiate from the point of impact.

Congenital. A condition present at birth.

Conjunctiva. The mucous membrane that lines the eyelid and the front of the eyeball.

Convection. Heat transferred by currents in liquids or gases.

Cornea. The clear transparent covering of the eye.

Crepitus. A grating sound produced by bone ends rubbing together.

CRT. Capillary refill time. For example, "Capillary refill time is 3 seconds."

Cyanosis. Bluish discoloration of the skin, mucous membranes, and nail beds indicating inadequate oxygen levels in the blood.

Diabetes. A disease resulting from inadequate production or utilization of insulin.

Distal. Farther from the heart.

Electrolyte. A substance that, in solution, conducts electricity: Common electrolytes in our body are sodium, potassium, chloride, calcium, phosphorus, and magnesium.

Embolism. An undissolved mass in a blood vessel; may be solid, liquid or gas.

Epilepsy. Recurrent attacks of disturbed brain function; classic signs are altered level of consciousness, loss of consciousness, and/or seizures.

Eversion. A turning outward (as with an ankle).

Giardia. A genus of protozoan, a simple unicellular organism that causes an illness that is often characterized by diarrhea.

Globule. Any small rounded body.

Hematoma. A pool of blood confined to an organ or tissue.

Hyperglycemia. High blood sugar.

Hypoglycemia. Low blood sugar.

Intercostal. The area between the ribs.

Irrigate. To flush with a liquid.

Kilocalorie. A unit of heat; the amount of heat needed to change the temperature of 1 gram of water 1 degree centigrade.

LOC. Level of consciousness.

Meninges. The three membranes that enclose and help protect the brain.

MOI. Mechanism of injury for an accident.

Morbidity. The state of being diseased.

Occlusive dressing. A dressing impermeable by moisture.

Palpate. To examine by touching.

Paraplegia. Paralysis affecting the lower portion of the body and both legs.

Paroxysmal. A sudden, periodic attack, spasm, or recurrence of symptoms.

PFD. Personal flotation device (life jacket)

Plasma. The liquid part of blood.

Prodromal. The initial stage of a disease.

Quadriplegia. Paralysis affecting all four limbs.

Rales. Crackly breath sounds due to fluid in the lungs or airways.

RR. Respiratory rate. For example, "RR is 18 and unlabored," or "RR is 22 and shallow and regular."

SCTM. Skin, color, temperature, and moisture. For example, "Skin is pale, cool, and moist," or "Skin is red, hot, and dry."

Seizure. A sudden attack of a disease as in epilepsy.

Signs. An indication of illness or injury that the examiner observes.

Sprain. Trauma to a joint causing injury to the ligaments.

Strain. A stretched or torn muscle.

Symptoms. Pain, discomfort, or other abnormality that the patient feels.

Tendinitis. Inflammation of a tendon.

TRS. Township, range, and section. A grid system used as a legal description of location. The coordinates are available on many topographic maps.

Varicose veins. Distended, swollen, knotted veins.

Vasoconstriction. Narrowing of blood vessels.

Ventricular. Referring to the two lower pumping chambers of the heart, the ventricles.

Vertigo. The sensation of objects moving about the person or the person moving around in space.

Virus. A microscopic and parasitic organism dependent on the nutrients inside cells for its reproductive and metabolic needs.

Wheezes. Whistling or sighing breath sounds resulting from narrowed airways.

BIBLIOGRAPHY

Askew E. W. "Nutrition for a Cold Environment." *The Physician and SportsMedicine.* 17, No. 12 (1989) 76–89.

Auerbach, Paul. *Management of Wilderness and Environmental Emergencies.* 4th ed. St. Louis: Mosby, 1995.

Ayvazian. A. "Women on Wilderness Expeditions: Special Concerns." Amherst: Hampshire College, School of Natural Science, unpublished manuscript, 1981.

Bowman, Warren D. *Outdoor Emergency Care.* Denver: National Ski Patrol System, Inc., 1988.

Chisholm, J. A. "Backcountry Guide to Lower Extremity Athletic Injuries." Lander, WY: National Outdoor Leadership School, unpublished manuscript, 1986.

Dumont-Herskowitz, R. "Outward Bound, Diabetes and Motivation: Experiential Education in a Wilderness Setting." *Diabetic Medicine.* 7, No. 10, (1990), 1–6.

Forgey, W. *Hypothermia, Death from Exposure.* Merrillville, Indiana: Camp Supply Books, 1985.

——. *Forgey's Wilderness Medicine.* 5th edition. Merrillville, Indiana: Camp Supply Books, 1999.

——. *Wilderness Medical Society Practice Guidelines.* Merrillville, Indiana: Camp Supply Books, 1995.

Gentile, Douglas A., John A. Morris, and Tod Schimelpfenig. *Wilderness Injuries and Illness.* Annals of Emergency Medicine July: 1992.

Hampton, B., and D. Cole. *Soft Paths: How to Enjoy the Wilderness Without Harming It.* Harrisburg: Stackpole Books, 1995.

Houston, C. S. "Altitude Illness in 1989." Proceedings, National Outdoor Leadership School Wilderness Education Conference. Lander, WY: Sept. 1989.

——. "High Altitude: Illness and Wellness." Merrillville, Indiana: Camp Supply Books, 1993.

——. "Going Higher: The Story of Man and Altitude." Burlington: Free Press, 1983.

Klauber, L. *Rattlesnakes.* Berkeley: University of California Press, 1982.

Mitchell, J., and G. Bray. *Emergency Services Stress.* Englewood: Brady, 1990.

Pozos R.S. and L. Wittmers, Jr., *The Nature and Treatment of Hypothermia.* Minneapolis: University of Minnesota Press, 1983.

Pozos, R. S., and D. O. Born. *Hypothermia, Causes, Effects, Prevention.* Piscataway: New Century, 1982.

Schussman, L. C., and L. J. Lutz. "Mountaineering and Rock-Climbing Accidents." *The Physician and Sports Medicine.* 10, No. 6 (1982), 53.61.

Serra, J. "Management of Fractures and Dislocations in the Wilderness Environment." Syllabus, Wilderness Medical Society Annual Meeting. Jackson, WY: Sept. 1988.

Shlim, D. R., and R. Houston. "Helicopter Rescues and Deaths Among Trekkers in Nepal." *JAMA.* 261, No. 7 (1989), 1017–1019.

Stewart, C. E. *Environmental Emergencies.* Baltimore: Williams, 1990.

Tilton. B., and F. Hubbel. *Medicine for the Backcountry.* Globe Pequot Press, 1999.

Tilton. B. *The Wilderness First Responder.* Globe Pequot Press. 1999.

Wilkerson, J. A., C. C. Bangs, and J. S. Hayward. *Hypothermia Frostbite and Other Cold Injuries.* Seattle: The Mountaineers, 1986.

Wilkerson. J. *Medicine for Mountaineering.* Seattle: The Mountaineers, 1993.

Williamson, J. *Accidents in North American Mountaineering.* New York: The American Alpine Club, 1989.

INDEX

Page numbers in italics indicate illustrations.